THE NEW INQUISITION

OTHER BOOKS BY ROBERT ANTON WILSON

1972   Playboy's Book of Forbidden Words
1973   *Sex and Drugs: A Journey Beyond Limits
1973   The Sex Magicians
1975   ILLUMINATUS! (with Robert Shea)
          The Eye in the Pyramid
          The Golden Apple
          Leviathan
1977   *Cosmic Trigger: The Final Secret of the Illuminati
1978   *Neuropolitics (with T. Leary and G. Koopman)
1980   The Illuminati Papers
1980-1 The Schrodinger's Cat Trilogy
          The Universe Next Door
          The Trick Top
          The Homing Pigeon
1981   Masks of the Illuminati
1983   Right Where You Are Sitting Now
1983   The Earth Will Shake
1983   *Prometheus Rising
1985   The Widow's Son
1986   *The New Inquisition
1987   *Wilhelm Reich in Hell
1988   *Coincidance
1989   *Ishtar Rising
1990   *Quantum Psychology
1991   *Cosmic Trigger II

* Published by New Falcon Publications

THE NEW INQUISITION

Irrational Rationalism
and the
Citadel of Science

by

Robert Anton Wilson

1995
NEW FALCON PUBLICATIONS
TEMPE, ARIZONA, U.S.A.

International Standard Book Number: 1-56184-002-5
Library of Congress Catalog Card Number: 86-83176

First Edition 1987
Second Printing 1987
Third Printing 1991
Fourth Printing 1995

Cover Design by Studio 31
Cover Painting: Paul Bockli

The paper used in this publication meets the minimum requirements of the American National Standard for Permanence of Paper for Printed Library Materials Z39.48-1984

Address all inquiries to:
NEW FALCON PUBLICATIONS
1739 East Broadway Road Suite 1-277
Tempe, AZ 85282 U.S.A.
(or)
1605 East Charleston Blvd.
Las Vegas, NV 89104 U.S.A.

With the unknown, one is confronted with danger, discomfort and worry; the first instinct is to abolish these painful sensations. First principle: any explanation is better than none . . . The search for causes is thus conditioned by and excited by the feeling of fear. The question "Why?" is not pursued for its own sake but to find a *certain kind of answer* — an answer that is pacifying, tranquilizing and soothing.

Nietzsche, *The Twilight of the Idols*

A rose by any other name
Would never, never smell the same
And cunning is the nose that knows
An onion that's been called a rose.

Wendell Johnson, *Your Most Enchanted Listener*

If you see a two-headed pig, keep your mouth shut.

Irish proverb

Other Controversial Titles From New Falcon

TABLE OF CONTENTS

Introduction — i

ONE — **Models, Metaphors & Idols** — 1
(with comments on primate psychology
and quantum mechanics)

TWO — **Skepticism & Blind Faith** — 31
(with comments on book-burning,
biological surrealism and Game Rules)

THREE — **Two More Heretics &
Some Further Blasphemies** — 67
(with comments on werewolves
and similar Forbidden Things)

FOUR — **The Dance of Shiva** — 101
(with comments on Bell's Theorem, Po
and mysterious fires)

FIVE — **Chaos & the Abyss** — 137
(with comments on phantom kangaroos
and blasphemies against Reason)

SIX — **"Mind", "Matter" & Monism** — 159
(with comments on coincidence and
the Damnedest Heresy of all)

SEVEN — **The Open Universe** — 191
(with further comments on energy
fluctuations and "spooks")

EIGHT — **Creative Agnosticism** — 223
(with further comments on the human brain,
and how to use one)

INTRODUCTION

This book speaks of a New Inquisition, a New Idol and a New Agnosticism.

By the New Inquisition I mean to designate certain habits of repression and intimidation that are becoming increasingly commonplace in the scientific community today. By New Idol I mean to designate the rigid beliefs that form the ideological superstructure of the New Inquisition. By the New Agnosticism I mean to designate an attitude of mind which has elsewhere been called "model agnosticism" and which applies the agnostic principle not just to the "God" concept but to ideas of all sorts in all areas of thoughts and ideology.

The agnostic principle refuses total belief or total denial and regards models as tools to be used only and always where appropriate and replaced (by other models) only and always where not appropriate. It does not regard any models, or any class of models, as more "profound" than any other models, or any class of models but asks only how a model serves, or fails to serve, those who use it. The agnostic principle is intended here in a broad "humanistic" or "existential" sense, and is not intended to be narrowly technical or philosophical only.

This book is deliberately polemical because I believe models, as tools, should be tested in that kind of combat which Nietzsche metaphorically called "war" and Marx called dialectical struggle. It is deliberately shocking because I do not want its ideas to seem any less stark or startling than they are.

Some of what I say here may *seem* to contradict and repudiate ideas espoused in some of my earlier works. In fact, it does not. I still support a high-technology society rather than a more primitive one; I still refuse to join those who glamorize the middle ages (which I regard as a time of madness and superstition); I still advocate space colonization, longevity research and other goals that seem Faustian (or worse) to *lauditores temporis acti* such as Theodore Rossack and the Pop Ecologists. Above all, I still think the scientific establishment being satirized here is not nearly as nefarious as various religious establishments, especially those of Christianity and Islam. In criticizing what I call Fundamentalist Materialism—a term I coined over ten years ago, and have used in many articles and a few books—I am opposing the Fundamentalism, not the Materialism. (This point will be clarified as we proceed.)

Some terms which may be unfamiliar to certain readers are used frequently in this book. They are defined briefly here, and will be explained further, by context and example, as the argument unfolds.

EMIC REALITY: the unified field made up of *thoughts, feelings and apparent sense impressions* that organizes our inchoate experience into meaningful patterns; the paradigm or model that people create by talking to each other, or by communicating in any symbolism; the culture of a time and place; the semantic environment. Every emic reality has its own *structure*, which imposes structure upon raw experience.

ETIC REALITY: the hypothetical actuality that has not been filtered through the emic reality of a human nervous system or linguistic grid. If you have anything to say about Etic Reality *without using words or any other symbols,* please send a full description of it to the author at once.

INFORMATION: as used in mathematical information theory, this denotes the amount of unpredictability in a message; information is, roughly, what you do not *expect* to hear. In this sense, information may be "true" or "false," but is always a small surprise. *Resistance to new information* measures the degree of Fundamentalism in a culture, a sub-culture, or an individual.

NEUROSEMANTICS: the study of how symbolism influences the human nervous system; how the local reality-tunnel programs our thoughts, feelings and *apparent* sense impressions.

REALITY-LABYRINTH: existence regarded as a multiple-choice intelligence test; the sum total of reality-tunnels available to an open-minded or non-Fundamentalistic human at a given time and place.

REALITY-TUNNEL: An emic reality established by a system of coding, or a structure of metaphors, and transmitted by language, art, mathematics or other symbolism.

SYNERGY: those behaviors of whole systems which cannot be predicted by analysis of parts or sub-systems. A term popularized by Buckminster Fuller and roughly equivalent to Holism. Cf. *Gestalt* in psychology and *transaction* immediately following:

TRANSACTION: used here in the sense of Transactional Psychology, which holds that perception is not passive *re*-action but active, creative *trans*-action, and that the "observer" and the "observed" must be considered a synergetic whole.

The scientists quoted at various points are responsible only for their own attributed speech or writings. All ideas not so attributed are to be blamed always and only on the author.

During the writing of this book, I had the opportunity to discuss the ideas herein through fruitful interaction and discussion with audiences who attended seminars and workshops. I wish to thank all those who helped organize these tours, especially Jeff Rosenbaum, Joe Rothenberg, Kurt Smith and Laura Jennings. I also wish to thank the staffs of Esalen Institute (California), Naropa (Colorado), Ojai Foundation (California), De Kosmos (Amsterdam) and Sphinx (Basel).

Above all, I thank my wife Arlen, for her patience and loving support.

CHAPTER ONE

MODELS, METAPHORS AND IDOLS

(with comments on primate psychology and quantum mechanics)

How is the quark more real than figurative? And is not the very term *quark* coined from that most metaphoric and creative of works, *Finnegans Wake*? And when physicists, with tongue in cheek, apply terms like *color* and *charm* to quarks, can we believe they are oblivious to their own creative acts?

Roger Jones, *Physics as Metaphor*

All that is, is metaphor.

Norman O. Brown, *Closing Time*

The late R. Buckminster Fuller—architect, engineer, poet, mathematician and gadfly—used to astonish audiences by remarking casually in the middle of a lecture that everything we see is inside our heads. If the consternation of the audience was voluble, Fuller would stop and explain, by drawing on the blackboard the diagram encountered in the elementary optics part of any first year physics course:

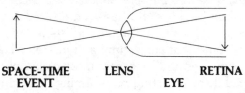

SPACE-TIME   LENS   RETINA
EVENT   EYE

The upward arrow on the reader's left represents an "object" or, in more precise terms, a space-time event. The light rays from this existential knot or energy cluster travel to the lens of the eye which, like all lenses, reverses them and the retina then registers the reversed "image." We do not see things upside down because the retina is part of the synergetic eye-brain system and *before* we have a conscious perception of the energy-knot the brain has already interpreted and edited the signal into its system of classification, which includes turning it around to mesh with the general geometrical coordinate system the brain uses to "file" data.

Some people think they understand this the first time it is explained to them. Others, around the hundredth time it is explained, suddenly cry "Eureka!" and think they *really* understand it at last. In my experience teaching seminars on this area, nobody gets the full meaning of it until some experiments are performed which make it a vivid experience. Here is one such experiment which the reader is urgently implored to duplicate:

Ask a friend to cooperate and then obtain a newspaper you have not already glanced over. Sit in a chair and have the friend, holding the newspaper so that you can read the front-page headlines, walk slowly away, across the room, until the headlines are blurry for you. Have the friend turn a page to ensure that you cannot read the headlines. Then have him, holding the newspaper in the same position, read a headline out loud. You will then "see" the headine clearly.

I repeat: reading about such a demonstration does not make the principle as clear and deeply understood as *actually performing* the demonstration.

Aristotle, without knowing the modern laws of optics, understood this general principle well enough to point out once that *"I see"* is an incorrect expression and really should be *"I have seen."* There is always time, however small, between the impact of a signal on our eye and the "perception" or "image" in our brains. In that interval the brain *imposes* form, meaning, color and a great deal else.

What is true of the eye is true of the ear and of other senses.

On the face of it, once this has been pointed out, there seems no escape from an at least partial agnosticism—i.e. from recognition that all ideas are somewhat conjectural and inferential. Aristotle escaped that conclusion, and until recently most philosophers and scientists have escaped it, by asserting or assuming or hoping that a method exists whereby the uncertainty of perceptions can be transcended and we can arrive at certitude about general principles.

Since Hume—*at least* since Hume—this Faith had gradually broken down. Various philosophers have expressed this collapse of certainty in different ways, but in essence the modern relativist position can be simply expressed by saying that there is no way of deriving certain conclusions from uncertain perceptions, for the same reason that there is no way of obtaining *a definite sum* if every figure in an account is estimate such as "about two pounds" "about a pound and a half" "about six or seven pounds" etc. *If perception is not absolute, no deduction from perception can be absolute.* No matter how ingeniously one juggles with approximations, they do not magically turn into certainties; at best, they become the most accurate possible approximations.

Again: consider this well-known illustration, to be found in most general psychology texts:

If you see the line on the bottom as longer than the line on the top, your brain, working on habitual programs, has deceived you. The V and reverse-V decorations seduce the eye-brain system into seeing inaccurately. You have just had a mild hallucination.

The processes (optical and neurological) by which "miracles" and "UFOs" are created *and by which you "create" the chair across the room from you* right now, are fundamentally similar to what just happened when you looked at those lines. If you think the chair is somehow more "objective" than a poem by Dylan Thomas or those pixillated lines, you might try the expensive experiment of hiring three painters and three photographers to come in and make you a "realistic portrait" of the chair. You will find that, in the photos as much as in the paintings, a personality has somehow given a meaning or a richness to the "object."

Now, this is not to endorse what might be called Absolute Relativism—the idea that one generalization is as good as another. Some generalizations are *probably* much more accurate than others, which is why I have a lot more faith in the chair I am sitting on than I have in the Virgin of Ballinspittle. But these generalizations remain in the area of *probability*. They never attain the certitude claimed by the Pope, Dr. Carl Sagan and the priests of other Idols.

"The" Greeks as we say, or "the" ancient Greeks—the handful of ancient Greeks whose ideas we encounter in University, actually— were well aware of this fallibility of perception, and an illustration well-known in Athens in its Golden Age went like this: take three bowls of water. Make one of them quite hot, one medium-temperatured, and the third quite cold. Put your right hand in the hot bowl for a while and your left hand in the cold bowl. Then put both hands in the medium bowl. The same water will feel "cold" to your right hand and "hot" to your left hand. (Again, *doing* the experiment teaches more, neurosemantically, than merely reading about it.)

Nonetheless, the Greek philosophers, or some of them, still thought there was a path to certitude. They called it the path of Pure Reason. The argument for PR goes that, even if sense data is fallible, we have a higher faculty which is not fallible and which knows truths *a priori*. This has collapsed over the centuries for a variety of reasons, but chiefly because the things philosophers thought they knew this way have often turned out to be simply not true. For instance, even as late as the age of libertarian free thought in the 18th Century, Kant still thought PR "knew" intuitively that Euclidean geometry was *the* true and only geometry. Nowadays, mathematicians have several varieties of non-Euclidean geometry, all of which are equally valid (consistent) and all of which are as useful as Euclidean geometry, although in different areas.

In the 13th Century, Thomas Aquinas thought he had the infallible method of arriving at certitude—a combination of PR and Holy Writ. This is still believed in backward countries like Ireland or Portugal, but is not generally accepted in civilized nations because PR itself has been proven fallible, as noted, and because there are many varieties of HW around—Buddhist, Hindu, Taoist, Jewish, etc. as well as such modern products as *Oahspe* and the *Urantia* book—and there is no known empirical test to determine which HW is the "real" HW.

In the 19th Century, Kierkegaard circled back to the pre-Aquinas era of Christianity and suggested, again, that the way out of this perpetual relapse into uncertainty is a "leap of faith." Kierkegaard was such an intricate writer that any criticism of him will be denounced as superficial by his admirers, but in essence his argument is something like that of the present book (and of Nietzsche), which is that all the other methods of seeking certitude have a *concealed* "leap of faith" in them, which their devotees conveniently "forget" or overlook. So Kierkegaard asks: why not admit frankly that we are taking a "leap of faith"?

My answer to that is that there is an alternative which appears more reasonable to some of us; namely to avoid the "leap of faith" and remain agnostic about all methods, although *willing to learn* from them in an open-minded way. The justification for this is entirely empirical and only probabilistic, of course. It is that those who have taken a flying "leap of faith" generally look rather silly within a few generations, or sometimes even within a few years.

There remains, of course, Scientific Method (SM), the alleged source of the certitude of those I call the New Idolators. SM is a mixture of SD (sense data: usually aided by instruments to refine the senses) with the old Greek PR. Unfortunately, while SM is powerfully effective, and seems to most of us the best method yet devised by mankind, it is made up of two elements which we have already seen are fallible—SD (sense data) and PR (pure reason) can *both* deceive us. Again: two fallibilities do not add up to one infallibility. Scientific generalizations which have lasted a long time have *high probability*, perhaps the highest probability of any generalizations, but it is only Idolatry which claims none of them will ever again have to be revised or rejected. Too many have been revised or rejected in this century alone.

Certitude is seized by some minds, not because there is any philosophical justification for it, but because such minds have an emotional need for certitude.

For instance, run your eyes down the following list of propositions and play the Aristotelian either/or game with them: mark each one "true" or "false" (since no "maybes" are allowed in the strict Aristotelian game).

1. Water boils at 100° Celsius.	T	F
2. pq equals qp	T	F
3. The infamous Dr. Crippen poisoned his wife.	T	F
4. The Communists are plotting to enslave us.	T	F
5. The Nazis killed 6,000,000 Jews.	T	F
6. Marilyn Monroe was the most beautiful woman of her time	T	F
7. There is a tenth planet in our solar system, beyond Pluto.	T	F
8. Colorless green ideas sleep furiously.	T	F
9. Francis Bacon wrote *Hamlet*.	T	F
10. *Lady Chatterley's Lover* is a pornographic novel.	T	F
11. *Lady Chatterley's Lover* is a sexist novel.	T	F
12. The Pope is infallible in matters of faith and morals.	T	F
13. Beethoven is a better composer than Mozart.	T	F
14. Ronald Reagan wrote *Hamlet*.	T	F
15. God has spoken to me.	T	F
16. The following sentence is false.	T	F
17. The previous sentence was true.	T	F
18. All human beings are created equal.	T	F
19. Capitalism is doomed by its internal contradictions.	T	F
20. My spouse has always been faithful to me.	T	F
21. I am probably not as smart as I think I am.	T	F

We will return to these propositions later and find other lessons to be learned from them, but for now it is sufficient to notice that *emotional preferences* and *fixed ideas* did become somewhat perceptible in a few cases, for almost every reader, even when, or especially when, the evidence for or against the proposition is dubious or controversial. It is amusing to reflect that other readers no doubt experienced a similar insight into their own bias but on entirely different items on the list (Only an astronomer who has spent a long time looking for the possible tenth planet would feel strong bias there, probably, but a large percentage of married persons feel a definite bias when confronting item 20 . . .)

What I call Idols are projections of these inner compulsions of human psychology. When an Idol "speaks" (through its priests) it only says what the Faithful *want* to hear.

The more technical criticism of PR can be found in such books as Morris Kline's *Mathematics: The End of Certainty*, Hofstadter's *Godel, Escher, Bach* and the section on Godel in Newman's *The World of Mathematics*.

Simplified, it goes like this:

All thought consists of manipulations of symbols according to Game Rules. The combination of symbols and rules (for manipulating the symbols) makes up a *system*. When stripped down to their bare mathematico-logical bones, all systems appear to be either trivial or dubious. If trivial, they are certain, but we cannot learn much from them because they "refer" to very little. As soon as a system becomes less than totally trivial, and "refers" to more and more, a species of *infinite regress* enters it and it becomes increasingly uncertain: we have to prove, as it were, an endless series of steps *between* Step A and Step B *before* we can go on to Step C.

There is a hilarious example of this regress, from Lewis Carroll, in Hofstadter's book mentioned above. A simplified analogy is this, which I once heard:

"I never eat animals because they are our brothers," said an American student of Buddhism, to a Zen *roshi*.

"Why shouldn't we eat our brothers?" asked the *roshi*.

The student had a simple system which can be abbreviated:

Animals are our brothers.

We should not eat our brothers.

Therefore, we should not eat animals.

Once any step of this is analyzed critically, a new argument begins; and that argument in turn can be analyzed at any point, and so the infinite regress is created. In "common sense" or in the context of probability, many such challenges appear absurd and can be disregarded, but any system that claims *certainty* must answer *all* challenges. Since this would take an infinite amount of time, it has not yet been performed, and the foundations of every mathematical-logical system are increasingly regarded as *formal*—Game Rules—and not as eternal "laws of thought" as they seemed to be to philosophers from Aristotle to about the time of Kant.

This applies to the structure of systems of PR in itself. When we combine PR with SD (sense data) another problem arises—the fallibility of SD already discussed. A third problem is that there are many systems of PR available—e.g. in describing separation we have to choose between Euclidean geometry, Gaussian-Reimannian geometry, Lobachevskian geometry, Fullerian geometry, n-dimensional Hilbert space, etc.—and we can only judge which system of PR should be combined with SD by scrutinizing the results of further SD (by experiment), which gives us high probabilities but still no certainties. Any system of PR/SD which has worked in the past may be replaced if new SD no longer fits its grid, or if a different system of PR gives a new "perspective" which seems more useful operationally or practically.

Or, as Einstein once said—quoted by Korzyski in *Science and Sanity*— "Insofar as the laws of mathematics are certain, they do not refer to reality; and insofar as they refer to reality, they are not certain."

In daily life and in "common sense," we use this agnostic *caution* most of the time and "expect the unexpected" and "keep our eyes and ears open," etc. We only *rush to judgment* when we are under time-pressure to make a quick decision *or when our prejudices are involved*, as in political and religious controversy.

When there is no existential pressure for quick decisions, only prejudice asserts certitude.

The following diagram is adopted from Professor O.R. Bontrager of University of Pennsylvania Department of Psychology and from the general principles in Blake's anthology, *Perception*, University of Texas, 1952.

| I | II | III | IV | V |

Stage I represents an energy-event in the space-time continuum, in the Einsteinian sense. This can be a sub-atomic process, a horse running in a field, a Laurel and Hardy movie projected on a screen, the nuclear engine called "the sun" transmitting light and heat to us across 93,000,000 miles, or any other kind of event possible in space-time. This is often called *Etic Reality*, or non-verbal Reality.

The first arrow represents *part* (not *all*) of the energy in the original energy-event traveling toward some perceptor organ belonging to you or me or some critter like us.

Stage II represents the activity of the perceptor organ after being "hit" or tickled or somehow excited by the *part* of the energy that reaches said organ. Please note that *all* of the energy is not absorbed by the organ even in extreme cases—e.g. when we are hit by a hammer, we still do not absorb *all* the energy in the hammer.

Even at this stage—even if nothing further was required for

perception—we would still be dealing with *part*, not *all*; we would be dealing with abstraction, uncertainty, fallibility.

The second arrow indicates *part* of what happens after the perceptor organ is stimulated, by *part* of the energy flowing to us from the space-time event. In this arrow we are representing very, very many signals traveling to many parts of our organism.

Stage III represents this organismic reaction, which can be quite complex. For instance, if the energy-packet happens to be the signal, "Your mother has been raped and murdered by terrorists," the stomach and tear-ducts and heart at least will be involved in processing the signal, as well as the neural and neuro-endocrine systems.

Try to imagine, for instance, some of the probable organismic reactions, including bile and adrenalin production, in those Fundamentalist Christians who have been hardy enough to have worked their way through the first few pages of this opus; or in a Feminist confronted with the signal, "No woman has ever written a first-rate symphony;" or in a Marxist listening to a Margaret Thatcher speech; or in a midget reading a collection of midget jokes which are "really" quite funny—to non-midgets; or in a Jewish scholar trying to read objectively through the writings of those Revisionists who claim the Holocaust never happened.

It is obvious that along with *subtraction* (or abstraction: receiving part not all of the external energy), perception also involves a kind of *addition* of pre-existing emotions, which is what Freud meant by "projection."

The next arrow indicates the transmission of all this to the brain. Obviously, what the brain receives is *already* highly colored by the subtractions and additions we have indicated; but the brain itself, except perhaps in the newborn infant, already has a set of *programs*, or a "filing system" for classifying such incoming signals.

Stage IV indicates the "percept" as it is usually called, the mental "image" or "idea" that emerges after the brain has processed the original energy plus additions and minus subtractions.

The final, two-way arrow indicates the most subtle and nefarious stage of this neurological programming, the feedback between the incoming energy (plus additions and minus subtractions) and the *language system* (including symbolic, abstract languages like mathematics) which the brain happens to use habitually.

The final precept in humans is always verbal or symbolic and hence coded into the pre-existing *structure* of whatever languages or systems the brain has been taught. The process is not one of linear reaction but of synergetic transaction. This finished product is thus a *neurosemantic* construct, a kind of metaphor.

This discovery that language is basically metaphoric, which emerged gradually in the early 19th Century, inspired Emerson's famous dictum that we speak to each other in "fossil poems." Thus, to *want* something is to be empty—*want* and *vacant* come from the same root. Speaking of all desires as "*appetites*" brings us back to the same metaphor. Even "to be"—the most abstract word in normal use—comes from an Indo-European root which evidently meant becoming lost in the woods. That was as abstract, I guess, as an early human could feel; when no longer lost, when other people were found again, he or she would no longer simply "*be*" abstractly but become embroiled again in a more complex state, namely *social* existence and its Game Rules. A *villain* is a person without property (and Marxists should have given us many more exegeses on the class-bias in our languages). *Man* is the general human being, as Feminists keep telling us, because of the gender-bias in our language. A humorous story of sexual nature is a "dirty joke" because ascetics and puritans have left their own programs embedded in our speech; but Saxon words for body functions are "dirtier" than Norman words because of a plurality of puritan-economic-racial prejudices.

Even "*the*" is a metaphor—it assumes the world *is* divided the same way our minds divide it—and seems to have been a very hypnotic metaphor indeed. In terms of human tragedy and suffering, think of what has been provoked by generalizations about "*the* Jews" and "*the* blacks." More subtly, remember that "*the* length of *the* rod" seemed to be a perfectly meaningful and "objective" phrase until Einstein demonstrated that a rod has various lengths—$length_1$, $length_2$, etc.—depending on its velocity and depending also on the relative velocity of the galoot who is trying to measure it.

And what about "is" in the sense of Aristotelian identification—as in A *is* a B? This appears very useful mathematically, *because the members of a mathematical set exist abstractly, i.e. by definition,* but what happens when we apply it to non-mathematical, sensory-sensual events? Consider such pronouncements as "This *is* a great work of art," "This *is* meaningless drivel," "This *is* Communism," "This *is* sexism," "This *is* fascism." To reflect the currently acceptable principles of neurology, such statements should be a bit more complicated—e.g. "This seems like a great work of art to me," "This seems like meaningless drivel to me," "This seems like

Communism to me," "This seems like sexism to me," "This seems like fascism to me."

Of course, if some pedantic bastard like me points this out, people will say that the latter formulations are what they *really* mean and that the Aristotelian "is" was used only for convenience or brevity. But if you observe people carefully, you will note that language does indeed have hypnotic effects, and that one who has said "This is Sacred" will treat the non-verbal event as if it *really* is Sacred, and those who say "This is Crap" will act as if the event *really is* Crap.

Roger Jones's *Physics as Metaphor* spends most of its time trying to make clear to the reader the transactional or poetic element in so seemingly factual a statement as

This table is three meters long.

In case Dr. Jones's point still seems obscure or excessive, consider the celebrated "cock-eyed room" designed by Dr. Albert Ames. This is discussed in Blake's *Perception* mentioned above and has often been shown on educational television. This room is designed so that the brain, using its ordinary programs and metaphors, will classify it as an ordinary room. It is not ordinary, however: it has walls and ceiling and floor designed at odd angles which optically produce in educated humans the same signals as a "normal" room. (Some evidence suggests that children under 5 years of age are not taken in by this illusion.)

Something very amusing and instructive happens—something which may relate, I think, to UFOlogy and other "crazy" topics—if two men of the same size enter the cockeyed room and walk to opposite walls. What the brain "sees" is that one man "miraculously" grows taller, becomes a virtual giant, while the other man "shrinks" down to a dwarf. The brain, it seems, having classified the room as normal, stubbornly clings to that program, even at the cost of having to classify new signals into a virtually supernatural event.

Incidentally,

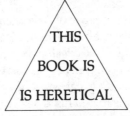

If you didn't notice something a bit peculiar in that triangle, look again. If you still don't see it, look a third time.

More subtle and alarming issues arise when we consider the *structure* of a *system* of metaphors interlinked into a code or language.

Descartes who tried, or says he tried, to doubt everything, found that he could not doubt the proposition "I think, therefore I am." That was because he lived before the discoveries of 19th Century linguists. Nietzsche, who was trained in that field before becoming a philosopher or a social menace or whatever he became, noted that Descartes couldn't doubt that proposition because he only knew Indo-European languages. It is an Indo-European coding convention that a verb must have a substantive noun before it—than an action *must* be attributed to some alegedly isolated and allegedly reified Actor. It is this convention which still makes us say "It is raining," even though we no longer believe in Zeus or any other rain-god and would be hard put to say what else the "it" might refer to.

These *linguistic structural* factors explain the notorious inability of even genius to translate a poem from one language to another, except very approximately. They may also explain some of the great conflicts in the history of philosophy—Prof. Hugh Kenner has wittily argued that Descartes, thinking in a French even more latinate than today's, would perceive *un pomme grosse et rouge* and conclude that the mind starts from general ideas and then discovers particulars, whereas Locke, thinking in English, would perceive the same sort of space-time event as *a big red apple* and decide that the mind starts from particulars and then assembles general ideas.

In Chinese, the characters which literally translated into English would be *jade/sun + moon* comes over to us, once we know that *sun + moon* means among other things brightness, as "the jade is bright" or more elegantly "the jade shines." And *student/sun + moon* becomes a surprisingly familiar metaphor—"the student is bright." But *heart + liver/sun + moon* has baffled every translator of Confucius.

Even a Chinese, reading this in English, can rediscover or re-experience the hidden poetry of his own language by thinking about why this Confucian term is so hard to transmit cross-culturally. An English speaker, similarly, can relive the forgotten poetry of our own language by trying to translate into some other speech such familiar phrases as "tight-fisted," "open-hearted," "radiant health," "walking the straight and narrow," "under a cloud," "fiery tempered," "those legalistic asses."

And what about "matter," the Idol of the Fundamentalist Materialists? This is a metaphor, too, a petrified poem, and is related to *meter* and *measure* (and, oddly enough, to *mother* also). Somewhere, somehow, out of the organismic (holistic) activity of metering and measuring, somebody invented the metaphor, the substantive noun, of that-which-is-measured. In the same way, out of the experiences which Nietzsche once called "this leaf" and "that leaf" and "the next leaf"—which semanticists call $leaf_1$, $leaf_2$, $leaf_3$ etc.—the substantive noun, or poem, of "leaf" or "*the* leaf" was created. That the process was very poetic indeed and even metaphysical is indicated by the fact that Plato either believed, or has been understood to have believed, that "the leaf" really exists somewhere.

Most Materialists, similarly, either believe, or are very easily misunderstood as believing, that "matter" exists somewhere.

But nobody has ever experienced this poem or abstraction "matter," anymore than anybody has ever experienced "the leaf." Human experience remains limited to $measurement_1$, $measurement_2$, $measurement_3$ etc. and $leaf_1$, $leaf_2$, $leaf_3$ etc.

Specific space-time events are encountered (and usually endured); substantive nouns are conventions of coding, or metaphors.

If "matter" is a metaphor, what of the "space" and "time" in which it is conventionally assumed either to move or stand still?

That these are also metaphors is easily seen from the fact that modern physics, since Einstein, has found it profitable to replace them with the more elegant metaphor of "space-time"; and that, using this more modern metaphor throughout this chapter, I am yet comprehensible even to those who are more accustomed to the pre-Einsteinian metaphors of "space" and "time" as separate substantives.

The conventions of coding or *systems of metaphor* that make us human are known as "culture" or "cultural configuration" in anthropology. The systems used in science at a given date are known as the *models* of that period, or sometimes all the models are lumped together into one super-model which is then called "*the*" *paradigm*. The general case—the class of all classes of metaphors—is called a group's *emic reality* (by Dr. Harold Garfinkle who has built a meta-system called ethnomethodology out of the sub-systems of anthropology and social psychology) or its *existential reality* (by the Existentialists) or its *reality-tunnel* (by Dr. Timothy Leary, psychologist, philosopher and designer of computer software).

That these terms are sometimes overlapping and sometimes distinct can be illustrated with a few real and hypothetical examples.

To cite Bucky Fuller again, Mission Control at Houston is often heart asking astronauts "How are things going up there?"—even when the astronauts are *below* Houston at the time. The technicians at Houston have a post-Copernican *model* most of the time, but their *emic reality* or *reality-tunnel* retains pre-Copernican metaphors implying both Earth's flatness and its centrality. According to Fuller, who may sound excessive at this point, this neurosemantic *dissonance* between model and metaphor could some day lead to a serious blunder.

Fuller, from 1928 on, always wrote and said "Universe" instead of "the" Universe. When questioned about this, he would explain that it is consistent with modern scientific models to regard Universe as process and *"the"* implies medieval notions of stasis and thing-ification.

Prof. X, let us say, "is" a Marxist (i.e. accepts that label). As such, he accepts also a determinist *model* of human behavior. Nonetheless, he will often exhibit irritation or downright anger at people with non-Marxist or anti-Marxist opinions. He has a *model* that claims these people must be what they must be, but his *reality-tunnel* still contains neurosemantic reactions appropriate to the earlier theological model of "free will."

In terms of one kind of sociological *model*, a common event in any large city can be described as follows: A group of people agree to meet at a certain hour on a certain day to make noise. Other people arrange to be there, to listen to the noise. The meeting happens as scheduled, the noise continues for over an hour, and everybody exhibits behavior indicating that the ritual was satisfactory to them.

According to another type of sociological *model*, favored by phenomenologists and ethnomethodologists, we need to know that the noise was called Symphony No. 9 in D by Beethoven before we can begin to *understand* what has happened, which is that in the *emic reality* or *existential reality* of these people something has occurred which contains *meaning, beauty, grandeur* and *affirmation of life*.

Prof. X, who is Japanese, shares the same *model* of gravity as Prof. Y, who is Swedish, because they are both physicists; but Prof. X still lives in a Japanese reality-tunnel when relating to family and friends and Prof. Y is in a Swedish reality-tunnel when outside the lab in Swedish society. This is why, when not discussing physics, Prof. X might seem stiff or formal to Prof. Y, who might in turn seem rude or even crude to Prof. X.

Stanley Laurel throws a pie which hits Oliver Hardy in the face. In the physicist's model or reality-tunnel (the two overlap in this case) the best description of what has happened is Newton's F equals ma (Force equals mass times acceleration). In the anthropological reality-tunnel, what has happened is a continuation of the Feast of Fools or Saturnalia or the tradition of the royal fool who is immune from the tabu against rebellion in comic form. To some Freudians, the best reality-tunnel is that the Son's rage against the Father is being expressed symbolically. To some Marxists, it is the worker's rage against the boss. Etc.

It begins to seem that no *one* "reality-tunnel" is adequate for the description of all human experience, although *some* reality-tunnels are better for *some* purposes than others are.

I have spoken of Fundamentalism and Idolatry several times; now I may define these terms. Idolatry is my label for that stage of semantic innocence in which the inferential and metaphoric nature of models and reality-tunnels is forgotten or repressed or has not yet been learned; the stage of innocence or arrogance in which *Stage V on our perception diagram, somebody's edited final version of a perception ("Emic Reality"), is confused with Stage I, the energy-event or Etic Reality "out there"* in what is traditionally *assumed* to be a more-or-less Euclidean space.

To the Idolator, events *"really are"* what they appear to be as coded into his or her favorite reality-tunnel. Any other reality-tunnel, however useful it may appear to others with different pruposes and different interests, must then be "mad" or "bad"—delusory or fraudulent. Anybody who disagrees with such an Idolator *must be*, by definition, a loony or a liar.

This mentality underlies all Inquisitions, and I call it Fundamentalism when it appears as an active social ideology.

History and anthropology reveal that humans have "made do" or at least survived with an incredible variety of metaphor-systems or *emic* realities. In our own Western civilization, only 600 years ago everybody was living/sensing existence through the Thomist model with a man-like "God" at the top of everything, choirs of "angels" "thrones" and "dominions" descending therefrom, humans wandering about on a flat earth in the middle, and a burning "hell" full of "demons" beneath. Some of the denizens of County Kerry, and evidently some Hollywood screenwriters, are still in that reality-tunnel, which is just as *"real"* from inside as Beethoven's grandeur is in the *existential* reality of those inside the classical music coding system.

Around the world today are millions livng in the Marxist reality-tunnel, the vegetarian reality-tunnel, the Buddhist reality-tunnel, the nudist reality-tunnel, the monetarist reality-tunnel, the Methodist reality-tunnel, the Zionist reality-tunnel, the Polynesian totemistic reality-tunnel etc.

Of course, this position "is" relative relativism, not absolute relativism. We say again that some reality-tunnels seem better, in some ways, than others. One would not wish to live in a nation dominated by the Nazi reality-tunnel, for instance; and that is called a *moral* choice. The Einsteinian reality-tunnel "is" better, in the dimension of predicting more accurately, than the Newtonian reality-tunnel; and that is called a *scientific* choice. James Joyce seems to "be" a great writer *to me* than Harold Robbins; and this is called an *esthetic* choice.

In every case, however, a human organism, and specifically a human nervous system—in the biological model, a specialized kind of primate nervous system—has made the choice. The *scientific*, the *esthetic* and the *moral* are not always distinct, either—as can be seen by studying the arguments, anywhere, for and against building a new nuclear power plant. Even in the scientific area, no choice is purely "objective" anymore, if it ever was, because—as we shall soon see—there are a variety of alternative models available these days in the advanced fields, and the choice between them always includes such factors as "simplicity" and "elegance": two very subjective factors, indeed.

And, of course, in historical perspective, any choice between reality-tunnels is *always* made on the basis of insufficient data, because we have no way of knowing what new data will be discovered the next day, the next decade or the next century.

As Persinger and Lafreniere write in *Space-Time Transients and Unusual Events*, Nelson-Hall, 1977, page 3:

> We, as a species, exist in a world in which exist a myriad of data points. Upon these matrices of points we superimpose a structure and the world makes sense to us. The pattern of the structure originates within our biological and sociological properties.

To the extent that we remain conscious of this process of superimposing structure (programming our emic reality) we will behave liberally *and will continue learning throughout life*. To the extent that we become unconscious of this process, we will behave Fundamentalistically or Idolatrously and will never again learn anything after the hour at which we (usually unconsciously) elevate a generalization into a dogma and stop thinking.

If we are fully *hypnotized* by a reality-tunnel, we may even become, in conventional terms, a bit mad. In such a state of mania, we might even burn books that contain heresy against our Idols, or fake the data to support our prejudices, or find ourselves compelled to explain increasing amounts of discordant data by accusing vast amorphous conspiracies of having "cooked" the data, or we might even become *sincerely convinced* that anybody who sees or hears or smells or tastes or otherwise senses anything inconsistent with our Idol must be hallucinating.

In such a state, we appear "beyond reason"—i.e. beyond the normal parameters of social discourse. The only places for us, then, are in a quiet and restful home in the country, surrounded by kindly doctors, or in the Vatican, or in the Committee for Scientific Investigation of Claims of the Paranormal.

Basically, thusfar in this chapter we have been discussing some of the imperatives of what might theologically be called primate psychology, although we prefer to refer to it, less metaphysically, as primate neurology.

Human beings appear, in the biological model, as very unique primates, but primates nonetheless. Specifically, the usual primate program about territory and property can be seen mirrored in any domesticated primate[1] (human) community in the plethora of "NO TRESPASSING" signs.

Most primates mark their territories with excretions; domesticated primates mark their territories with *ink excretions* on paper (treaties, land titles, etc.). From the biological perspective, every national border in Europe, for instance, marks a place where two rival gangs of domesticated primates fought until exhausted and then left a territorial mark.

Due to the unique capacity of domesticated primates (evidently including chimpanzees, according to some recent reports) to learn neurosemantic systems (codes: languages), it becomes possible for these unique mammals to "own" (or think they "own") *symbolic territories* as well as physical territories. These symbolic territories are usually called "ideologies" or "belief systems"—in our preferred terminology, reality-tunnels.

Domesticated primates battle not only over physical territories but over these "mental" or neurosemantic territories: York versus Lancaster becomes the Red Rose versus the White. "Communism" versus "Free Enterprise." The Big Endians versus the Little Endians. Etc.

If a donkey kicks a donkey, as some cynic once remarked, that is a matter between two donkeys, but if a Spaniard kicks the King of France, all the citizens of those nations may become involved in the kind of territorial frenzy known as "war." This will be proceeded by a great deal of what an extraterrestrial would call "*noise*"; those who have entered the Western Linguistic reality-tunnel will recognize the "noise" as including signals concerning "national honor," "an unforgivable outrage," "our duty to our nation," "cowardly appeasers who would crawl on their bellies," etc. etc. These "noises" are as *real and meaningful*, to those in that existential reality, as the "noises" of Beethoven's Ninth are to those in the Classical Music reality-tunnel.

Mark Twain once remarked that anti-semitism reminded him of a cat he once knew who sat on a hot stove once and never sat on a hot stove again. "What's wrong with that?" asked an anti-semite, falling into Twain's trap. "The stupid cat never sat on a cold stove either," Twain replied. This illustrates the generalization that mammals seem incapable of criticizing or examining their neural programs. To a dog or a cat or a monkey, some act or event or thing that seemed "bad" once will always seem "bad" and it, or anything that looks like it, will be attacked or fled. Such programs are created by processes known as *imprinting* and *conditioning*, which seem quite mechanical, in that observing them can yield predictions that will be verified, as precisely in many cases, as the predictions of Newtonian mechanics.

Domesticated primates (humans) seem also to function largely on *imprinting* and *conditioning*, and mostly they share the mammalian inability to criticize or examine these neurological programs. These mechanical reactions interact with a linguistic (emic) reality-tunnel to produce a characteristic vocabulary, from which *behavior* can often be predicted mechanically. If one hears the metaphors and/or cuss-words of the Ku Klux Klan, one can guess how a Black human will be treated in that group. If one hears the language system of Radical Feminism, one knows how a male human will be regarded. If one hears the noises of Fundamentalist Materialism, one knows how an allegation of "ESP" will be received. Etc.

It appears that *some* domesticated primates, over the aeons, have not precisely evolved but have learned *how to criticize and examine their own neurological programs*. Members of this group cannot be mechanically predicted. They exhibit, at times at least, what looks like "growth" or "creativity," although it is possible for Fundamentalist Materialists to insist that this "*is really*" random behavior or behavior whose determinants had not yet been understood.

Leaving aside these experiences or hallucinations of "creativity" and "growth" or self-criticism and self-overcoming—we shall return to them—it appears that most of what I have been calling Idolatry and Fundamentalism can be biologically described as normal primate behavior—mechanical imprinting and conditioning combined with normal territorial pugnacity.

And in that case—unless some real possibility of *creative* thought exists—only mechanical primate programs will determine how we evaluate any incident or event, from the chair across the room to yarns about bleeding Catholic statues or charmed quarks or UFOs.

Artists, like mystics, are forever insisting that we do not *look* closely enough at the world, that we do not *see*, etc. In our terms, this means that we follow conditioned programs so much that we do not stop to exercise our potential creativity. The artist tries to jar us out of this conditioned or hypnotic state by showing us a normal thing in a new way. The mystic tries to jar us by telling us to sit and look at a wall or an apple or something until—through the stress of social and sensory deprivation—we stop "seeing" what we always saw and start "seeing" in a new way. We are using neither the artistic nor the mystic method here but are trying to look at those things which are normally ignored or dismissed—to look at them without first placing one of our habitual Idols in the way of our vision—

And then, when we look back at the normal world again, at that chair across the room, will it *still* be quite normal for us?

The late J.B. Priestly often animadverted upon what he called *the Citadel*—the scientific-technological elite which both supports and is supported by our military-industrial *alpha males*. The Citadel, in most countries, gets millions of pounds for every twopence doled out to the humanities, the social studies or the arts; it devotes most of its time and intellect to the task, as Bucky Fuller used to say, of delivering more and more explosive power over greater and greater distances in shorter and shorter times to kill more and more people. For this reason, the Citadel increasingly frightens most of us and there is a vast, somewhat incoherent rebellion against it all around the world. This rebellion takes the form, most of the time, of return to some earlier philosophy or reality-tunnel, although within the scientific community there is also a rebellion which is seeking a *new* reality-tunnel, which is usually called the New Paradigm.

The Citadel has always been arrogant and intensely territorial. After all, it grew out of the science and philosophy of the 18th-19th centuries, and has inherited many qualities of that epoch, including anti-religious bias (the Citadel had to fight the Church to find its own place in the world) and also including tacit allegiance to the political powers that support and *feed* it. Since I regard the rank-and-file of the Citadel as domesticated primates—a term both scientific and satiric, which I also apply to myself and my friends—I am not surprised or appalled by its territorial pugnacity. The Arts Department is equally territorial in its own way. I *am* appalled, I admit, by the cold-bloodedness with which the Citadel detachedly hatches greater and greater potential holocausts— but that is a subject for another book, concerning the *humanitarian* objections to the Citadel. In the present book, I am concerned with the *libertarian* objections to the Citadel—with the evidence of its increasing intolerance and inquisitorial attitude toward all old or new paradigms which conflict with its own favorite reality-tunnel.

In casting a Swiftian eye on the modern Laputa, I am not advocating any specific old or new paradigm; I am merely advocating agnosticism and tolerance of dissent, for the usual reasons that political libertarians advocate those attitudes. As Lord Acton said, all power corrupts, and I think the Citadel has acquired enough power and corruption to become, at times, as dangerous to open enquiry and free speculation as the Church ever was.

Of course, "the Citadel" is a metaphor, a rhetorical convenience. Many of the most creative scientists of the past half-century have dissented vehemently from official Citadel dogma and even engaged in Heresy[2]; and a surprising number of "Scientific" Materialists are not scientists at all but cranky Village Atheists left over from horse-and-buggy days.

We will now consider the rather peculiar case of a cat who is dead and alive at the same time.

This flexible feline first appeared in Volume 23 of *Der Naturwissenschaft* (1935) and is the progeny of Dr. Erwin Schrodinger, Nobel laureate in physics.

Some of you will be relieved to know that this cat is only theoretical.

Others will find "cold" or at best lukewarm comfort in that, because—just as, once you have entered the emic reality of Western classical music, Beethoven means *something*, even if he perhaps does not mean as much to you personally as Bach or Mozart—once you have entered the reality-tunnel of quantum physics, Schrodinger's damned cat means *something*, even if no two quantum physicists I have met can agree what the deuce the cat does mean.

This is the case: inside the atom, or below the atomic level, are various thingamajigs—we cannot be more specific—which are sometimes called waves and sometimes called particles. If the reader has digested the earlier part of this chapter, that can be translated: the thingamajigs can be usefully described in a wave model part of the time and in a particle model the other part of the time.

If we want to know what one of the sub-atomic thingamajigs is doing or where it is going, we find "the" answer in one of the equations for which Dr. Schrodinger won the Nobel prize. The equation—and the nonmathematical reader need not be alarmed at this point— happens to look like this:

$$\frac{\partial \Psi}{\partial t} = -\frac{\hbar}{2m}\nabla^2 \Psi + V(x,y,z)\,\Psi$$

The first side of the equation $\frac{\partial \Psi}{\partial t}$ means the rate of change in time (t) of Ψ ; we will explain Ψ , soft of, in a moment. The other part of the equation tells what that rate of change is. We need not, in this book, concern ourselves about all of the symbols. The x, y and z are merely the spatial coordinates which even the most nonmathematical may remember vaguely from analytical geometry classes in secondary school, while $\hbar$ would require a lengthy essay on quantum mechanics to be explained fully. For the purposes of ordinary understanding (if we are not to embark on careers as quantum physicists) it is enough to note that all the symbols on the right denote properties of the sub-atomic system in question, and then to note that they are all multiplied by the mysterious Ψ .

For the sake of ordinary simplicity in the lay sense (*not* mathematical simplicity) we can regard the right-hand side of the equation as

A Ψ +B Ψ

—which is to indicate, more clearly, that all the symbols in the first half of the expression are multiplied by Ψ and so are all the symbols on the left half.

So what is Ψ ?

Ψ is the symbol for the components of the "state vector." Note that the word "components" is plural. When I asked a friendly physicist, Saul Paul Sirag, for a definition of the state vector that would be accurate but also comprehensible to non-physicists, I got the following from him:

> The state vector is the mathematical expression describing one of *two or more* states that a quantum system can be in; for instance, an electron can be in either of two spin states, called "spin up" and "spin down." The amusing thing about quantum mechanics is that each state vector can be regarded as the superposition of other state vectors.

The important part of that definition is the part Sirag italicized. Any state vector, Ψ , has two or more components. This underlies the one generalization about quantum mechanics that every layperson has heard of by now—their indeterminacy. Physicists cannot predict what a quantum system will do; they can only calculate the probability that it will arrive at each of *two or more* possible states. This equation is used in calculating such probabilities. It gives us probabilities, not certainties, because Ψ is itself uncertain, or has more than one possible value.

This indeterminacy was a hard pill for physicists to swallow; it was even hard for Dr. Schrodinger, who worked out the mathematics of it. This is where the two-valued cat comes in. Schrodinger invented the cat problem as a way of bringing to the forefront of debate and philosophical analysis among physicists the question of what this quantum indeterminacy means to our ideas of actuality.

The case assumes a cat in a box, together with some sort of lethal device, such as a pistol or a poison-gas pellet, which may discharge and kill the cat. The device will discharge and kill the cat at some stage of a quantum decay process. We want to know, at a given second, t, if the device has gone off and killed the cat yet. We solve the equation—and we find, in the "best possible case," where all the other functions are known, that that damned Ψ function, the state vector, is still in two states. The answer is then that the cat is both dead and alive at that moment.

Of course, common sense "knows" that this cannot be true—if we open the box, we will find either a dead cat or a living cat, not some monster in a mixed dead-and-alive state—

But mathematical quantum physics does not "know" this—it only "knows" that the state vector is in "a mixed state" (the expression is actually used) and therefore it predicts that the cat is in a mixed state, too—

So: do we believe mathematical physics or do we believe common sense?

Readers familiar only with one form or another of Fundamentalism will assume I am about to answer that question. I am not. As I said, Schrodinger first published the problem fifty years ago. That's half a century. In that time, the majority of physicists have arrived at no consensus about it. They are still arguing.

The argument for trusting common sense in this case sounds much of a muchness with the epistemology of the present chapter. The models of physics are abstractions from experience. They are coded into symbolisms, here technically called *formalisms*, which are useful at a time and in a given area of investigation. When formalisms is generalized—when the model is extended—and the results are "obviously" absurd, as in the Schrodinger's cat example, then we need to remember that the model is only a human invention or emic tool and not identical with *etic* (non-verbal) actuality.

You might say that those who hold this view are close to my position that if we believe a model in all cases we have become Idolators of the model.

The opposite position—and there are intermediate positions, too, as we shall see—starts by reminding us that that which is "obvious to common sense" is not always true. It adds that most great scientific breakthroughs were profound shocks to common sense at first—Copernicus was unbelievable to those who "knew" and felt deeply that they were standing on an Earth that did not move; Darwin was equally stunning to those who *knew* they were not primates; Einstein was almost incomprehensible at first to those who *knew* that a rod has only one length which is "objective"—

The proponents of this view usually add also that quantum mechanics has been one of the most fruitful areas in modern science; it underlies not only about half of modern physics (including the nuclear weapons that terrify us) but is crucial to many other fields, including television and computers and molecular biology. Those who argue this way say that we should dare, at least as an exercise, to think about the possibility that what the quantum model seems to imply may indeed be the case. If the quantum equations *mean nothing*, why does the technology based on them work?

The development of this view is known as the multiple-universe theory, or the EWG Model—named after Everett, Wheeler and Graham, who first proposed it—and says that each state vector does produce two or more results. Since these cannot all be in one universe, there are then many universes. In effect, anything that *can* happen, *does* happen—somewhere or other in some space-time continuum.

The latest spokesperson for this view is John Gribbin, physics editor of *New Scientist*, who writes forthrightly enough in his *In Search of Schrodinger's Cat*, Bantam, New York, 1984, p. 238:

> There is a live cat, and there is a dead cat; but they are located in different worlds. . . . Faced with a decision, the whole world—the universe—split into two versions of itself . . . (This theory) sounds like science fiction, but it goes far deeper than any science fiction, and it is based on impeccable mathematical equations, a consistent and logical consequence of taking quantum mechanics literally.

John Archibald Wheeler, one of the greatest living quantum physicists, helped create this model, but now says he no longer believes it. Dr. Bryce de Witt, who has written that he could not take this theory seriously when he first encountered it, has now become one of its leading advocates. Other physicists, whom we will discuss when we return to this topic in more detail, have found other ways around or under or over that damned dead-and-alive cat.

When our knowledge of the mathematical basis of physical structures is in this state—when physicists cannot agree with each other about what is a real possibility and what is a flight of fantasy— any Fundamentalism seems a bit premature.

SOMBUNALL. . .

Is this a new wonder-drug? The latest computer from Japan? The Swahili word for water-closet? Another borrowing from *Finnegans Wake*?

Sombunall is, I think, a word we badly need. It means *some-but-not-all*.

We have already pointed out that perception involves abstraction (or subtraction)—When we look at an apple we do not see all the apple but only part of the surface of the apple—And our generalizations or models or reality-tunnels are made up of coordinations or orchestrations of these abstractions—

We never know "all"; we know, at best, *sombunall*.

Now, to return to my frequent occupation of writing science fiction, imagine a world in which German did not contain the word "*alles*" or any of its derivatives, but did include some form of *sombunall*.

Adolph Hitler would never have been able to say, or even think, most of his generalizations about all Jews. At most, he would have been talking and thinking about sombunall Jews.

I don't claim this alone would necessarily have prevented the Holocaust—I am not about to offer some form of linguistic determinism to rival Marx's economic determinism or Hitler's own racial determinism, but—

Holocaust mentalities are *encouraged* by all-ness statements.

They are *discouraged* by sombunall statements.

Imagine Arthur Schopenhauer with a *sombunall* instead of *all* in his vocabulary. He could still have generalized about sombunall women, but not about all women; and a major source of literary misogyny would have vanished from our culture. Imagine the Feminists writing about sombunall men, but not about all men. Imagine a debate about UFOs in which both sides could generalize as much as they wished about sombunall sightings but there was no linguistic form to generalize about all such sightings.

Imagine what would happen if, along with this semantic hygiene, the Aristotelian *is* were replaced by the neurologically-accurate "seems to me."

"All modern music is junk" would become "sombunall modern music seems like junk to me." Other dogmatic statements would become, e.g. "Sombunall scientists seem to me ignorant of art and culture," "Sombunall artists seem to me ignorant of science," "Sombunall Englishmen seem to me a bit pompous," "Sombunall Irishmen seem to me to drink a lot" . . .

Idols would suddenly shrink back into models or reality-tunnels; we would remember that we created them, or that our ancestors did. We might become suddenly startlingly sane.

It's only a suggestion.

Medieval Idolatry consisted of metaphors that were called Revealed Truth. Modern Idolatry consists of metaphors that are called Objective Truth. In both cases *human linguistic structures*—complicated primate chatterings—have, in effect, become Gods, and whoever questions them is considered a blasphemer and the priests seek to destroy the impiety. That's how books get burned, in Florence in 1300 (or in New York in 1956, as we shall see).

To replace one set of metaphors with another set of metaphors may be an advance in predictability, and hence in technology, but it does not necessarily create an advance in intelligence.

To regard metaphor *as metaphor* and not as a kind of God might create a real advance in intelligence, and in behavior.

Every reality-tunnel or neurosemantic system encourages us to "see" (and give importance to) *some* information—to pay close attention to a certain kind of signals. The astronomers who believe in the tenth planet beyond Pluto (for mathematical reasons) are, for instance, looking very closely at signals from that part of space-time. A painter is looking very closely, meanwhile, at a different class of signals, involving a different space-time game. A poet, or a certain kind of poet, is more interested in sounds and connotations than in purely visual stimuli. Etc.

Every reality-tunnel, alas, also tends to *discourage* attention and alertness to some other classes of signals. I am annoyed when the phone rings while I am writing. Bobby Fisher, the American chess champion, allegedly interrupted a political discussion on one occasion to ask irritably, "What the hell does that have to do with chess?" As C.P. Snow once pointed out, most artists not only don't know the Second Law of Thermodynamics but aren't even ashamed of their ignorance in that case; it is simply irrelevant, they think.

Due to the territorial imperatives of primate neurology, some information is not only ignored but actively resisted. Denial, anger or even desire to punish the messenger who brings "bad news" are well-known traits of our species. To the extent that we are aware of this tendency, and try to combat it in ourselves, we will make efforts to *seek* unwelcome signals—e.g. by reading periodicals of the groups whose reality-tunnels oppose our own, as Bertrand Russell often recommended. To the extent that we ignore or forget this primate tendency in ourselves, we will lapse into Fundamentalism, Idolatry and the Inquisitorial mode of behavior.

Civil liberties are profoundly counter-intuitive. It takes an effort of imagination and good will to remember that those we despise deserve the same legal rights as those who agree with us.

At least a partial agnosticism is necessary before we can sincerely and consistently pursue the goal of "equal justice for all."

You have a new dog and you wish the dog to treat you (rather than another member of your family) as "Master." The first rule is to *feed* the dog regularly, and, if possible, in early months, make sure no other member of the family ever feeds the dog.

In ethological jargon, the dog will *imprint* you as the equivalent of Top

Dog in a wild dog pack, or the closest analog to that Top Dog in a domesticated canine-primate ambience.

Similarly, all brainwashers use this principle—usually unconsciously—by feeding their victims. This is necessary to keep the victims alive until their minds have been re-conditioned, of course, but it may also be a re-imprinting technique. We are mammals, too, and we tend to imprint as Top Dog those who feed us when we are helpless. The "paradoxical" sympathy for terrorists often reported by those who are held captive may also grow out of this neurological tendency to make a Top Dog out of *whoever* feeds us.

It is shocking, to some, to think that this may also be the origin of the infant's love for its mother.

One cannot help wondering how much of the reality-tunnel of the Military-Industrial Empire gets imprinted or conditioned upon the Scientific Citadel which is fed by it.

1   My reasons for regarding humans as domesticated animals are given in my *Prometheus Rising* (Falcon Press, 1983) and dramatized comically in my science-fantasy trilogy *Schrodinger's Cat* (Sphere Books, 1981). Here it can be said briefly that as the *alpha male* of a wild primate pack evolved into the "king" or "Executive" of a human social group, a class-and-caste system was produced which gave birth to those traits called "alienation" (Marx), "repression" (Freud), "slave morality" (Nietzsche) *"anomie"* (Durkheim); all of these are names, in other models, for what I name *domestication*. See also the discussion in Buckminster Fuller's *Critical Path* (St. Martin's Press, 1981) of the evolution from mammalian *alpha male* to the "Great Pirates" who have domesticated and fleeced the sheep-like masses throughout history. We will discuss this further in the last chapter, in explaining why men are easily led to a place where it is statistically certain that some of them will have their legs blown off.

2   Among physicists, Einstein had a personal "Cosmic Religion," which sounds like pantheism to me; Schrodinger, Oppenheimer and Bohm have all been influenced by Oriental mysticism; Bohr said his favorite philosophers were the mystic pragmatist, William James, and the Christian existentialist, Kierkegaard, and took a Taoist religious symbol for his Coat of Arms when knighted by the Danish court. The English astronomers, Jeans and Eddington, both became mystics; the American astronomer, Hynek, dissents from Citadel dogma by insisting UFOs are worthy of serious investigation; Edison

became a Spiritualist, and two other electrical pioneers, Tesla and Marconi, insisted, despite ridicule, that they had received intelligent signals from outer space. America's most respected anthropologist, Margaret Mead, fought tooth and nail to get the heretical parapsychologists admitted to the American Association for the Advancement of Science. The great biologist-mathematician, J.B.S. Haldane, preferred Marx's dynamic Dialectical Materialism to Fundamentalist Materialism and studied Yoga seriously. Etc.

CHAPTER TWO

SKEPTICISM AND BLIND FAITH

(with comments on book-burning, biological surrealism and Game Rules)

Thou shalt not make unto thee any graven image, or
likeness of any thing that is in the heaven above, or that is
in the earth beneath, or that is in the water under the earth:
Thou shalt not bow down thyself to them, nor serve them

Exodus 20:4-5

Religious Fundamentalists of the extreme sort often take the above verse literally and regard all art as a Sin against God. Religious Liberals, on the other hand, are aware that a sentence with a colon in the middle must be read as a whole. They say, reasonably, that the above text is not forbidding the making of images and likenesses in itself; it is forbidding the act of *worshipping* an image or likeness. In terms of logic, the author (Moses or God, as you will) does not condemn p *or* q—making an image *or* worshipping it—but p *and* q—making an image *and* worshipping it.

That's a bit of a relief to those of us who like to make images. As an artist (to the extent that a novelist may still be called an artist these days) I make images, or metaphors, or parables—call them what you will— but I do not bow down and worship them, nor do I expect my readers to comport themselves in that undignified manner.

Nonetheless, any image or metaphor can quickly become an Idol if it is not immediately identified as an art-work; Bacon and Nietzsche (among others) have animadverted on that subject before me.

It is the thesis of this book that since the passing of the Old Idolatry and the Old Inquisition, we have seen, without recognizing what was happening, the rise of a New Idolatry and a New Inquisition. Of course, that thesis is a polemical position, a wild satirical exaggeration, a fancy bit of rhetoric.

Of course.

Nonetheless, in the following pages I will examine scandals that most people would rather forget and look into yarns that the comfortable would rather ignore. You might call this an expedition into the philosophical unconscious, where materialist society buries its repressed *fantasies and fears.*

I suspect that I shall make myself unpopular.

I shall exhibit learned men behaving with the bigotry of Mississippi lynch-mobs, distinguished scholars conspiring to suppress dissident opinions, savants acting like circus clowns or hooligans.

I shall regale you (or annoy you) with creatures who pass (almost) as wolves but who are not wolves—signs and wonders in the sky, very few of which are conventional enough to be called flying saucers—cats with wings, a two-headed goat and a talking mongoose—flying furniture, levitating mammals, phantom trains—a lady who seems to have climbed Mount Everest in high heels—and a man who might have made a rain storm with a non-existent energy before the defenders of Reason burned his books and threw him in prison. I will resurrect buried heresies, defend the indefensible, try to think about the unthinkable.

Of course, *most* of this is merely offered as intellectual *entertainment*, as philosophical comedy in the manner of the Greek sophists who would argue absurd propositions just to baffle and bewilder the orthodox. I hardly expect the ordinary, common-sense reader to take much of it seriously—anymore than the average reader of 1905 would consider for a moment that space and time might be relative to the observer.

Personally, I am not brave enough, or mad enough, to believe all of what follows. I utter sarcasms: I raise subversive doubts: I turn Idols upside-down and ask embarrassing questions about the King's New Clothes—but it is all in the spirit of fun. Honestly. No more malicious than *Gulliver's Travels* actually.

But I quote the warning of the linguistic philosopher, Josiah Warren: "It is dangerous to understand new things too quickly."

I might *possibly* be a little bit serious, part of the time.

The priests who serve the Citadel—the scientific-technological Elite of our time—are paid workers, on salary, and most of their earnings derive from the military-industrial complex that owns, and governs, most of the world, and wishes to own, and govern, the rest of the world as well.

One does not have to be a dogmatic Marxist to accept some of the Marxist reality-tunnel—sombunall of it—and wonder if the priests of the Citadel have a *vested economic interest* in supporting the axioms of their employers and of imperialist-materialist philosophy in general. For instance, it has been hazardous to economic self-interest in some cases to wander even as far from Fundamentalist Materialism as to accept the "heresy" of Dialectical Materialism. To embrace a non-violent religious sect means, in many cases, that one is obliged by conscience to resign from the Citadel.

These are potent, if tacit, factors in determining the reality-tunnel within the Citadel.

Most of the employees of the Citadel are white and most are male. These are other potent sources of bias and one can even predict from them what sort of ideas, in general, are regarded as "unthinkable" within the Citadel.

To deny that these economic-statistical factors influence the models and reality-tunnels in the Citadel is to contradict the major findings of the last hundred years of sociology, anthropology and social psychology.

That the philosophy of Fundamentalist Materialism is the only known philosophy that justifies the behavior of the military-industrial complex is hardly a coincidence. Christianity, Buddhism, Existentialism, and most other philosophies regard the materialist-militarist elite as *monstrous.*

Back on page 7 I asked you to play the Aristotelian Logic game and classify some propositions as "true" or "false."

The first of these propositions was "Water boils at 100 degrees Celsius."

Within the Aristotelian game, with only two choices, it is probable that most of us would classify this proposition as "true." Since the invention of the thermometer, most people have found this statement true.

That is because most people have lived at or near sea-level, historically.

Those who live in the Alps, the Rocky Mountains or the Himalayas— and those scientists who have done research at such altitudes—realize that the statement needs to be modified before we can call it true. It should say "Water boils at 100 degrees Celsius *at sea-level on this planet.*"

Similarly, the second proposition—"pq equals qp"—is only true, or valid, within ordinary algebra. It is not true in the equally valid (self-consistent) algebra invented by William Rowan Hamilton.

It is possible that "truth" only exists when one has already specified the *context or field* within which one is speaking.

The third proposition—"The Communists are plotting to enslave us"—may require even more pedantic analysis before we come to any conclusion about it. I leave it for the reader to ponder a while longer before I return to this subject. . .

Perhaps what I am doing in this damned crazy book is demonstrating a new quasi-Newtonian law *in psychology*—a law whereby every mental action produces an equal and opposite mental reaction, so that every Idol, or obsession, if worshipped devoutly enough (and humorlessly enough) gradually turns into its own opposite.

In particular, we will see evidence that *skepticism* and *blind faith* often turn into each other if somebody is logical enough, or mad enough, to pursue them to that point of pure abstract consistency where ordinary common sense is left behind in the rush for certitude.

It is obvious that every dogmatic faith produces around itself a secondary layer of doubt, denial and outright skepticism—about rival faiths. The most bigoted Bible Fundamentalist, for instance, is capable of quite corrosive cynicism about the miracles of Buddha. The most fanatic Marxist is also a cynic, about the infallibility of the Pope. The Ayatollah Khoumeini believes every word of the *Koran*, he says—but he is downright atheistic about the pronouncements of the U.S. State Department. This is universal: every faith, every acceptance, creates a necessary doubt, or rejection, or things outside the faith. Every Idol is jealous of other Idols.

Less obviously, the humorless or obsessive or crusading skeptic has his or her own blind faith, a psychological scotoma that is unconscious and therefore unacknowledged. To deny dogmatically is to say that something is *impossible*. But to assert this is to claim, tacitly, that you already know *the full spectrum of the possible*. In a century in which every decade has brought new and astonishing scientific shocks, that is a huge, brave and audacious faith indeed. It requires an almost heroic self-confidence and an equally gigantic ignorance of recent intellectual history.

The only escape from this trap, as far as I can see, is to be skeptical about one's own skepticism: which is what I mean by "the New Agnosticism."

Fall 1984 *The Skeptical Inquirer* (journal of the Committee for the Scientific Investigation of Claims of the Paranormal) Vol IX No 1, p 44, article by Professor Mario Munge—"Likewise telepathy may be a fact after all—though not clairvoyance, precognition, or psychokinesis, all of which conflict with basic physical laws." Leaving aside Prof. Munge's odd tolerance about telepathy—Black Heresy to get printed in *that* journal!—note well what his sentence says and what it implies. It seems to me that it implies that he already knows all the laws of the universe, or all the *important* ones; and that is what I mean by a huge and audacious faith.

To you and me and the man and woman in the street it is now obvious that nobody in the past ever knew all the laws, or all the important laws; the scientists of 1904 were astounded by the discoveries of 1910; those of 1914 by the discoveries of 1920; etc. From this we have learned a certain mild agnosticism or open-mindedness; we are prepared to be startled by new discoveries. Prof. Munge is not so prepared; he knows in advance what is possible and what is not possible. Few theologians these days dare to speak with that kind of dogmatic Authority. Prof. Munge's "skepticism" has become a blind faith, a faith that he *knows* in 1984 what may and may not be proved in 1990.

Since this book is a venture in guerilla ontology—an attempt to enlarge our concept of the thinkable, in the tradition of Nietzsche, surrealism, Pataphysics and Charles Fort—it will predictably be denounced violently by the Citadel and by those self-described skeptics, like Prof. Munge, who have a blind faith in current Idols, accepted paradigms and the local tribal reality-tunnel in general. Because I have a vulgar taste for a little baroque rhetoric now and then, I shall continue to call these high priests of the modern Idol, the *New Inquisition*, and refer to their dogmatic reality-tunnel as the *New Fundamentalism*.

These are not intended solely as terms of abuse such as all polemicists try to hang around the necks of their opponents. I wish to distinguish between liberals and fundamentalists, in science as well as in religion, and even in general philosophy. For instance, one who has had his mind enlarged or ruined by a good course in epistemology might come out a fundamentalist, or absolutist, Humean—convinced that all proof is impossible and no idea is any more valid than another. But a wiser and less logical student might become merely a liberal Humean—one who holds that no proof is absolute but some ideas are more plausible than others, e.g. "If it rains, the streets will get wet." Similarly, there are liberal Theists everywhere these days, who will cheerfully admit there is no undeniable argument for God's existence, but still think the case for God a little better than the case against God. And, of course, there are fundamentalist Theists, survivors of the Old Inquisition, who would happily burn at the stake anybody who has any doubts on the matter at all.

The *liberal* materialist, then, I define as one who holds that materialism is a "relative best bet" among competing philosophies, or the most plausible model around, whereas the *fundamentalist* materialist— either out of ignorance of philosophy or out of sheer bravado or out of blind faith—proclaims that materialism is the One True Philosophy and that anyone with doubts or hesitations about it is insane, perverse or a deliberate fraud. This One True Philosophy is the modern form of the One True Church of the dark ages. The fundamentalist materialist is the modern Idolator; he has made an image of the world, and now he kneels and worships it.

Fundamentalist science is similar to other fundamentalisms. Lacking humor, charity and some measure of self-doubt, it behaves intolerantly, fanatically and *savagely* to all "heretics." Eventually, like all closed ideological systems, it becomes comical and overtly ridiculous—and that shall be my main demonstration.

Because it provides a certain drama, or a certain low comedy, I shall write as if the New Fundamentalists are firmly entrenched in power structures everywhere in the modern world and really act like a New Inquisition toward those who reject their Idol. I confess again that this rhetoric is, like all polemics, exaggerated and wicked. Really. The men of the Citadel have never burned books, or conspired to suppress books, or faked evidence to support their own prejudices, or engaged in calculated smear campaigns against those who differ from them. They are honorable men, all honorable men. Of course.

Nonetheless—see *The Quest for Wilhelm Reich*, by Colin Wilson, Grenada Books, London—

In October 1957, agents of the U.S. government went to the Orgone Institute Press in New York City; they seized all the books; they loaded the books into a comandeered garbage truck; they drove to the Vandivoort Street incinerator; they burned the books.

This was not "back in the dark ages"; it was only a few years ago. It did not happen in a fascist or Marxist dictatorship but in a nation whose constitution specifically forbids that pyromaniac way of disposing of unpopular ideas. And it was not instigated by religious fanatics but by those "scientific" fanatics whom J.B. Priestly dubbed the Citadel.

The books were by Dr. Wilhelm Reich, a former student of Freud and a political radical. Dr. Reich had been a Communist briefly and a Socialist for a while and eventually developed his own Ideology, called Work Democracy, which can be briefly described as more-or-less similar to the Guild Socialism of Chesterton, the Anarchism of Kropotkin and the Libertarian Marxism currently fashionable among rebels against orthodox Marxism. Dr. Reich also believed that all Ideologies, including his own, were unworkable until a Sexual Revolution of psychological (not political) nature occurred and people were no longer ashamed of their bodily functions.

Dr. Reich annoyed the American Medical Association by taking an extreme "psychosomatic" position, holding that almost all illness was caused by *repression*, in both the Freudian and political senses—i.e. that domesticated primates had been trained to a kind of masochistic submissiveness that literally made them sick, both "physically" and "mentally." Reich also annoyed the powerful American Psychoanalytical

Association by claiming that Freudian therapy did not cure anything in itself and needed to be supplemented by what is now called "body work"—various techniques to relax the muscles and normalize the breathing. Worst of all, he mortally offended the Citadel by insisting that all nuclear energy (even in "peaceful" industry) was unhealthy for humans, and, to ensure his unpopularity, he directly challenged the New Fundamentalism by alleging the existence of a new energy characteristic of living beings, which he called *orgone*, which was suspiciously like the "vital force" posited by anti-materialists such as Bergson and Bernard Shaw.

The propaganda war against Reich had been led by Martin Gardner, a Scientific Fundamentalist whom we shall meet many times in these pages. Mr. Gardner has an infallible method of recognizing real science and of recognizing pseudo-science. Real science is what agrees with his Idol and pseudo-science is what challenges that Idol. Colin Wilson has written, "I wish I could be as sure of anything as Martin Gardner is of everything." Not all the Popes of the 20th Century collectively have dared to issue as many absolute dogmas as Mr. Gardner; no man has had such superb faith in his own utter correctness since Oliver Cromwell.

Mr. Gardner's papal bulls against the Reichian heresy are very interesting, and very typical of fundamentalism when enraged, in that one finds a strong, very strong implication that Dr. Reich was insane and hallucinating, although this is never stated directly and unambiguously. It is even possible for a defender of Mr. Gardner to claim that that sentence is unfair, because Gardner never explicitly said Reich was as crazy as a dancing mouse—he merely says, e.g. that Reich's books sound "like comic opera." Nonetheless, the *suggestion* of mental unbalance is heavily present in everything Gardner wrote about Dr. Reich. This *suggestion* is almost always implied in fundamentalist diatribes against those who do not accept their Idol. One might say that they are not *sure* you must be crazy to disagree with them but they strongly suspect it.

To the best of my knowledge, having followed the literature of the Reich controversy for nearly 30 years, there is no place in Gardner's writings where he claims that he repeated Dr. Reich's experiments and obtained results contrary to Reich's claims. As an agnostic, I suppose it is possible that Mr. Gardner did make this assertion somewhere, but if he did so, he must have so asserted in a very obscure periodical, with a very low circulation, and the reports of his experiments have not been reprinted in any publication findable by me. It appears, from available sources, that Mr. Gardner did not conduct any experiments to test Dr. Reich's claims. It appears that Mr. Gardner had, or thought he had, the same kind of knowledge as Prof. Munge—he *knew* what was possible and what was impossible, so he did not have to investigate.

While Mr. Gardner, and several others, denounced Dr. Reich in the media, members of the American Medical Association and American Psychoanalytical Association pressured the government to prosecute Reich as a crank or a "charlatan." Dr. Reich, either out of delusions of grandeur or out of principled commitment to libertarian ideals—take your choice—refused to admit that the government had any right to pass judgment on scientific theories, and as a result was convicted only of contempt of court. Nonetheless, the government followed this with the book-burning, and with *the destruction by ax of equipment in Dr. Reich's research laboratory*, and then threw him in prison, where he died of a heart attack after a few months. Reich's co-worker, Dr. Michael Silvert, subsequently committed suicide.

It would be comforting to think Reich *was* a nut, a raving cuckoo, as Gardner implies. That is the sane, conservative attitude to take. It is a bit unnerving to think that books that get burned in democratic nations might have something valuable in them, like the books that get burned in undemocratic nations.

Still—burning books is a bit *thick*. It leaves a bad smell, to those of us raised on Burke and Jefferson and Mill.

And Reich was not the only victim of the New Inquisition. There have been others. We wll meet them as we go along.

The New Idol might be as blind and savage as the old?

Oh, no: I admitted that was only melodramatic rhetoric.

But —

Just suppose Dr. Reich was even partly or occasionally right. After all, even a stopped clock is right twice a day. But the Citadel burned all of his books, all. Thirty years of scientific research dumped into a flaming garbage incinerator, a burnt offering to the Moloch of orthodoxy. The books included *The Impulsive Personality*, *The Function of the Orgasm*, *Character Analysis*, *The Mass Psychology of Fascism*, *The Sexual Revolution*, *People in Trouble*, *The Murder of Christ*, *The Cancer Biopathy*, and others. Thirty years of reports on psychotherapeutic practise; sociological observations of Nazi and Communist party members and their work situations and family relations; laboratory research on bio-electrical charge and discharge in orgasm; clinical studies of the psychology of cancer and asthma patients; dozens of alleged experiments with the alleged "orgone" energy. All of it burned, consumed.

I have no idea how much of that 30-some years of work was sound, how much unsound. I know that the Reich orgasm formula of four stages of physiological excitation and relaxation has been confirmed by Masters and Johnson, and that his analysis of the fascist personality has been widely accepted by other psychologists, and that many of the therapeutic techniques he pioneered are widely in use in the United States—such as teaching the patient to scream and weep and strike out with the fists. I do not, from that, deduce that *all* of Reich's ideas were correct. I think it might take perhaps two decades of work, by several independent scientific groups, to sort out how much of the "orgone" theory is sound and how much it is perhaps as loony as Gardner and the fundamentalist materialists claim. I see only one certitude in this whole tragedy of book-burning and independent intellect caged in a prison:

Thou shalt not blaspheme the new Idol.

I must emphasize that neither Mr. Gardner nor any of the other Fundamentalists who write diatribes against Dr. Reich were responsible for the book-burning, which was entirely the responsibility of the scientists and bureaucrats working for the U.S. government itself— the muscle of the Citadel, as it were. Nonetheless, the Citadel as a whole looked on, unmoved. *Only 18 psychiatrists in the whole country signed a protest against the book burning.*

Mr. Gardner himself, in the revised edition of one of his books—*Fads and Fallacies in the Name of Science*, Dover, New York, 1957—expresses repugnance at the burning of Reich's works.

Nonetheless, the New Inquisition rolled along. None of Dr. Reich's books could legally be printed in the U.S. until 1967. Those who would have liked to have formed an independent opinion of the scientific issues were legally unable to see or touch or even smell the *verboten* pages.

And the inquisitorial spirit continues today. While many psychologists admit some soundness in some of Reich's ideas, he is not "respectable" to the Citadel in general, and biologists and physicists never mention his alleged "orgone," except to sneer at it. This attitude survives despite that fact that nobody has yet published, in a major scientific journal—or any small journal known to me—experiments that refute or contradict Reich's claims. The Citadel feels no need to test Reich's ideas, it seems.

The intuitive certainty of Gardner and Prof. Munge appears to be widespread, almost omnipresent, in the Citadel. Everybody there "knows" Dr. Reich was wrong, so nobody bothers to investigate the matter.

There have been a few heretics, of course, but they have been ignored.

In 1962 appeared *A New Method of Weather Control* by Charles Kelley, privately printed. Kelley had been working for the U.S. Weather Bureau when Dr. Reich, just before his imprisonment, wrote to them that he would produce a rain storm in Maine to demonstrate the existence of his officially non-existent "orgone" energy.

The rain storm happened.

We have already explained that, of course—even a stopped clock is right twice a day. Besides, *it was only coincidence*. (Remember that phrase. It is the self-hypnotic chant by which the New Inquisition banishes all evidence it does not like. We will hear it often.)

But Kelley was intrigued by the man who made a storm with non-existent energy. He repeated Dr. Reich's weather-control experiments. His book has photos of his alleged results. The photos conclusively prove that Dr. Reich's experiments work, or else that Kelley is good at faking photos—as all photos that challenge the dogmas of the New Inquisition are *by definition* fakes, of course—

Still—the impulse to sin and heresy is in all of us—well, except for such stalwarts of Faith as Gardner and Munge—and some will dare to wonder: suppose Kelley did not fake those photos?

That's the way the powers of darkness seduce us. The path to hell is easy. You think a thought like that and the next thing—you are wondering about UFOs or "ESP" or even, God help you, astrology. You might end up meditating and eating vegetables.

The Reich controversy is not dead, even though the books were burned and the man was buried. Every few years a new book comes out by somebody, some spawn of the devil, who claims that, like Kelley, he repeated Dr. Reich's experiments and got positive results. In *Orgone, Reich and Eros*, sociologist Erik Mann describes his experiments with an orgone blanket that worked, or seemed to. In *Love and Orgasm*, Alexander Lowen, M.D. cautiously uses the vague expression "bio-energy" instead of the verboten "orgone," but says his work with patients confirms Reich's claims. In *Orgone and Me*, actor Orson Bean says he could *see* the damned "orgone" after being treated by an orgonomic physician, Dr. Baker. In *The Cosmic Pulse of Life*, retired Naval officer Trevor Constable has photos that either confirm Reich or show that Constable, like Kelley, knows how to fake photos.

They're all hallucinating, of course, except the ones with photos, who are frauds. Of course; of course. Knowing that, by definition, we don't have to go to the trouble of checking their claims.

Still—a few may have growing doubts at this point.

I don't know. I am not particularly interested, here, in how much of Reich was right or wrong. I present the Reich case as one illustration of how the current Idol, the orthodoxy of biological materialism, maintains itself. It does so all the way all orthodoxies and Idols have always maintained themselves. We will see more of this when we come to the case of Dr. Sheldrake, the English biologist who rediscovered the damned "orgone," or something a lot like it, and called it the "morphogenetic field."

Going back a bit, if "Water boils at 100 degrees Celsius" is only true at sea-level on this planet—and perhaps at a few similar places in space-time, but not *everywhere* in space-time—and if "pq equals qp" is only true (or "valid") within one kind of algebra—

Then, perhaps "truth" is only relative to a context of some sort?

Well, maybe. I don't expect everybody to jump to that conclusion at once. We are trying to move from a kind of first-plateau skepticism to a kind of second-plateau skepticism. We aren't going to leap blindly to *n*th-plateau skepticism quite yet.

However, we might remember the opinion of Sir Karl Popper, who holds that we can never establish Absolute Truth since that would require an infinite number of tests; Popper also argues that Absolute Falsity *can* be established, since a statement in *absolute* form is falsified once a single exception to it is found.

If we accept this view, which seems historically plausible, then the Aristotelian true/false game becomes relative to our knowledge at a particular time in history and should be modified *at least* to "Relatively True" and "Absolutely False."

For instance, unless we are excessively pedantic, "Ronald Reagan wrote *Hamlet*" should be considered Absolutely False. If we *want* to be excessively pedantic, we can rewrite this proposition as "Ronald Reagan wrote the version of *Hamlet* attributed to Shakespeare," and then it is Absolutely False, since we know of *at least one* (and, in fact, many) copies of "Shakespeare's" *Hamlet* that were in print before Mr.

Reagan was born. (We thus avoid the "tricky" possibility that Mr. Reagan wrote his own version of *Hamlet* in youth and then went stark staring sane and destroyed it—as I destroyed my own poetic effusions of youth—)

How about our proposition 3, "The infamous Dr. Crippen poisoned his wife"? We stipulate that "the infamous Dr. Crippen" is the Dr. Crippen that most readers are thinking of, the first man arrested by wireless telegraphy: *that* Dr. Crippen.

This proposition, like the ones about the boiling point of water and pq being equal to qp, appears at least Relatively True, to most of us. It is interesting, however, that we seem to have already passed through three *kinds* of Relative Truth.

"Water boils at 100 degrees Celsius" is "true" relative to the laws of physics at sea-level on this planet.

"pq equals qp" is *valid* (the word "truth" is seldom used in this area anymore) relative to *one* kind of algebra—the kind most people use in economic affairs. (It is not valid in the Hamiltonian algebra used in quantum mechanics.)

"The infamous Dr. Crippen poisoned his wife" is "true" relative to the rules of evidence in our legal system. Traditionally we express this by saying Dr. Crippen was proven guilty beyond a reasonable doubt. This kind of "proof," however, is not the *experimental* proof of physics nor the *formal* proof of mathematics; it is *legal* proof. At the risk of seeming even more pedantic and annoying than usual, I suggest that since scientific proof, mathematical proof and legal proof all have different *rules*, they refer to three kinds of "truth" or three kinds of demonstration. "The infamous Dr. Crippen was convicted of poisoning his wife" seems to be a fourth kind of statement, namely a historical "truth," and is (or seems to all but the *n*th-plateau skeptic) more certain than the "legal truth" that the blighter did poison his wife. The historical "truth" (Crippen was convicted) is based on *the assumption that we possess accurate records*, but the statement that Crippen *was* guilty is based on the additional assumption that the jury did not make a mistake in that case.

And what about proposition 4, "The Communists are plotting to enslave us"? That does not appear to be scientific "truth" *or* mathematical "truth" (validity) *or* even "legal truth." What sort of "truth" (*or* fallacy) is it?

That's a tough one. We had better postpone it again, while we continue our eccentric ramble from first-plateau skepticism to second-plateau skepticism.

The Citadel has a vigorous and versatile propaganda department in the United States called the Committee for Scientific Investigation of Claims of the Paranormal or CSICOP for short. You will not be surprised to learn that Martin Gardner and Prof. Munge are among its spokesmen. CSICOP's method of "scientific investigation" generally is to wage a campaign of vilification, in the media, against any researcher whose ideas they don't like.

What did I just say? That was polemical and unfair. I apologize. They are all honorable men.

Fate magazine (U.S.) October 1981:

32-page article, entitled "STARBABY," by Dennis Rawlins, a Harvard physics graduate who knows CSICOP from the inside. He was a co-founder in 1976, served on its Executive Council from 1976 to 1979 and was Associate Editor of their journal (originally the *Zetetic*, now the *Skeptical Inquirer*) from 1976 to 1980. Oh, I am fearful of writing this—this is a terrible Blasphemy even after such Damned Things as "orgone"—but—

Rawlins discovered in early 1977 that the first scientific study performed by CSICOP was, to put it mildly, erroneous. He calls the statistical techniques used "bungling." Professor Elizabeth Scott of the statistics department of University of California called it "misleading." Whatever one wants to call it, it was, as we shall see, a remarkable bit of unfeasible logic.

This was the case: the Fench statistician, Michael Gauquelin, had published a large-scale statistical sampling which seemingly confirmed some of the predictions of astrology. CSICOP had decided to refute this—Rawlins claims there was no doubt in anybody's mind, in CSICOP, that they intended to *refute*, not to examine impartially—and centered on one particular area, which has come to be known as "the Mars effect." Mars, relative to Earth, can be classified as occupying 12 positions in the sky at various times. Two of those positions can be regarded as "favorable" for the births of sports champions. If there is no validity in astrology, the chance of champions actually being born in those two positions ("Mars rising" and "Mars transiting") are 2/12 or approximately 17 percent. Gauquelin's statistics showed that the percentage of European sports champions born in those two time-zones was actually 22 percent.

Now, this deviation of more than 5 percent may not seem overwhelming to a layperson, but to a statistician it is meaningful. The odds *against* it occurring by chance are several million to one. Thus, if

Gauquelin's statistics are valid, either astrology is partially confirmed or some other explanation of the deviation is needed.

The CSICOP report claimed to have identified the factor that explained the deviation. This is known as "the Mars/dawn effect," and means simply that when Mars is "rising," relative to a position on Earth, it is around dawn at that place. The CSICOP report claimed to prove that the 22 percent of sports champions born then was not significant because 22 percent of *all humans* are born then—evidently because, for biological reasons, pregnant women are slightly more likely to go into final labor around dawn than at other hours.

The report did not prove this. It obtained this result by juggling figures—especially by reducing the total number of sports champions from 2088 to 303. This is what Rawlins calls "bungling" and Professor Scott termed "misleading." If CSICOP caught a parapsychologist or astrologer doing something similar they would call it "fraud" or "cooking the data." In any event, when the figures are corrected, and the full 2088 sports champions are considered, instead of the partial sample of 303, the statistics actually confirm Gauquelin instead of refuting him. The actual figures then are: 17 percent of all humans are born in the time-zone of the "Mars-effect," as chance predicts, and 22 percent of sports champions are born then, as Gauquelin had claimed.

As I say, Rawlins calls this "bungling." Some will have a stronger name for it. About what followed there seems to be no possibility of using "bungling" or general incompetence as an explanation.

Rawlins and Professor Scott, you will remember, discovered the statistical fallacy in the report before the end of 1977. All through 1978, Rawlins, a member of the CISCOP executive council, attempted to get this error corrected. He ran into a stone wall, and calls the behavior of other CISCOP executives a "cover-up" and compares it to the Watergate affair in politics.

The Committee refused to publish a letter by Rawlins about the matter, even though he was Associate Editor of their journal.

When Rawlins did a follow-up study, which amusingly enough did contradict Gauquelin, CSICOP was glad to publish it, but refused to allow him to include it in a section describing the error in their original report.

When Rawlins insisted that they print a sentence saying that part of his article had been censored, the other editors agreed verbally, and then removed the sentence without telling him. That is, they not only censored him but censored his attempt to tell readers they were censoring him.

When Rawlins insisted on a team of referees to judge the dispute, the executives did not allow an impartial team to be chosen, but selected their own referees. Nonetheless, the referees agreed that, when the errors were corrected, the original report did in fact confirm Gauquelin instead of refuting him, as Rawlins and Professor Scott had said from the beginning. The committee then refused to print the referees' report.

By 1979, Rawlins felt that he had seen so much dishonesty in this matter that he should speak out, but hesitated because "I didn't want to hurt rationalism." He went on struggling to get his corrections published, and finally realized that "realpolitik cynics were taking advantage of that reluctance" and exploiting his loyalty to the Cause. He tried to speak out at a press conference, and the executive council stopped the press conference before he could speak.

The executive council then met in closed session, with all members but Rawlins, and voted him out of the executive. They allowed him to continue as Associate Editor of their journal, however, and he went on struggling to get the correction published for another year. In 1980, he resigned from CSICOP in total disillusionment.

To summarize: CSICOP published a scientifically false report. They blocked all attempts by a member of their own Executive Council to inform members that the report was false. When their own selected referees agreed the report was false, they suppressed the referees' report. This went on over a period of four years (1977-1981) and if "bungling" explains the beginning of it, Rawlins's term "cover-up" certainly does not seem too strong for what followed.

Perhaps my wicked, polemical phrase the New Fundamentalism is not too strong, after all?

Fate September and October 1979, "The Crusade against the Paranormal," by Jerome Clark and J. Gordon Melton:

Another founding member of CSICOP resigned, or was ejected—accounts differ—but—

Prof. Marcello Truzzi, sociologist, from Eastern Michigan University, was editor of the CSICOP journal when it was called the *Zetetic*. He had a difference of opinion with the Executive Council, about whether dissenting views should be published. He says CSICOP isn't skeptical at all in the true meaning of that word but is "an advocacy body upholding orthodox establishment views." In other words, their alleged skepticism has become, as my paradox suggests, just another dogmatic blind faith.

Prof. Truzzi has started his own journal, now called the *Zetitic Scholar*, in competition with CSICOP's journal, now called *The Skeptical Enquirer*. He follows the normal procedure of what is usually considered adult debate among sane people: he prints articles on both sides of every question and allows open debate, unlike the *Skeptical Enquirer*, which only prints articles on one side, since they already know the truth. Their fury against him is what any student of priestcraft would expect.

Metamagical Themas, by Douglas Hofstadter, p 111-113:

Hofstadter, a good friend and admirer of CSICOP's Super-star Martin Gardner, gives his version of Prof. Truzzi's exodus. Truzzi wanted to publish articles on both sides of the Velikovsky controversy (which we will shortly examine). Gardner held that this would give Velikovsky "undeserved legitimacy," and insisted on the one-sided attitude which now prevails in CSICOP. (As a libertarian, I must admit that is incomprehensible to me. To attack a man's ideas, and then refuse to let him, or his defenders, answer the attack seems to me Idolatrous, if not fascist. To say that *after attacking him*, allowing rebuttal gives him "undeserved legitimacy" is a rationalization that, I think, only the most Faithful can believe, or even discuss with a straight face.) Hofstadter defends Gardner as well as he can, calling Velikovsky "obnoxious," but ends up admitting that he, personally, would prefer open debate. He still supports CSICOP, however.

CSICOP, meanwhile, isn't listening to Hofstadter. They still won't allow open debate in their journal. The heretical Jeffersonian view that even the "obnoxious" have the right to be heard hasn't percolated their craniums yet.

To return to our catalog of different *kinds* of propositions that human speech can utter— and remembering that any set of internalized propositions creates a reality-tunnel that edits experience—

Consider proposition 6, "Marilyn Monroe was the most beautiful woman of her time."

This can hardly be considered a scientific statement, since there is no such instrument as a pulchritometer which can give us a measurement in milivenuses comparing Ms. Monroe with, say, Jane Russell or Diana Dors. Nor is it a mathematical statement, obviously. It isn't a legal verdict, since no jury ruled on the case.

I suggest, following some ideas in semantics and modern logic, that

"Marilyn Monroe was the most beautiful woman of her time" should be considered a *self-referential statement*. That is, it refers to the nervous system of the speaker. Properly, it should be phrased as "Marilyn Monroe seemed the most beautiful woman of her time to me." Stated thusly, it is "true" (unless we want to be so tricky as to assume the speaker is deliberately deceiving us).

Such self-referential "truths" are valid for only one person at a time, or one group of persons, and do not refer to anything but the nervous system or nervous systems of thsoe who espouse them. This does not mean that they are "false," but only that they are even more relative (and subjective) than legal proofs, for instance, and that they are very, very different from scientific or mathematical "truths."

It seems that a potent source of error, and of potential dogmatism, enters our "thinking" when our language is *not pedantic enough.* "Marilyn Monroe was the most beautiful woman of her time" *seems* to be a statement about some "objective reality" and can easily lead to arguments with Sophia Loren fans; but "Marilyn Monroe seemed the most beautiful woman of her time to me" declares itself as a self-referential proposition and does not so readily get confused with "objective" statements.

Similarly, proposition 13, "Beethoven is a better composer than Mozart" might most profitably be considered a self-referential statement, which should be reformulated more correctly as "Beethoven seems a better composer than Mozart to me." Of course, music criticism—and art criticism in general—would be less lively and bitchy if this semantic reform were accepted; but it might make more sense.

According to the Logical Positivists, statements about the comparative beauty of Monroe and Loren, or Beethoven and Mozart, or Van Gogh and Picasso, etc. should all be considered "meaningless." We are not so stringent here. We grant that such statements are meaningful—to the people who make them. We are merely suggesting that, by calling them self-referential, we can avoid the errors and emotional tantrums that inevitably creep into conversation when it is tacitly assumed that they are statements of the same order as those about the boiling point of water or about pq and qp or even about whether Dr. Crippen poisoned his wife.

How about proposition 10, "*Lady Chatterley's Lover* is a pornographic novel"? It might be said that this was a legally true statement until the courts changed their minds about that, I suppose. It might also be said that this kind of statement is as self-referential as the ones about comparative beauty, and the courts in considering the matter at all were confusing the self-referential class with other, more objective classes. Alas, it is thoughts like that which have made me the sad case of aggravated agnosticism that I now am. Meanwhile, until a smutometer is invented, all such questions—about *Lady Chatterley*, or about Shakespeare, or about the films of Marilyn Chambers—are rather grossly different from questions about how many volts are in an electrical circuit.

Until pulchritometers and smutometers come on the market, it might be wise to regard statements about beauty and pornography as at least self-referential, even if we do not join the Logical Positivists in calling them totally meaningless.

But, then, how about proposition 11, "*Lady Chatterley's Lover* is a sexist novel"? If we call that a self-referential statement, too, we will make ourselves even more unpopular. As in the case of a new nuclear plant mentioned earlier, we seem to be entering here a borderline area where the "scientific," the "esthetic" and the "moral" cannot be disentangled to the satisfaction of any two commentators: where "objective" and "subjective" indeed overlap alarmingly.

Perhaps recognizing that problem, rather than claiming to solve it, is itself a step toward clarity?

22 February 1981 *New Sunday Times* (Malaysia)—a boy, aged fifteen, has been running "an abnormally high temperature" for ten years, since he was five. Doctors find nothing wrong with him, and he is not ill or distressed. Neighbors call him "fireboy," it says.

What are we to make of a yarn like this? Some, I suppose, will believe it, and some will attribute ti to TUUR—The Ubiquitour Unscrupulous Reporter—the gent who is responsible for all bizarre and sensational newspaper stories.

I don't know. I just wonder a bit. Since there is nothing "psychic" or "extraterrestrial" or otherwise spooky about this, I imagine most readers will wonder a bit. Perhaps this means that there is no Taboo against thinking about this kind of oddity?

26 February 1981 *Straits Times* (Singapore)—an 18-month old infant girl in Mianyang, southwest China, also has an abnormally high temperature. Unlike the Malaysian "fireboy" she was born with this condition. Alleged doctors have allegedly examined her and allegedly found no medical problem.

The Ubiquitous Unscrupulous Reporter strikes again?

Maybe. Then again, since no Taboo is breached, many might

consider this a possible oddity rather than an obvious hoax.

Phenomena, by Michell and Richard (Thames and Hudson, 1977) p 24—in 1934 an asthma patient named Anna Monaro developed a *blue* luminescense around her breast, when she was asleep and only when she was asleep. Many doctors were involved in trying to explain this mystery but no single explanation was acceptable to all of them so they argued endlessly while Signora Monaro continued to glow. The case is discussed in London *Times* for May 1934.

Reich's orgone is supposed to be blue—but that was only Reich's hallucination, of course—

Phenomena, same page, citing Father Thurston's *Physical Phenomena of Mysticism,* says many Catholic saints have been reported glowing in that amusing manner. That's a lot of Papist superstition, of course, but still—one of Thurston's cases, St. Lidwina, only glowed while asleep, like Signora Monaro. Some might think a bizarre detail like that, which sounds less like the "miraculous" than the merely enigmatic, is not helpful to the notion of Divine Intelligence. It looks more like Divine Idiocy—or like a natural phenomena we don't, presently, understand— something a liberal materialist, as distinguished from a fundamentalist, might be willing to think about—

I am not advocating specific ideas here. I am trying to bring to full consciousness the kind of half-conscious *decisions* which determine, for each of us, which thoughts are "thinkable" and which are "unthinkable."

Somehow, in passing from abnormal temperatures to blue luminescense and "haloes," we seem to have crossed a line, and, for most readers, skepticism is increasing. I wonder why that is? Is it possible that what I call the New Idol so dominates the modern world that even those who read a subversive book like this are still uneasy about becoming too blasphemous, too heretical?

Remember: I am not asking you to believe these yarns at all. We know how much nonsense gets published these days, do we not? I am merely asking that you observe in yourself the *strength* and *immediacy* of the impulse to deny at once. Does this impulse vary according to the weight of the circumstantial evidence (such as it is) or according to how much your own imprinted and conditioned reality-tunnel is challenged?

If you say "St. Lidwina did not glow," you are making a seemingly objective statement about events you presumably were not around to examine personally. If, on the other hand, you say "I doubt that St. Lidwina glowed" you are making a true report on how your nervous system operates—how your imprinted and conditioned reality-tunnel judges things it has not observed. Which of these statements appears more in accord with current neurology and perception psychology?

7 September 1871 New York *Herald*—Nathan Coker, a blacksmith of Easton, Maryland, was immune to pain from fire—*but not to other kinds of pain*. The *Herald* alleges that Coker demonstrated this immunity to various scientific investigators by performing such feats as holding hot pokers to his skin without flinching and swilling molten lead in his mouth, spitting it out without any burn marks on tongue or lips.

That's as bad as Reich and his damned orgone, I know. Those who have been indoctrinated, or bulldozed, or religiously converted, by fundamentalist materialism, will never consider it for a minute—it's as "impossible" as the alleged firewalking of the Polynesians. It *has* to be the work of the Ubiquitous Unscrupulous Reporter, who was employed by the *Herald* in 1871.

Phenomena, by Michell and Rickard, *op. cit.* p 30-31—several eye-witness accounts of the *verboten* and impossible fire-walking.

The eye-witnesses were all fools or liars, of course. Of course.

One of the firewalks described (p 30) was supervised and observed by medical authorities from the University of London.

Well, then, they were all tricked or deluded, of course. All scientists who report things repugnant to fundamentalist materialist dogma have been tricked or deluded *by definition*. See the endless polemics in *The Skeptical Enquirer* against those scientists who cannot see accurately what is directly in front of their faces and have to be corrected by CSICOP members far from the scene who know *a priori* what is and is not "possible." See especially the interminable diatribes of CSICOP's James Randi against Drs. Puthoff and Targ, physicists of Stanford Research Institute (Palo Alto) who allowed Uri Geller into their laboratory and then reported that which Mr Randi, who was not there, *knows* passionately could not have happened.

Winter 1984 *Fortean Times* No. 42, p. 10-12: a so-called "poltergeist" in the home of the Resch family of Columbus, Ohio. According to the moderately superstitious, a *poltergeist* "is" a ghost of some sort; according to the extremely superstitious it "is" demon out of hell (see *The Exorcist*); according to parapsychologists, it "is" usually an explosion of emotional energy in "psychokinetic" form by a disturbed individual, usually adolescent; according to fundamentalist materialism, it "is" all trickery or fraud, of course. Whatever this one was, it allegedly threw clocks and candlesticks and other furnishings around, made the lights flash off and on at odd intervals, and even heaved a telephone across the room in the presence of a photographer from the Columbus *Dispatch*. (The photo is in the cited *Fortean Times*, p. 11.)

Then Mr. Randi of CSICOP arrived and, without entering the house, announced that it was all a fraud. The Resch family, offended, refused to let Mr. Randi into the house, whereupon he left, presumably still knowing it was all fraud.

Like Mr. Randi, I never got into that house; unlike him, I am therefore unsure of what was happening there. *Maybe* it was all fraud.

Fortean Times cites from *Columbus Dispatch* the words of an electrician, Bruce Claggett, who was called in by the police to deal with the on-and-off light problem. Says Mr. Claggett, "I was up there three hours, and the lights were just turning themselves on all over the place. I tried taping over the switches, but as fast as I would tape them in the down position they'd come back on."

That *might* give pause to one whose Faith was not as passionate as that of Mr. Randi and his colleagues in CSICOP. It might even provoke curiosity?

30 August 1921 London *Evening News*—a child with a wolf's head born in Avigon, France. He died within five days.

Probably an exaggeration. The head was only a *little* wolfish . . .

The *News* says he also had lobster-claws in place of hands.

What do *you* think, dear reader? Is that one *more* or *less* likely to be a fraud than the "*poltergeist*" in Columbus, Ohio?

For the wolf-headed boy, we have few details; for the "*poltergeist*" we have a photo (that might be faked) and the name of an electrician as witness (but he might be fictitious, if The Ubiquitous Unscrupulous Reporter was working in Columbus that year). If we have to guess which story is more unlikely, do we guess on the basis of these details, or on the basis of a prejudgment that a teratological infant of the sort described is not quite as absurd as a "ghost"?

If you are willing to think the events in Columbus are possible, do you also tend to believe the ghost explanation, or the demon theory, or the "psychokinetic" force? Why?

10 June 1933 London *Sunday Dispatch*—a cat with wings. It was allegedly found by Mrs. Hughes Griffith of Summerstown, Oxford. Mrs. Griffith allegedly took it to Mr. Frank Owen, allegedly of the Oxford zoo, who allegedly examined it and allegedly decided the wings were real.

Once again: the ubiquitous unscrupulous reporter?

There is a photo of the winged cat with the story.

Well, then, the unscrupulous reporter was aided and abetted by an unscrupulous photographer this time? We all *know*, of course, that Kelley's photos of "orgone" effects on trees and clouds are fakes, and so are all UFO photos, and the photo of the levitating telephone mentioned on the previous page was a fake, too—at least according to those who *know* what is impossible.

I suppose this photo might very well be a fake.

That's because it's easier for me personally to imagine a genetic donnybrook producing a boy with a wolf's head and lobster claws (or head and hands so disfigured as to look wolfish and lobsterish) than to imagine a genetic *katzenjammer* weird enough to produce wings on a cat.

Fortean Times No. 34 (Summer 1981)—letter from Sid Birchby who recalls that damned winged cat in Oxford in 1933. Mr. Birchby says that the zoo keeper pronounced the wings real but that the cat could not fly.

Mr. Birchby also tells of a *second* winged cat reported in the 23 September 1975 Manchester *Evening News*. This one was originally found as a kitten and the wings took a year to develop fully, whereupon they allegedly measured 11 inches from shoulder to tip.

Birchby says this story was also accompanied by a photograph.

Well, then, at least two pixilated reporters have found two equally nefarious photographers and, for inexplicable reasons, have faked winged cat stories with supporting winged cat photos? It must be the same vicious and malign humor that causes others to fake UFO photos year after year, I guess. We will see as we go along that these desparate characters are not merely pranksters, but indeed seem to be part of some Vast International Conspiracy, because they continually produce fakes that support one another's fakes. Just as the wicked Darwinians do—according to the faithful Creationists.

It's not that I believe in the boy with a wolf's head or in these winged cats—or in astrology or "orgone" for that matter—but that I wonder a bit. That is my heresy; that is why I cannot buy into fundamentalism. I wonder a bit.

18 October 1931 London *Sunday Dispatch*—a two-headed goat. It was born in Boizana, Italy, and did not survive long. It ate with both heads, or so the story alleges.

19 December 1932 London Evening *Standard*—a *girl* with two heads,

born six weeks earlier, was being studied at the Soviet Institute of Experimental Medicine in Leningrad.

She ate with both heads. Like the goat in France. It says.

22 December 1931 London *Morning Sun*—a mule in Weenan, Natal, had given birth to its second foal. The first, allegedly born seven years earlier, was allegedly already a healthy stallion.

Now, to the ordinary reader this yarn is not as startling as the winged cats or the two-headed goat, but to biologists this is the worst blasphemy I have uttered thus far. See any biology textbook: they'll not only tell you mules are infertile, but they'll explain why. Mules are hybrids and hybrids *must be* infertile according to basic biological laws. Just as the seeming psychokinesis in that house in Columbus is impossible according to Prof. Munge's basic physical laws.

The *Sun* story goes on to say that the authenticity of the births is vouched for by Dr. Ernest Warren of the Natal Museum. The mother was actually a mule, Dr. Warren says, and not a small horse who looked like a mule.

Dr. Warren must be a GS—a Gullible Scientist, like the fools from the University of London who thought they saw a man walk on fire without being burned, or like Drs. Puthoff and Targ of Stanford Research Institute, who think they saw Uri Geller do things which James Randi knows by definition could not have been done. When TUUR, the ubiquitous unscrupulous reporter, does not devise these blasphemies out of whole cloth, he always has a GS in cahoots with him. Or an MS—a Mad Scientist, who hallucinates, like Dr. Reich.

19 April 1931 London *Evening News*—inquest on one John Charles Clarke. The coroner allegedly said that the alleged Clark's alleged blood was *black*—"coal black, of the consistency of tar," were his words.

Maybe Mr. Clarke smoked too much. Or maybe the coroner was drunk as a barn owl. Maybe it's just "genetic copying error." Maybe it's TUUR, sending us up once more.

Or maybe the idea of absolute laws is just a projection of the emotional *need* for certitude in some kinds of people?

4 March 1931 Brighton *News Chronicle*—*millions* of mice (it says) "coming from no one knows where" to invade the Nullabor Plain, through which the Trans-Australian Railway runs. A station master at Loongana is quoted: "Everywhere one looks one sees thousands of mice, which seem to have come out of the sky. They are eating everything in their advance and attacking furniture and bedding."

Seem to have come out of the sky . . .

Oh, no. That must have been just a colorful expression the station-master used. We are considering blasphemies against basic biological laws, to begin with; we are not ready for blasphemies against Prof. Munge's basic physical laws yet.

25 May 1889 *Toronto Globe*—reports from Simcoe, Ontario, claiming that a cow on the farm of Mr. John H. Carter had given birth to a calf and two lambs.

Like that allegedly fertile mule in Natal, this is more awful to the experts than to ordinary readers. As Charles Fort commented, it would not be more repugnant to biological orthodoxy if the damned cow had given birth to a calf and two bicycles.

Worse: the *Globe* sent a reporter to the scene. By Murphy's Law or the Law of the Perversity of Things in General or some such cosmic cussedness, this reporter just happened to be another incarnation of that arch-demon TUUR. The lying bastard said he examined the blasphemous brood and two out of three of them were definitely lambs but had cow-like hair on their breasts instead of wool.

25 May 1889 *Daily Mercury* (Quebec)—they sent their own reporter to Simcoe. He also alleges that he saw the same High Crime against Revealed Law with his own eyes.

Coincidence again—the only two reporters sent to the scene just happened to be members of the Vast International Conspiracy that is devoted to faking reports of those things that the New Fundamentalists know could not have happened.

As a philosopher, or a public nuisance—the two terms have been interchangeable since the time of Socrates—I think our judgment about this yarn especially, and about the others in general, really rests on the degree to which Platonism still dominates Western thought unconsciously. I think what we are asking ourselves in each case is whether Absolute Laws are being violated or not; if a story doesn't directly contradict such Absolute Laws, then we tend to think, however bizarre or unusual it may be, it *might* be possible, but if it does contradict Absolute Laws, then we "*know*" (or think we "know") that it is impossible.

The New Fundamentalism usually calls itself Science when it wishes to impress and put on some swank; it more bluntly calls itself Materialism when it is pugnaciously seeking quarrels with mystics or poets or such oddballs; but I think it can accurately be called the latest variety of neo-Platonism.

What are Absolute Laws supposed to be? They are supposed to be spaceless, timeless, eternal and unchanging—just like Plato's Ideas or forms. How can we know these ectoplasmic entities? Not by science in the grubby, nitty-gritty sense in which I, or the woman in the street, or modern physicists, know science; for that kind of science—the kind we see in the real world—only produces models which are good for a time and place, and it discards these models as soon as better models are created.

Absolute Laws in the Platonic sense cannot be known scientifically— as Plato himself realized. They can only be "known" (or imagined) by intuition or by some Act of Faith. Empirically and existentially, nobody knows today, right now, if we have any Absolute Laws in our intellectual common market. All that we *know* is that we have some models that work a lot better, practically, than some of the older models we have discarded.

If the so-called "laws" contained in our models are only generalizations based on *our experience until this date*—if they are not spaceless, timeless, eternal and given by some divinity or other—then things that do not fit our current models should not be rejected *a priori*. They should be studied carefully, as clues that might lead us to better models tomorrow.

The position that rejects this and claims to know with certitude which alleged "laws" are Absolute goes far behind materialism, which is only, properly speaking, a theory that the metaphor of "matter" is the best metaphor to use in organizing our models. It goes all the way to Platonism, even if its advocates seldom consciously realize this.

Our understanding of "matter" changes continually, particularly in this century; and the majority of physicists seem to think "matter" itself belongs in the dubious quotes with which I decorate it habitually, since "matter" currently appears as a kind of temporary knottiness in energy. We do not know "all" about "matter," and we know that we do not. A philosophy of materialism *per se* need not dogmatically reject any data *a priori*, since any data might, if verified, teach us more about "matter."

The only philosophy that can dogmatically reject *a priori* any data is the Platonic philosophy of spaceless, timeless, eternal Ideas, or Absolute Laws.

The New Fundamentalists are not as far separated from the Old Fundamentalists as they like to think they are.

Returning to the perversely miscellaneous propositions considered on page 7—which the reader was encouraged at that point to force into

the straight-jacket of Aristotelian true/false logic—we have suggested
that some of the propositions seem Relatively True (in a context), some
seem to rest on one kind of "proof" and some on other kinds of "proof"
and some appear to be best categorized as self-referential, i.e.
statements about one's own neurosemantic reactions. Let us look at
some of the remaining propositions from that list.

7. "There is a tenth planet in our solar system, beyond Pluto," can
neither be verified nor refuted at the date I am typing this. (It is a
measure of scientific acceleration in our time that it might be verified or
refuted by the time this reaches the bookstores, incidentally.) Logical
Positivists once wanted to call propositions of this sort "meaningless,"
but that position has crumbled, and most modern logicians would
probably agree with the terminology of Dr. Anatole Rapoport who
calles such statements *indeterminate*.

An indeterminate proposition cannot be verified or refuted at the *date*
when we confront it, but there are clear scientific processes by which it
can be verified or refuted at some *future* date. The tenth planet beyond
Pluto, in this instance, will be discovered, or won't be discovered, when
the space telescope goes into orbit in the near future. The existence of
advanced life-forms beyond Earth may not be verified or refuted for a
thousand years or longer—or it may be verified tomorrow, if the
"Space Brothers" beloved in UFO lore suddenly land *en masse*—but at
present it remains similarly indeterminate.

It shows What Is Wrong With Me, I guess, that I consider most of
the newspaper yarns in this chapter equally indeterminate. I honestly
don't know how to form a judgement about them—which may be why
I prefer the easier task of forming judgements about why some people
want earnestly to believe in them and others *want*, with equal fervor, to
deny them.

Of course, 8, "Colorless green ideas sleep furiously" fits the classic
Logical Positivist (and Linguistic Analyst) category of truly "meaningless"
statements. That is because nobody can imagine a way of observing a
colorless green idea, even in the far future, or of learning its sleeping
habits. However, even here, a little pedantry is at least as amusing as it
is annoying. "Colorless green ideas sleep furiously" is *meaningless* as a
philosophical or scientific proposition, but I did not pick it at random. It
is quite meaningful *in another sense*. Prof. Noam Chomsky uses it to
illustrate a technical point in linguistics, namely that we can recognize a
correct grammatical structure even when we can't recognize any
sensible message in the grammar.

Most modern logicians would classify 15, "God has spoken to me" as equally meaningless in the above sense. Partially, I agree. Partially, I think it more accurate, and compassionate, to regard this as a badly-formulated *self-referential* statement. That is, just as "Beethoven is better than Mozart" is a bad formulation of the self-referential proposition "Beethoven seems better than Mozart to me," it may be most helpful to consider "God has spoken to me" as a bad formulation of the correct proposition, "I have had such an awe-inspiring experience that the best model I know to describe it is to say that God spoke to me." I think this is helpful because the proposition is only false if the person is deliberately lying, and because it reminds us that similar experiences are often stated within other paradigms, such as "I became one with the Buddha-mind" or "I became one with the Universe." These have different philosophical meanings than "God has spoken to me," but probably refer to the same kind of etic (non-verbal) experiences.

What, then, do we make of 12, "The Pope is infallible in matters of faith and morals"? Some would call this meaningless, since it can neither be verified nor refuted, and some would see it as a badly-formulated self-referential proposition ("I accept the Pope as infallible in matters of faith and morals.") I would suggest that it might be better to consider this a Game Rule. That is, it is a Rule which one must accept if one wishes to play the Roman Catholic game; if one rejects it, one is automatically excluded from the Roman Catholic game. Similarly, "The Umpire's decision is binding" is a Rule of the Game of Baseball and "You may not eat pork" is a Rule of the Game of Orthodox Judaism.

Therefore, I think it makes sense to regard proposition 18, "All human beings are created equal" as a Game Rule of liberal democracy. Certainly, this is not a scientific statement, since some humans are measurably taller, or measurably have higher IQs, or write better poetry, etc. And to describe "All human beings are created equal" as *self-referential* misses its point, since it is not merely a paraphrase of "I wish to treat all human beings as equal." It is a proposal for what type of society we (or some of us) wish to have. Therefore, it should be considered a Game Rule for that type of society, precisely as the Pope's "infallibility" is a Game Rule of Roman Catholicism.

Proposition 16, "The following sentence is true" presents a new kind of problem. Once again, the proposition can hardly be classed as true or false in itself, and we have to judge its truth or falsity *in a context*. Fortunately, the context is specified, and is Proposition 17, "The preceeding sentence is false."

In this case, the context seems to confuse us instead of enlightening us. The first sentence is true if false, and false if true.

Such systems are traditionally called paradoxes; I prefer to borrow a term from Mr. Hofstadter and call them Strange Loops.

The classic Strange Loop, of course, is the notorious Cretan who informs us that Cretans always lie.

A more modern instance is the barber who shaves every man in town who does not shave himself.

If Proposition 16 is true, it is false. If the egregious Cretan is telling the truth, he is lying. If the barber shaves himself, he does not shave himself. The most wonderful of Strange Loops (to me) is Bertrand Russell's class of all classes that are not members of themselves; if it is a member of itself, it isn't, but if it isn't, it is.

Such Strange Loops are not merely philosophical comedy or games by which logicians annoy one another. As I have argued in *Prometheus Rising*, and as has been argued by Bateson and Ruesch (*Communication: The Social Matrix of Psychiatry*) and Watslavick (*How Real is Real?*) and many others, a great deal of personal and social irrationality seems to result from people accepting Strange Loops into their thinking. I personally suspect that much of what I call the New Inquisition results from the Strange Loop

A. All ideas deserve equal protection under the law.

B. Some ideas do not deserve equal protection under law.

The New Fundamentalists have some dim respect for Rule A, which is deeply embedded in modern Western culture, even while their Faith drives them to act on Rule B. This leads them to remarkable flights of Irrational Rationalism.

A great number of "mental illnesses" seem to result from the Strange Loop

A. I must obey my parents' Game Rules.

B. I must obey my society's Game Rules.

When the parental and social Game Rules differ very greatly, some degree of "mental illness" is almost inevitable.

In logic, there is no escape from a Strange Loop. In pragmatic life, there is an easy escape—reject one part of the system. *Sombunall* can be very helpful there. A disturbed patient is beginning to recover, for instance, when the last Strange Loop is modified to:

A. I must obey sombunall of my parents' Game Rules.

B. I must obey sombunall of society's Game Rules.

Proposition 5, "The Nazis killed 6,000,000 Jews" presents us with even more disturbing problems, because it is believed by almost everybody and rejected by a vehement minority called Holocaust Revisionists. The case for Holocaust Revisionism is that there is a Vast Worldwide Conspiracy that has faked all the evidence which the rest of us naively accept.

Holocaust Revisionism or HR can hardly be called "false" in a historical sense because it is not part of the History Game; it rejects the rules of evidence that historians play by. This can be seen by comparing it with the thesis that President Richard Nixon never existed and all evidence of such a man was faked by another Vast Worldwide Conspiracy. One cannot disprove either HR or NR (Nixon Revisionism) since all historical evidence relevant to the dispute is *defined* as tainted.

I think it is safest to regard HR as another Strange Loop. By assuming all inconvenient evidence is faked, one opens an infinite regress, and one can logically ask next if the evidence that Holocaust Revisionists exist might have been faked (i.e. did the ethnomethodologists or other sociologists interested in "breaching experiments" on reality-tunnels manufacture the books and pamphlets of HR as an experiment, to see if we would *believe* people would write such documents seriously?)

I leave it an open question whether Creationism (which alleges the evidence for evolution has been faked) is another Strange Loop.

Nonetheless, there have been fakes, or deceptions, in political history; there have been fakes in art; there have even been fakes in science, such as Piltdown Man. I think a Strange Loop only appears when the charge of fake involves a conspiracy of such size that *all* evidence becomes suspect since a conspiracy of that magnitude can in principle deceive us about anything.

It is amusing to note that the New Fundamentalists are always skating near this kind of Strange Loop in their criticisms of so-called "ESP" research, which is now over 100 years old and has involved literally thousands of scientists everywhere in the civilized world. To call *all that research* fakery would immediately open a Strange Loop and probably an infinite regress as well. The Fundamentalists sense this, and use the word "faking" only part of the time, and speak of "blundering" or "incompetence" or, best yet, "inadequate controls" the rest of the time.

Nonetheless, I myself sometimes sense a Strange Loop in such polemics, because when I consider the amount of *fakery, blundering, incompetence* and *inadequate controls* that are alleged in such critiques, I start wondering about how much of that sort of thing may go on in other areas of research, and my agnosticism accelerates to a point where I even wonder about the Creationists' case against evolution . . . I only pull myself back to comfortable common sense again when I realize that, continuing that way, I will soon be wondering if everybody I have ever met might be a robot programmed to behave as a human, or if some of my own science-fiction plots might be real . . .

No: I stand firm in second-plateau skepticism, most of the time. Skepticism of *n*th degree is an exhilarating place to visit (for a novelist) but I do not want to live there.

At this point, it might be illuminating (or annoying) to repeat our little quiz, without the Aristotelian true/false game this time, and including our additional categories beyond true-false. (See page 63.)

Do you prefer to shift some propositions from "true" or "false" into one of the other categories? Do you think this is just pedantry, or that applying such a multiple-choice approach to life generally might clarify thought at times and even free some creative energies? Do you agree with my suggestions or do you think some propositions should be moved from the categories I assigned them into another category?

And, most important in the context of this book:

Do you think Inquisitions are more likely to flourish in an Aristotelian true/false game or in this kind of multiple choice game?

Like *sombunall*, this is not an attempt to solve all our philosophical and psychological problems once and for all. I'm not bright enough to do that. This is just a suggestion. Some of you might find it useful.

Some of you might also want to look back over our news stories, or yarns, and move them "true" or "false" into one of the other categories.

In *Messengers of Deception* (And/Or Press, Berkeley, 1977), Dr. Jacques Vallee suggests that UFOs may be produced by a Vast Worldwide Conspiracy. Dr. Vallee does not seem paranoid, and does not insist on this model; he merely asks us to consider it, as one possible model for a phenomenon that is not well understood by most of us. The Vast Worldwide Conspiracy, in this case, is assumed to be an intelligence agency, and its aim is to create *disinformation*—to confuse and befuddle other intelligence agencies.

PROPOSITION	RELATIVELY TRUE	FALSE	SELF-REFERENTIAL	"MEANING-LESS"	INDETER-MINATE	STRANGE-LOOP	GAME RULE
1. Water boils at 100° Celsius.	☐	☐	☐	☐	☐	☐	☐
2. pq equals pq	☐	☐	☐	☐	☐	☐	☐
3. The infamous Dr. Crippen poisoned his wife.	☐	☐	☐	☐	☐	☐	☐
4. The Communists are plotting to enslave us.	☐	☐	☐	☐	☐	☐	☐
5. The Nazis killed 6,000,000 Jews.	☐	☐	☐	☐	☐	☐	☐
6. Marilyn Monroe was the most beautiful woman of her time.	☐	☐	☐	☐	☐	☐	☐
7. There is a tenth planet in our solar system, beyond Pluto.	☐	☐	☐	☐	☐	☐	☐
8. Colorless green ideas sleep furiously.	☐	☐	☐	☐	☐	☐	☐
9. Francis Bacon wrote *Hamlet*.	☐	☐	☐	☐	☐	☐	☐
10. *Lady Chatterley's Lover* is a pornographic novel.	☐	☐	☐	☐	☐	☐	☐
11. *Lady Chatterley's Lover* is a sexist novel.	☐	☐	☐	☐	☐	☐	☐
12. The Pope is infallible in matters of faith and morals.	☐	☐	☐	☐	☐	☐	☐
13. Beethoven is a better composer than Mozart.	☐	☐	☐	☐	☐	☐	☐
14. Ronald Reagan wrote *Hamlet*.	☐	☐	☐	☐	☐	☐	☐
15. God has spoken to me.	☐	☐	☐	☐	☐	☐	☐
16. The following sentence is false.	☐	☐	☐	☐	☐	☐	☐
17. The previous sentence was true.	☐	☐	☐	☐	☐	☐	☐
18. All human beings are created equal.	☐	☐	☐	☐	☐	☐	☐
19. Capitalism is doomed by its internal contradictions.	☐	☐	☐	☐	☐	☐	☐
20. My spouse has always been faithful to me.	☐	☐	☐	☐	☐	☐	☐
21. I am probably not as smart as I think I am.	☐	☐	☐	☐	☐	☐	☐

Dr. Vallee also suggests that *some* UFO "believers" and *some* UFO "skeptics" may be part of the conspiracy, working together to spread confusion and cover up other activities of the parent Agency.

This hypothesis also opens a Strange Loop, if you consider it; yet some second-plateau skeptics will not regard it as impossible or unthinkable.

In a critique of this particular Vast Worldwide Conspiracy theory, I have suggested that recent scientific "discoveries" such as quasars and Black Holes may also be faked in this manner. Since the Citadel of Science is, as I keep reminding you, owned by military-industrial cliques, it might seem desirable to announce and publicize "discoveries" that never happened: this would bedevil and bamboozle the other side in the Cold War and lead their scientists to waste a great deal of effort and time in what might be called snark-hunting.

I am only joking again. Of course. But . . .

Spokesmen for the New Fundamentalism, who have their own favorite neologisms, often speak of "the New Irrationalism." By this term they designate an attitude of mind which suspects the scientific community as a whole of engaging in the kind of deceptions which the New Fundamentalists attribute only to parapsychologists and other heretics. I agree that many of the claims of the New Irrationalism are as absurd as my little flight of fantasy about quasars and black holes, but I think the Citadel has created this Strange Loop for itself.

If Prof. X is paid by the government to invent weapons to kill people, some will inevitably wonder about the moral character of Prof. X.

If Prof. Y claims that Prof. Z the parapsychologist is untrustworthy, some will wonder if Prof. Y himself can be trusted fully, and if science is truly "impartial."

In a world of TOP SECRET stamps and FOR YOUR EYES ONLY, some will inevitably wonder *how much* is being hidden from them by the Citadel, as the Manhattan Project was hidden in the 1940s and C.I.A. drug research was hidden in the 1960s and 1970s.

As long as the Cold War exists, the New Irrationality will have its own kind of rationality, just as Establishment-salaried Rationality has its own irrationalism.

Against the paranoia that easily infests either Establishment dogma and anti-Establishment dogma, the only defense I see is agnosticism, well-flavored with a sense of humor, and an awarenes of one's own fallibility. I suspect a great deal, but as long as Government Secrets exist, I am not *sure* of anything.

A while back, I mentioned "breaching experiments," in which sociologists and/or psychologists test the rigidity of a reality-tunnel by subjecting people to experiences that contradict their reality-tunnels.

One of the most interesting collections of breaching experiments around is *Studies in Ethnomethodology* by Harold Garfinkel (Prentice-Hall, Englewood, N.J., 1967).

In one experiment, students who lived at home with parents were asked to observe their parents from an alien viewpoint: to look at these middle-aged people as a boarder rooming at the house would look at them. Students found this both amusing and alarming, although it is a rather elementary exercise in Buddhist detachment.

In a more exciting experiment, the same students were asked to *act* as if they were boarders while at home. This led to considerable melodrama, and some hysteria, even though the students were meticulously polite and well-behaved, as "good" boarders should be. Nonetheless, some parents were frightened, and even suggested psychiatric treatment for the students, just because inarticulate Game Rules were being breached.

In a third experiment, students pretended, while in conversation with persons not members of Garfinkel's class, not to understand certain "common sense" assumptions about cause and effect, location in space-time, etc. In all cases, persons trying to explain "common sense" to these *faux-naifs* showed distinct irritability and anxiety like that Socrates provoked by always asking "What do you mean?" and "How do you know?"

The irritability and anxiety some readers of this book are beginning to feel?

This is another area in which the "scientific" and "moral" can not be easily separated. Some regard breaching experiments as immoral and even as dangerous. Richard de Mille, in particular, has charged (without details) that there are rumors that some breaching experiments have led to murders, suicides and psychotic breakdowns.

Consider the following multiple-choice test:

	TRUE	FALSE	INDETER-MINATE	MEANING-LESS	GAME RULE	STRANGE LOOP
This book is, in part, a breaching experiment	□	□	□	□	□	□

Incidentally, how many of you have a Security Clearance high enough to be *absolutely sure* Dr. Vallee's theory of the UFO Conspiracy isn't true?

Nicola Tesla: Prodigal Genius, by John O'Neill, Neville Spearman, London, 1979—

Tesla invented the alternating current electrical systems now in use throughout most of the world. He also invented and patented over 100 other electrical devices that helped create the modern industrial state. Between the 1890s and 1910, he was one of the most respectable, successful and influential scientists of his time, and earned over $1,000,000—a huge sum in those days.

After 1910, all that stopped.

Tesla's works were not burned, like Reich's; he was not imprisoned; he was not persecuted in any way. He merely became—unfashionable. For some reason, nobody would invest further in his research or his inventions.

There is a great mystery about the Tesla matter, and he has become a hero—a cult-figure—to many parts of the counter-culture. It is widely suspected that he was the victim of a commercial conspiracy, and that his proposed worldwide electrical grid would destroy all monopolies by making energy free to anybody who planted an antenna in their backyard.

It is hard to form an objective opinion about this. Tesla's grid has never been tested. We don't know if it would do all he claimed.

One can only be agnostic in a case like this.

Nonetheless, Tesla was considered a genius by his contemporaries, and he has been ignored by the Citadel for over 70 years now. One can only wonder why.

It is interesting that Tesla, like Reich, was profoundly opposed to nuclear energy, and claimed that even in "peaceful" uses nuclear power was dangerous to humans. The people who finance the Citadel do not like that idea.

As I say, one can only wonder. When so much science is TOP SECRET, one can never really be sure.

But Dr. J. Robert Oppenheimer was ejected from the Citadel, colorfully slandered and publically "disgraced" for opposing the development of the Hydrogen Bomb. And Oppenheimer, like Tesla, was considered a genius by those in the field, before his ideas became—unfashionable.

CHAPTER THREE

TWO MORE HERETICS AND SOME FURTHER BLASPHEMIES

(with comments on werewolves and similar Forbidden Things)

It is venturesome to think that a coordination of words (philosophies are nothing more than that) can resemble the universe very much.

Jorge Luis Borges, *Labyrinths*

The case of Dr. Immanuel Velikovsky:

The Citadel didn't burn his books, but they tried. This was back in the 1950s but many still remember the scandal. For those who have forgotten, complete dossiers are available from *Kronos*, Box 343, Wynnewood, Pennsylvania 19096. The dossiers show that publishers were harassed and threatened if they dared to publish Velikovsky; they were told they would be boycotted. One publisher was frightened enough to break a legally-binding contract which had already been signed. Dr. Velikovsky's books survive—you and I and other heretics may consult them if we are curious about this matter—*only* because the New Inquisition is not as powerful as it would like to be.

Kronos is a publishing house devoted to defending Dr. Velikovsky's models. Perhaps they exaggerate the degree of threat and harassment used by his opponents?

May 1980, Conference of the American Association for the Advancement of Science, paper on "Pathological Science" by Dr. Ray Hyman of Washington State University. He talks at length about what he calls the "conspiracy" to suppress Dr. Velikovsky's books. He says the conspiracy was "more pathological" than Dr. Velikovsky's heresies.

Incidentally, Dr. Hyman is a member of CSICOP, the group against which I have engaged in so much wicked sarcasm. I mention this fact lest any careless reader think I wish to denounce that whole society in a lump. No: my irony is directed, as always, only at *sombunall* of any miscellaneous association of individuals, never at *all*. It is the Fundamentalism in any group, or any individual, that causes me alarm; and nobody's Fundamentalism alarms me as much as my own, whenever I spot a bit of it skulking around in the back rooms of my skull.

Fortean News, No. 36, Winter 1982—"Anomalistics," by Dr. Wescott of Rutgers State University—Dr. Velikovsky predicted in the 1950s that Venus would be found to be terribly hot when Orthodoxy insisted it was cold. The Venus fly-bys found it hot as hell.

Coincidence, of course. We know it is coincidence, because we know that the Honorable Men of the New Inquisition would not conspire to suppress books unless the books were totally nefarious.

Still citing Wescott, *Fortean News*, same issue:

Velikovsky predicted in the 1950s that Jupiter would be found to produce radio emissions. Such emissions have recently been found.

Coincidence again—like the rain storm that came when Dr. Reich thought he was firing his non-existent "orgone" at the clouds.

Or maybe Dr. Velikovsky was a lucky guesser.

But maybe, just maybe, *sombunall* of Dr. Velikovsky's model may have been bang on target, and maybe, just maybe, the New Inquisition may be, in *sombunall* cases, as blinded by intolerance as the old inquisition?

After all, what was Dr. Velikovsky's heresy? Did he dare to conduct experiments about "extrasensory" and "psychic" things and then publish experimental results which those far from the laboratory *know* in advance could not be accurate? Did he dare to speculate about UFOs or "ESP" or that impossible and eternally cursed "precognition"?

No. Velikovsky only suggested that evolution did not proceed smoothly and uniformly. He argued that there have been planetary catastrophes—that comets have wreaked havoc on Earth in the not-too-distant past, by passing close enough to tumble us about.

It is extremely unlikely (to me) that a tiny, microscopic blasphemy like that could bring down the full fury of the New Inquisition. Hardly. I suspect it was Dr. Velikovsky's *methods*, not his conclusions, that pushed the panic button of the Fundamentalists.

Dr. Velikovsky examined the myths of the ancients and speculated that they might contain a few facts—*sombunall*, in our terms. Facts exaggerated, facts distorted in re-telling, facts embellished by poets, but facts that could still be deduced by comparing various myth systems and noting what they have in common. For instance, there are over 120 flood legends in addition to the one in the Old Testament. They come from every part of the world—Asia, Africa, Australia, Russia, Scandinavia, Ireland, North America, South America, Polynesia. Throw out the local details and you have one constant: the idea that there was once a flood. So maybe there was? And maybe a comet created it?

That doesn't seem terrifying to you? Or you've read Locke and Mill and think a person should be allowed to think and to publish his or her thoughts?

The terror might be this: *if one Bible story is even partially confirmed, the whole damned religious business might come back and be at our throats again.*

I redundantly remind you again that this book is not, *per se*, advocating any particular heresies, but only examining *why* certain ideas are *taboo* and *verboten*, and why otherwise rational people conspire to suppress them. I regard this work as mostly a contribution to the sociology or sociobiology of *panic and stampede behavior* among domesticated primates, or—more politely—resistance to bizarre information.

Think of this "thin entering wedge" of Soviet dictatorship perceived by those sincere Tories who "see" communism in any bill to feed the starving. Think of the "thin entering wedge" of Papal tyranny "seen" by those who rioted in the streets of London in 1780 when Parliament considered a bill to allow Roman Catholics the same civil rights as other English citizens.

Think of the New Inquisition's fury against any scientist, however formerly reputable, who dares to assert statistical evidence of that damnable "ESP," and remember that *"ESP" even if it exists does not require a "spiritual" or "mentalistic" explanation.* Nicola Tesla, the great inventor of numerous electrical devices, either had "ESP" or had the delusion that he had it; but Tesla remained a materialist, albeit a liberal one, all his life. (See *Nicola Tesla, Prodigal Genius,* by John O'Neill, op.cit. page 49.) "ESP" may travel on a quite material wave, such as an electrical wave, if it exists at all. But—but—but—I think the anxiety is—if we allow "ESP" into the category of the thinkable or possible, who knows what other "spooky" stuff might ride in on its tail?

Similarly, with Velikovsky: let in Noah's flood, and the next thing you know the Holy Ghost and the virgin birth might be back.

In fact, in the argument between Mr. Hofstadter and Dr. Truzzi previously quoted (*Metamagical Themas,* p. 111), Hofstadter states that Velikovsky "claimed his views reconciled science and the Bible." For all I know, Dr. Velikovsky did claim that, some time or other, but it is irrelevant to judgment about his claims for a variety of reasons:

1. Newton also thought his model reconciled science and the Bible. Many others have had similar notions. The value of a model depends on its scientific utility, not on whether its spokespersons *think* it supports or contradicts the Bible.

2. Those who think a scientific theory supports the Bible may be right or wrong; those who think a scientific theory contradicts the Bible may also be right or wrong. That is a tangled branch of scriptural exegesis and has nothing to do with the scientific validity of the theory itself.

3. Many readers of Velikovsky, whom I have met, are not aware that he said, or is thought to have said, that his views support the Bible. These readers, who are not notably stupid, have rather an opposite impression. They think Velikovsky "supports" not the Bible but the general idea that *some* myths of all peoples are based on historical events. In other words, this group of readers did not get the message "The

Bible is true" but the rather different message, "Some myths contain some truth." This is hardly unthinkable; since the excavation of Troy, Homer is now recognized as containing *some* truth—sombunall.

4. Bible Fundamentalists are as enraged at Velikovsky as the New Fundamentalists. His *comet model* explains (or tries to explain) events (or alleged events) which *they* prefer to explain with *the "God" model.* And, indeed, if we accept the "comet" model, we don't really need the "God" model in this case. An idea that creates equal fury in *two opposed groups of Fundamentalists* can only be considered propaganda for *one of those groups* by those members of the other group who are so Fundamentalistic that their prejudice totally obliterates ordinary reasoning in them.

5. To proceed from "Something like Noah's flood once happened" to "The whole Bible is true" is not very logical, and I can't find anything like it in any book of Velikovsky's that I've read; and it would be just as logical, and just as illogical, to proceed from "Something like the Polynesian flood story once happened" to "The whole Polynesian mythology is true," and Velikovsky does not say that either as far as I have read him.

Dr. Velikovsky, incidentally, thought that a comet big enough to cause all the flood legends would have to be an unusually large comet. I heard lots of Fundamentalist argument, back in the 1950s, about why such a giant comet was impossible, but—

Since then the great explosion in Siberia in 1905, which unleashed 10^{23} ergs of energy, has become a matter of great controversy, especially since some Russian scientist—or some Russian "pseudo-scientist" as the Fundamentalists would say—suggested that the blast might have resulted from the crash of a nuclear-powered UFO, or alien spaceship.

To the hard-core Fundamentalists, UFOs are just as *verboten* as "ESP," so some other explanation was needed. A variety of ideas have gone around, but the most popular one—the model urged on television by Dr. Carl Sagan, one of the more urbane members of CSICOP—is that the Siberian explosion was caused by the crash of a comet.

A comet that unleashes a 10^{23} ergs is a mighty big comet.

If a monster of that size could hit us only 80 years ago, what others might have passed this way in the past 8,000 years, or the past 8 million years?

"Punctuated evolution."

That's the name, or a name, for the currently acceptable model which holds that, in contrast to old Uniformitarian doctrine, evolution might have been effected by catastrophes. Almost any recent article about dinosaurs, for instance, will propose that some catastrophe—usually, the suggestion is of a near-by super-nova—might have caused the extinction of those huge reptiles.

But when Velikovsky was condemned such *punctuation* was unthinkable. The chief argument against him, by those who argued at all and did not just fling cuss-words like "pseudo-science," was that Uniformitarianism was so established, so certain, that it was "absurd" or at least "unnecessary" to re-examine it at all.

How to Build a Flying Saucer by T.B. Pawlicki, Corgi Books, Ealing, 1973:

Mr. Pawlicki is a construction engineer, not an Astronomer or Physicist. Nevertheless, he claims the right to think, and to publish his thought. Fundamentalists might almost forgive him his other heresies for the sake of his beautiful first chapter, which explains in concrete detail how Stonehenge and similar monuments could be built with Stone Age technology, with no Ancient Astronauts helping at all.

Alas, in his third chapter, Mr. Pawlicki defends a neo-Velikovskian or quasi-Velikovskian model of the solar system. He argues that if Uniformitarianism were strictly true—if there were never any local catastrophes—the planets should exhibit a great deal more uniformity than they do. Mr. Pawlicki cites Funk and Wagnall's *Encyclopedia* as his source for the following oddities:

Jupiter has five times the angular momentum of the sun.

Venus rotates backward on its axis, and radiates more energy than it receives from the sun.

Earth's moon does not follow the same kind of orbits as the moons of all other planets; in fact, the Earth-moon system acts more like a double-planet system than a planet-satellite system.

The polar axes of Earth and Mars are both tilted $30°$ from the planes of their orbits, although all the other planets are not.

Jupiter, like Venus, radiates more energy than it receives from the sun.

The axis of Uranus is at right angles to the plane of the rest of the solar system.

The inner satellite of Neptune revolves backwards and the outer one has the most eccentric orbit in the solar system.

Pluto is so odd in so many ways that many astronomers do not think it's a planet at all but another satellite of Neptune that somehow wandered away.

Most of these oddities will be confirmed by standard works of popular astronomy, where they are treated as puzzles that remain to be explained. Perhaps the angular momentum of Jupiter—five times that of the sun—is the greatest puzzle of all. If the planets came out of the sun in some uniformitarian manner and evolved uniformally, they should each have an angular momentum less than that of the sun, and adding them altogether should still yield a sum less than that of the sun. One of them should not have an angular momentum *five times greater* than its source, anymore than a piece of pie should be *five times bigger* than the pie.

All of these observations are consistent with catastrophic models or "punctuated evolution"; all are extremely awkward for uniformitarians.

Mr. Pawlicki didn't even mention the asteroids. According to Bode's "law"—an emperical observation, with no basis in known laws, but nonetheless an observation that fits the rest of the solar system fairly well—there should be another planet between Mars and Jupiter. There isn't. Instead there are thousands and thousands and thousands of asteroids. It isn't regarded as heresy to speculate that these might be chunks left over from some planetary catastropohe.

If one planet might have been smashed to several thousand pieces by one catastrophe, of unknown origin, why is it "obnoxious" (Mr. Hofstadter's word) to speculate that another planet (ours) could have been thumped about a bit by another catastrophe, possibly a comet?

The only answer I can see is that no speculation is obnoxious to an open mind but all new and challenging speculations are obnoxious to Fundamentalists.

Incidentally, I have spent a lot of time talking to people who take Velikovsky seriously, and they have not yet convinced me that his particular catastrophe happened exactly as he described it. I don't really care about that. What I do care about is the threat to my own free speech—and *yours*—posed by the mentalities that tried so hard and so long to suppress Dr. Velikovsky's right to think and to publish.

Maybe—just maybe—the taboo breached by Velikovsky is this:
We are not supposed to think about Planetary Catastrophes.

While the Citadel is building more and more nuclear missiles for the Military-Industrial Empire, it is apt to provoke anxiety or guilt or uneasy sensations in general to think about the subject of Planetary Catastrophe. The people who do think about that are likely to resign from the Citadel—or get expelled, like Dr. Oppenheimer—or even to march around with picket signs, making a nuisance of themselves.

5 February 1980 *Weekly World News* (U.S.A.)—police in Roanoke, Virginia, arrested a man (name withheld) for standing on a roof, naked, howling and barking like a dog.

He was wearing a dog collar and he bit officer E.L. Mills while being arrested. Police said the man and a group of dogs had been digging up gardens. "It wasn't just the man who thought he was a dog," said Officer Mills. "The dogs seemed to think he was a dog, too. It was uncanny."

So TUUR is still alive and well, and living in Roanoke?

Maybe that's not necessary. This can be considered "only" a case of mental pathology, even if an especially weird one.

March 1905 *Occult Review* (England): Account of a man in Wales seen turning into a wolf. The witness was Mrs. Mary Jones, a revivalist preacher.

Oh, well, the *Occult Review*—and a woman preacher—

Same magazine, same article—another man in Wales, same year, seen turning into a wolf. This time there were two witnesses, both males.

Must have been "dual hallucination." If one person sees a blasphemy, that is simple hallucination. Two people—dual hallucination. Many, many people—"mass hallucination."

I don't doubt that there "are" hallucinations, or things that can most usefully be modelled by the theory of hallucination, even dual hallucination and mass hallucination, but, once this is granted, why be selective with such labels?

One witness sees a caterpillar turn into a butterfly—hallucination. Two witnesses see it—dual hallucination. Many, many witnesses— mass hallucination.

We don't take that step, I think, because we have a *theory* to explain insect metamorphoses, but we have, at present, no *theory* to explain primate-lupine metamorphoses.

If the Old Inquisition had been as semantically agile as the New Inquisition:

Galileo sees spots on the sun—hallucination. Two more observers see the spots—dual hallucination. Many, many observers—mass hallucination.

I don't see how science could grow if we did not occasionally admit that things which contradict old theories may be significant and may require new theories. Everything inconvenient cannot be dismissed as "hallucination."

But still—*werewolves*? I am only joking again. Of course.

William Seabrook, *Witchcraft: Its power in the world today* (White Lion Publishers, London, 1972) pp 153-154—he and two friends, in a psychic experiment, saw a woman in trance turn into a wolf.

But then—this was in a semi-darkened room—they turned on the light and found that, like the gent in Roanoke, she was only doing a very good imitation of a wolf.

Well, that's a relief. Maybe in those two Welsh cases nobody looked closely enough.

I am merely trying to show that, in the present primitive condition of this backward planet, we are still governed by imprinting and conditioning—that all of us, like Mr. Gardner and Mr. Randi, find it literally impossible to think, even for a nanosecond, about certain ideas—that you and I think we are more tolerant than Mr. Randi or Mr. Gardner until we confront that which is strictly intolerable for *us*—

But back to Mrs. Jones, the lady who saw the first of our alleged primate-lupine metamorphoses:

See London *Times* for 1905, Manchester *Guardian* same year, Barmouth *Advertiser* (Wales) same year—dozens, scores, of stories of mysterious lights seen in the night sky in or near towns where Mrs. Jones was preaching. These lights were seen by all classes, educated and uneducated, believers and unbelievers. Reporters (scrupulous or otherwise) wrote of seeing the lights themselves. If it happened today, it would be called a "UFO flap"—

So, just as Falstaff was not only witty himself but inspired wit in others, Mrs. Jones was not only hallucinatory but inspired hallucinations?

It is accepted by all schools of philosophy that the world presents only *appearances* to us. Facts are deduced from the appearances, according to the various factions, by PR (pure reason) or by a combination of PR and SD (sense data) in tandem, or by PR and SD aided and abetted by creative intuition, but in any case, they are *deduced*, not given. Hume and Nietzsche seem to be alone in claiming that what *is called* a "fact" is just another appearance which somebody has *decided* to believe is a fact.

26 February 1905 *News of the World* (London)—while the lights, or appearances of lights, were flying, or appearing to fly, in Wales, other appearances were happening there, in a butcher shop in Portmadoc.

These appearances included what appeared to be teleportations and levitations. 12 January 1905 Barmouth *Advertiser*—something that appeared to be a "ghost" in a house in Barmouth. 11 and 12 February 1905 *Daily News* (London)—mysterious knockings, or the appearance of what appeared to be knockings which appeared to be mysterious, in a house in Lampeter, Wales. 15 February 1905 Liberpool *Echo*—what appeared to be lights *inside* a house in Rhymney, Wales, together with what appeared to be the sounds of more mysterious knocking.

23 February 1905 Southern *Daily Echo* (Wales)—more of what appeared to be lights and levitations and teleportations and knockings in a house in Crewe, England. These were particularly nasty appearances. A young maid dropped dead of fright.

To the religious, or superstitious, these appearances seem like "ghosts" or "demons." To the parapsychological heretics, they might have been "explosions of psychokinetic force," which may or may not mean something. To the New Inquisition, they *are*, beyond doubt, hallucinations or frauds.

I wonder a bit, as usual. I especially wonder about that poor maid who allegedly died of fright.

Mrs. Jones went on preaching, and people continued to see lights, or the appearance of lights, in the night sky. 18 January 1905 Liverpool *Echo* gives details of the sociological fallout of this mass hysteria, or this mind/matter agitation, or whatever it was: shop girls in the midst of waiting on customers would suddenly start clapping hands and singing. In one town a man went from store to store handing in things he claimed he had stolen; shopkeepers said the items had *not* been stolen from them. Bands of young people rushed into orthodox churches, disrupting the services with ecstatic singing and hand-clapping.

Nietzsche would have said the Dionysian spirit was abroad in Great Britain that year. Freud, who read and enjoyed Nietzsche, would say in his own language that unconscious forces were errupting. Jung, influenced by both Freud and Nietzsche, would say the Dionysian archetype was escaping from the collective unconscious, accompanied by *synchronicities* (uncanny coincidences).

Then this: 28 February 1905 Blyth *News*—the body of Barbara Bell, 77, found "scorched" by "intense flames" in a room that was otherwise undamaged by fire and showed no evidence of fire.

Meanwhile, the lights, or UFOs, or angels, or demons, or at least the *appearances* continued spreading from Wales to England throughout

1905. The lights were positively identified as swamp gas by one expert, but then they were positively identified as luminescent insects by another expert. Other experts, who hadn't seen them, continued to identify them as good old "mass hallucination." ·

Charles Fort, *The Books of Charles Fort*, Dover, New York, 1974, p 660 ff.—all the while the lights and "hauntings" and religious hysterias were going on in 1905, in Northumberland something was mysteriously killing sheep. It was assumed to be a wolf.

A man "seen" turning into a wolf in Wales—another man (or the same man?) "seen" turning into a wolf, also in Wales, by two witnesses—something thought to be a wolf killing sheep a few miles away—I fear me, I fear me, but some readers, unintimidated by materialist dogma, or hypnotized by other dogma, are going to imagine a connection here.

A wolf was finally shot in Northumberland.

It did not turn into a human being as it died.

I'm sorry.

I know some of you would like it to have turned into a human, because you prefer certain old Idols to the New Idol. And some materialists would like me to quote a story from the *East Jesus Holler* saying it *did* turn into a human, because that would show that I am willing to stoop to *anything*—

No: it did not turn into a human. But, then, I am not trying to do anything else in this book except hold up a mirror to that part of human psychology in which anxiety increases perceptibly (or is replaced by anger) when we even *approach* the line at which Taboo might be broken. I am trying to show that every *emic reality* or mind-construct is a way of segregating appearances, so that those which fit our personal reality-tunnel can be accepted as "real" facts and those which do not fit are quickly discarded as "only" appearances.

Among the appearances in Wales and England that year of 1905 were the maid who was frightened to death and the old woman who burned in an otherwise unburned room.

Sombunall of what was going on in Great Britain in 1905, I think, can be safely classed as "mass hallucinatoin" and "hysteria."

Sombunall, I think, requires a further explanation, which Fundamentalist Materialism cannot provide—but which, maybe, a liberal materialism might someday provide—

Try this multiple choice test:

	TRUE	FALSE	INDETER-MINATE	MEANING-LESS	GAME RULE	SELF-REFER-ENTIAL	STRANGE LOOP
Wales exists	□	□	□	□	□	□	□
Strange lights exist	□	□	□	□	□	□	□
The National Debt exists	□	□	□	□	□	□	□
Quarks exist	□	□	□	□	□	□	□
Beauty exists	□	□	□	□	□	□	□
Size exists	□	□	□	□	□	□	□

All appearances seem to be facts, at first, to those to whom they appear.

If they are bizarre, if they don't fit our reality-tunnel, and if they go away quickly, we are happy to dismiss them as "only" appearances, or as misperceptions.

If they keep coming back, we wonder about our sanity, or we eventually accept them as "facts." As Norbert Weiner once said, the brain operates on Lewis Carroll's principle, "What I tell you three times is true." Redundance is the great persuader.

A fact allegedly *exists*; a non-fact allegedly *doesn't exist*.

But *existence* is something we can never know all about. It is a term in metaphysics, not in operational science.

It is awkward to think that bacilli and other small organisms did not exist until we invented microscopes to see them, or that other galaxies did not exist until, in the 1920s, we invented telescopes powerful enough to detect them. Similarly, the past does not exist any longer for us, in ordinary perception, but it exists—and so does the future—in the geometry of Minkowski's space-time continuum.

Bucky Fuller has another pedantic suggestion we might consider at this point. Since "existence" appears to be either meaningless (scientifically indeterminate forever) or some kind of Game Rule in disguise, we should not talk about it all, if we want to make sense. What we can talk about sensibly, Fuller says, is the *tuned-in* and the *not-tuned-in*.

The microscopic world was not *non-existent* but *not-tuned-in* before we had microscopes.

The beauty seen by a painter is not exactly non-existent for a money-oriented businessman but is not-tuned-in by him, because it is not relevant to his reality-tunnel.

What I perceive at a moment is not necessarily real or existent, for others, but merely what I am tuning-in at that moment. It may be my favorite day-dream.

If we talk always and only about the tuned-in and the non-tuned-in, we will make statements that are operationally and scientifically meaningful, although limited by our space-time coordinates. When we talk about existence and non-existence, on the other hand, we make statements that can never be totally confirmed and perhaps can never be totally refuted, which means we are making operationally meaningless statements.

Of course, like the other semantic reforms urged in this book, this introduces relativity into our speech and is profoundly repugnant to Fundamentalists.

What is tuned-in by Mr. A may not be tuned-in by Ms. B, but that does not mean that either of them is "crazy" or perverse. It merely means that every reality-tunnel encourages us to notice some things and ignore or forget other things.

What is not-tuned-in by the best scientific instruments of 1986 may easily be tuned-in in 1987, for all we know.

It is not impossible, however uncongenial the thought may be to the Citadel, that many "unscientific" reality-tunnels, explored by, say, painters, or poets, or musicians, or novelists, or "mystics," may be not non-existent but merely not-tuned-in by those who have not *practiced* for many years in tuning-in painterly or poetic or musical or novelistic or "mystical" brain circuits.

Omni Vol. 4 No. 11 (September 1982)—a new report from the Center for UFO Studies, Evanston, Illinois. The Center is run by Dr. J. Allen Hynek, astronomer, former UFO consultant to the Air Force. The report in this instance is written by Mark Rodeghier, astrophysicist. 440 UFO-related automobile accidents are studied. There were two features in common among all these cases:

Strange lights were seen in the sky.

And the motors of the cars mysteriously malfunctioned.

I will accept the lights as appearances, and as a neo-Humean I will even accept the motor failures as appearances in Hume's sense, but I suggest that any "Scientific Materialist" who accepts both motor failures and associated car accidents as appearances has gone a long way down the road toward the Buddhist doctrine of *maya*, which regards all data as appearances. At such a point, I fail to see much distinction at all between such a materialism and the most esoteric varieties of Oriental mysticism.

It is generally agreed that the United States had up to or over 500,000 troops in Vietnam during the 1960s and that these troops and their allies bombed, shot and napalmed over a million Vietnamese. There is some argument, still, about whether this invasion was either moral or necessary, but it is agreed that it happened. I suspect that it is agreed only because there is no organized Faith with a vested interest in asserting that the war never happened. If there were such a Faith, and if it were as devout and fervent as the New Fundamentalism, we would see endless books and articles proclaiming that the alleged movements of U.S. troops were yarns created by unscrupulous reporters, that the deaths of various Vietnamese were due to natural causes, that hoaxters and practical jokers had flown helicopters with U.S. Army markings on them, that whirlwinds had picked up napalm in one place and dropped it in another, and that—we have not studied CSICOP in vain—eye-witness testimony is "merely anecdotal," while statistical evidence has been "cooked."

This is not a wild fantasy. The Holocaust Revisionists use similar arguments to disprove the existence of Hitler's death camps. The human mind is ingenious enough to prove or disprove any proposition, *to its own satisfaction*, if not to the conviction of those who lack the Faith to believe it.

So: in 440 cases strange lights were seen in the sky and the motors of cars mysteriously malfunctioned. I deduce that in 440 cases where the motors of cars mysteriously malfunctioned, strange lights were seen in the sky. I even deduce that, while this *may* be "coincidence," it *may* also reflect a connection of some sort between strange lights and motor failures. I do not deduce that alien spaceships are involved. I don't know what the strange lights were, and I rather strongly prefer the non-judgmental label "Unidentified Flying Objects," which admits our ignorance, to the more popular label "alien spaceships," which rushes to certitude a bit to quickly for my agnostic taste.

But I wonder why the whole subject is under such heavy Taboo and why so many of the New Fundamentalists ot only reject the spaceship idea but reject the data as well and heap ridicule on anybody who reports such events.

I have personally met 17 UFO witnesses. I didn't seek them out—it just happens I travel a lot and lecture a lot and thus meet a lot of people. All 17 told me they had not reported their sightings to the government or the press. When asked why, all 17 said they were afraid of being called crazy.

So: I wonder—if the Center for UFO Studies found 440 cases of UFOs related to auto accidents, how many more such cases are there in which the witnesses were simply too prudent to talk about what they saw?

And if people in many cases are afraid to talk of what they have experienced, is it really wicked satire to say there is an Inquisitorial spirit abroad in the world today?

The Irish proverb quoted at the beginning—"If you see a two-headed pig, keep your mouth shut"—contains profound pragmatic wisdom. Maybe most people are shrewd enough to understand that, and the reports that get into books like this are a small, very small, cross-section of the Chaos that is actually going on around us.

Maybe.

Comptes Rendus 1887-182—an object that fell from the sky on June 20 that year in Tarbes, France. It was cut and shaped as if by intelligence and covered with ice.

Some of you *know* this Damned Thing only looked a little bit *as if* cut by intelligence because you know there are no intelligences beyond this planet, right? Me—I wonder a bit, as usual.

10 September 1910 *Scientific American*—a worked stone fell from the sky into the Yaqui Valley of Mexico. The author, Charles Holder, and a Major Burnham, examined it and agreed it had two concentric circles inscribed on it and some characters that Holder thought were Mayan. The stone was eight feet long.

Maybe Holder and Major Burnham were having one on the *Scientific American*.

Or maybe a whirlwind picked it up in the Mayan area of Yucatan and then dropped it in Yaqui Valley.

See? I told you, a few pages back, that it might be useful to invent such selective whirlwinds, if it were absolutely necessary to maintain certain Faiths at any cost.

27 April 1972 London *Times*—for seven hours two houses in Barmondsley were assailed by mysterious stones coming from an unseen source. Two children were injured, or thought they were injured, and every window was broken, or witnesses hallucinated that they were broken. Police were summoned early but could not catch any hidden vandal throwing the stones.

Can't see how a whirlwind could manage that. The hidden vandal must have been very, very clever, or else—TUUR occasionally sobers up long enough to get a temporary job with the London *Times*?

Flammarion, *The Atmosphere*, p. 34: a block of ice weighing four and a half pounds fell in Spain June 1829; another block of ice weighing eleven pounds fell in France October 1844; mass of ice three feet by three feet fell in Hungary May 1802.

When these abnormal blobs of ice fall these days—as they do: we shall see some cases later—the explanation is that they fell off the wings of an airplane; but there were no airplanes in 1802-1844.

Must have been a *segregating* whirlwind in each case. It ignored everything else in its path and only picked up ice.

31 July 1896 *Science*—W.R. Brooks of Smith Observatory reports an object passing slowly across the moon. He describes it as "round," just as many current UFO witnesses report slow-moving enigmas in the sky as "round."

And yet the UFO "skeptics"—that is, the True Believers in those models which declare UFOs impossible—insist, over and over, that no astronomer ever reported a UFO.

I guess they forgot about Brooks.

L'Astronomie 1886-70: *several* objects moving across the sun. Worse: they moved *in alignment*, just like modern UFOs often do. Seen on April 15 and again on April 25.

The "skeptics" forgot that, too.

Now, these last two cases sound a bit as if they might be spaceships (although I would not rush in haste to pronounce that verdict) but if the falling stones in Barmondsley were thrown by the crew of a spaceship, then extraterrestrials must have a damned peculiar sense of humor. In any case, I do not see a need for the spaceship idea, but I do see a need to think about such matters instead of mechanically affixing whatever label is most consistent with our reality-tunnel.

Messengers of Deception by Jacques Vallee, op.cit.—Dr. Vallee, now a computer scientist, started his career in France as an astronomer. He tells a shocking story in his first chapter—almost as bad as the story by Rawlins of Harvard about how he caught CSICOP, who are always accusing others of "cooking" data, "cooking" their own data—

Dr. Vallee says that, while working at an observatory in France, he saw two UFOs. The head of the observatory not only forbade him to write or speak of the subject, while employed there, but later went and destroyed the records of Vallee's sighting.

I can hardly believe it. I keep saying that the Fundamentalists are honorable men; I want to be charitable in my judgments; but—

It seems that when any model becomes an Idol its advocates begin to act like priests and inquisitors.

The UFOs were tuned-in by Dr. Vallee. By destroying the records, the administrator made sure they were not-tuned-in for future researchers in that observatory. Did that make them non-existent?

At this point, I recall a feature that once appeared in a San Francisco newspaper. Six people at random, on the street, were asked "Do you believe in UFOs?" Four said yes, and two said no. But if one read the answers carefully, as I did, it was obvious that none of them were replying to the question. They were replying to a different question— namely, "Do you believe in extraterrestrial spaceships?"

But a UFO is not an extraterrestrial spaceship. It is an etic event in space-time which some humans file in their reality-tunnels as a "spaceship"—and other humans file as "mass hallucination"—

Dr. Vallee, incidentally, regards Unidentified Flying Objects (UFOs) as still *unidentified*. He merely suggests that we should think about them open-mindedly, as I am trying to do. That is also the opinion of Dr. Hynek, of the Center for UFO Studies, whom I have mentioned earlier.

Such agnosticism may make sense to some of us but it is profoundly unsatisfactory to those Idolators of all faiths who already *know* what UFOs are.

Monthly Weather Review 32-365—On November 12, 13 and 14, 1902, it "rained" mud in Australia. There was a haze all the way to the Philippines and as far as Hong Kong.

That is not as "bad" as werewolves or spaceships on the face of it, but—try to think of a conventional explanation. Try, even—just as an experiment—to think about it without invoking 2000-mile-wide "mass hallucination" or claiming TUUR infiltrated himself into a science journal.

Monthly Weather Review 29-121—an even heavier fall of mud, and muck, in Europe February 1903. Most of it identified as water plus dust. A very eccentric whirlwind?

Journal of the Royal Meteorological Society 30-56—same case. They did their own analysis and say some of the muck was organic matter.

Organic matter?

Symond's Meteorological Magazine estimates that whatever it was—mud, muck, organic matter—it had fallen all the way from Ireland to Russia; over 10,000,000 tons of it are estimated.

Victorian Naturalist June 1903—it was back in Australia, and now is described as "red mud"—fifty tons per square mile—

Space-Time Transients and Unusual Events (hereafter STTUE) by Persinger and Lafreniere, *op. cit.* p. 35—July 1841 Lebanon, Tenn., fall of "fleshy material"; August 1841 Spring Creek, Tenn., fall of "flesh"; March 1846 Shanghai China, fall of hair and flesh; 1850, Virginia, fall of "several hundred pounds" of flesh—

Ibid, p. 34—July 1841, fall of fish, frogs and ice in Derby, England; December 1857—fall of lizards in Montreal, Quebec; August 1870—another fall of lizards, this time in Sacramento, Cal.

As Charlie Chaplin said once in a morbid context, "Numbers sanctify." The more I pile up such monstrosities, the more likely it is that some readers will start to believe them.

And yet the Fundamentalists are right, too, in their own way. *If* we already know all the laws of the universe, 100 alleged exceptions, just like one alleged exception, can be and should be dismissed as hoax or hallucination or misperception or some cuss-word that also means "it never happened."

But *only* if we already know all the laws of the universe. If perhaps we tend toward conceit and arrogance as a species and easily fall prey to thinking we know more than we do, in fact, know, then maybe we should *try* to keep an open mind.

Maybe it *is* all a matter of segregating whirlwinds, after all. Some whirlwinds select for ice, and some for fish, and some for lizards, and if we don't want to believe in the Vietnam war, some actually select for napalm—

19 September 1929 New York *American*—an alligator found and killed Hackensac, New Jersey, by one Carl Weiss.

Sorry: I'm violating my own principles. I should have said an appearance of something in space-time which Mr. Weiss categorized as an alligator.

23 September 1929 New York *Sun*—another appearance of something identified as an alligator was tuned-in near Wolcott, New York. A witness named Ralph Miles is quoted.

And when I tell the story that way I remember, alas, that space-time events do not come before us flaunting lables that say "FACT" or "APPEARANCE"—that *we* make that judgment, every second, and thus create our emic or existential reality—and that this is not just true of lesser mortals like you and me but of the High Priests themselves, maybe even including the High Priests of the New Inquisition—

Gentleman's Magazine August 1866—a crocodile found in Over-Norton, Oxfordshire, England. And the curious "coincidences" that haunt so many of these appearances—another crocodile had been killed there ten years earlier. Just as alligators are not normally found in New York and New Jersey but the two cases above are both from September 1929.

15 October 1982 New York *Post*—Hoboken, New Jersey, is haunted by a creature nicknamed "monkeyman." Described as hairy and ape-like and generally resembling Bigfoot of the Western states, but smaller. Oddly enough, this appearance is most frequently tuned-in by students in the schools.

Oh. Then it's just schoolboy humor.

But Bigfoot himself, reported by hundreds of witnesses over the decades?

Hunters-and-loggers humor, maybe.

The earliest Bigfoot report findable by me is in *La Scienza Nuova*, by Vico, 1735, attributed to the Chipeway Indians.

That must be Chipeway Indian humor, then.

Fortean Times No. 38 (1983)—two cycles of "monster" reports, or strange appearances, in St. Louis. First, several youngsters reported a creature "half man, half woman and with a bald head." Police Officer Bill Conreux says that he thought the students were sincere—but what does he know? Any Fundamentalist, far from the scene, is sure that it is remarkably easy for young people to deceive cops these days, although I don't know if any of them have tested that idea by personally trying to deceive a tough, inner-city cop. Anyway, Officer Conreux says that an *adult* (unnamed) had struggled with the creature, or the appearance, on one occasion. Shortly thereafter, reports of a *centaur*—half-man and half-horse—came in from over fifty witnesses.

Those folks in St. Louis must be smoking some freaky weed these days. They have not only tuned-in but turned-on.

3 May 1979 New York *Times*—a small elephant reported repeatedly in the Bay Ridge section of Brooklyn. Bay Ridge is a wealthy district, so the witnesses were not dismissed as loonies; the Bureau of Animal Affairs, the City Health Department and the ASPCA were all involved in looking for this alleged appearance.

The *Times*, which even Fundamentalists might admit has a very high reputation for scrupulosity, does not offer any conventional explanation in terms of an elephant missing from a local zoo or circus.

STTUE, Persinger and Lafreniere, p. 131—a "werewolf-like" appearance reported in Greegton, Texas, July 1958; "Bigfoot" in Fort Bragg, Cal. February 1966; gorilla-like critter in Lawton, Ok. February 1971—and this appearance was apparently wearing trousers according to some to whom it appeared.

Ibid. p. 139-140—another alligator, or alligatorish appearance, found frozen in a river in Janesville, Wis. February 1892; another alligatorish appearance found in the basement of a house in Newton, Kansas, August 1970; yet another alligatorish thing seen walking the streets of Windsor, Ontario, September 1970.

I don't see how even the most dextrous of segregating whirlwinds could have deposited that Beastie in the basement of the house in Newton, Kansas. Must have been TUUR again, then?

Ibid. p. 140—twelve cobras and a boa constrictor found in the same part of Springfield, Mo. 1953.

Charles Fort, the first great collector of this sort of anomalistic data, suggested, whimsically, that perhaps some sort of *teleportive force* just picks critters and other things up occasionally and then dumps them. I have a strong suspicion that Fort was not only whimsical but satirical, and that this "teleportive force" was just a parody of the segregating whirlwinds that other minds will try to convince themselves they can believe in when confronted with such reports.

But if it isn't teleportation or segregating whirlwinds what the merry hell is it?

And how many of us are so devout in our Faith in current paradigms that we really believe an endless succession of TUURs can really explain *all* this away? Including the Damned Thing that fell in Yacqui Valley according to *Scientific American* and the tons of unexplained mud and muck and organic matter recorded by *Monthly Weather Review* and the *Journal of the Royal Meteorological Society?*

Such data is so rare, some will say, that it is not worth any intellectual analysis.

But Charles Fort argued, at length, that such data is not uncommon at all; it is merely *repressed* by the same mechanisms of avoidance that Freud analyzed, the mechanisms that allow e.g. Roman Catholics and Marxists to "forget" things inconvenient to *their* emic realities.

We are certainly dealing with classic Freudian repression, bordering on hysteria, in some of our cases. The burning of Dr. Reich's books. The distortion of astrological statistics by CSICOP. The conspiracy to prevent the publication of Velikovsky's works. The destruction of Dr. Vallee's UFO's records by his superior at the observatory. Rational men and women do not do such things; only repression in the clinical sense—or acute anxiety—drives people to behave in that way.

Try an experiment that I have often performed. Go to a party, tell people you are a writer, and say you are writing a book on "paranormal" or anomalistic events. Ask if the people present have ever had any such experiences. Unless there is a Fundamentalist Materialist present to forcibly repress the relaxed conversational mood by hostile mockery and sarcasm, the most ordinary people will tell the most astounding tales.

From which I deduce that maybe these things are quite common after all, as Fort said, and the Fundamentalists will deduce, oppositely, that ordinary people do not know what the hell is going on around them unless the priests—pardon me, the *experts*—tell them what is really going on.

But try the experiment anyway, and see what stories you collect, and draw your own conclusions.

Let us take any year at random—say, 1922—and examine how such weirdity and downright blasphemy against Revealed Law can be found in that brief twelve-month period.

L'Astronomie 36-201—on February 15 at Orsay, France, an "unexplained" explosion in the sky, followed by another explosion in the sky 9 hours later. The latter was accompanied by an "illumination."

These were regarded as "unexplained" because no airplanes were lost at the time and no airplane wreckage was found.

Some will again heretically think of alien spaceships. I think simply that something unexplained happened—and that no upholder of the current model has, in the intervening 62 years, attempted to explain it. They have ignored it or forgotten it. One might almost be Freudian enough to suggest again that they have repressed it.

23 February 1922 *Nature*—another unexplained explosion "of startling intensity" over London. Again, no conventional explanation in terms of airplanes crashing or exploding.

Note that *L'Astronomie* and *Nature* are prestigious scientific journals—not the sort of places where TUUR would easily gain employment. And note also that, like the "UFO" reports from 19th Century scientific journals quoted a few pages back, these have simply been forgotten by orthodoxy. Is the Freudian term *repression* really too fanciful for such selective group amnesia?

12 March 1922 San Francisco *Chronicle*—mysterious rocks falling *slowly* in Chico, California. Meteorites do not fall slowly, and there is no other suggestion that these were meteorites. 16 March San Francisco *Call*—a "deluge" of the rocks falling on a crowd of curiosity-seekers. 15 March, San Francisco *Examiner*—Prof. Stanley of Chico Teachers College is quoted: "Some of the rocks are so large that they could not be thrown by any ordinary means."

So, then, TUUR was changing jobs rapidly that month, from one San Francisco newspaper to another—or there were three TUURS, part of the Vast International Conspiracy? And then Prof. Stanley, of course, was either a GS or an MS?

Or course, according to one of Galileo's laws, falling bodies such as rocks cannot fall "slowly" but most accelerate—fall faster and faster—unless interfered with by another force. So if we consider this Chico yarn at all, if we don't sweep it under the carpet by blaming it on TUUR, we will have to think about what kind of interfering force might account for such an oddity. And then—God help us—we can either rush in haste to such convenient but ill-defined concepts as "psychokinesis" or "teleportation," and be denounced as heretics—or, even harder, we can try to do some creative and original thinking, and then still be denounced as heretics.

Better to just forget it, then?

21 March 1922 Boston *Transcript*—a snow reported in the Alps—nothing odd about that—but this snow was accompanied by a fall, or an appearance of a fall, of caterpillars and huge ants along with the snow.

18 May 1922 Associated Press—particles of sooty matter falling for several days on the Virgin Islands. Regarded as unexplained because all local volcanos were inactive at the time.

29 May 1922 London *Daily Express*—an object, thought to be a craft or machine of some kind, fell into the ocean off Barmouth, Wales. Many witnesses. Unexplained, because no airplanes were reported lost at the time.

Some of the witnesses also said this Damned Thing fell slowly, in violation of Galileo—like those damned rocks in Chico.

5 September London *Daily News*—little toads reported falling, for two days, at Chalon-sur-Saone, France.

And all through 1922—see the "Index" to *The Books of Charles Fort*, under the date 1922—a continuous series of stories, in English newspapers, about a kind of *"poltergeist"* disturbance or "psychokinesis" or at least a series of mysterious occurrences that were happening all over England. Coal was exploding in English fireplaces. Some of it was so violently explosive that there were widespread charges that the coalminers, embittered by wage reductions, were putting dynamite in the coal. In some cases, however, the events or appearances were too strange to fit that theory. Some asserted that coal jumped out of the fireplaces and "ran" across the floor. An Inspector of Police had the impression that a piece of coal vanished from his hand, or dematerialized, while he held it. A physician, Dr. Herbert Lamerle, said he saw a *clock* vanish, or quickly become not-tuned-in.

Some of these appearances were truly horrific. One child died of fright—like the maid in Wales, 1905—and another had to be removed to a mental hospital.

All of these appearances in space-time occurred in one twelve-month period. Isn't it curious that, even after all the Relativism and Agnosticism we've been shamelessly wallowing in, all of us (including the author) still retain certain strong hunches (or prejudices) about which of them were *only* "appearances" and which were "real facts"?

And, incidentally—

We've already pointed out, in chapter one, that "matter" was originally a synergetic or holistic concept, *including the observer,* and not a reified or thingified Substance *outside* us—it meant, originally, that which we experience in making a measurement, remember?—and, in this connection, what do you suppose "fact" meant originally?

The Latin root, *facere* equals that which has been made. You can still see this holistic/interactive idea in such derivatives as *fact*ory and manu*fact*ure.

Dr. David Bohm notes in this connection (*Wholeness and the Implicate Order,* Ark Paperbacks, London, 1983, p. 142):

> Thus in a certain sense we "make" the fact. That is to say, beginning with immediate perception of an actual situation, we develop the fact by giving it further order, form and structure (we code it into our emic reality—R.A.W.). . . . In classical physics, the fact was "made" in terms of the order of planetary orbits . . . In general relativity, the fact was "made" in terms of the order of Reimannian geometry . . . In quantum theory, the fact was "made" in terms of the order of energy levels, quantum numbers, symmetry groups, etc.

It is passing strange that linguistic history brings us to the same view of *matter* and *fact* as is held in quantum mechanics—namely, that they are not separate "things" apart from us, but are holistic/transactions *involving* us. (It is even stranger that this is the view also of Buddhism.)

In any case, we are back to the second-plateau skepticism of Hume and Nietzsche. Facts are not presented to us, waving signs saying "We are the facts." We *make* facts by organizing appearances into reality-tunnels that suit our present needs, our problems-to-be-solved, our fears and fantasies, and our prejudices.

And just as the Fundamentalist Materialist classifies as "fact" that which fits its model, and dismisses as "mere appearance" that which does not fit, so, too the Fundamentalist Thomist mechanically accepts what fits the Thomist model and mechanically rejects what does not fit—and similar mechanisms perpetuate the Fundamentalist Samoan *tike*-worship reality-tunnel, and the Fundamentalist racist reality-tunnel, and the Fundamentalist male chauvinist reality-tunnel, and the Fundamentalist Ohio Presbyterian Republican reality-tunnel, and the Fundamentalist Iranian Islamic reality-tunnel—

And I repeat that we might all become startlingly sane, or at least much less stupid, if we tried, even occasionally, to look dispassionately and without prejudice at precisely those events which do not seem to fit our own favorite reality-tunnel or tunnels.

But the trouble with fundamentalists—of all sects, including those who are most angry at me just now—is also what is most attractive about them. I mean their modesty, their almost saintly humility. Nietzsche said once that we are all greater artists than we realize, but fundamentalists are too timid to think of themselves as great artists. They take no credit for what they have invented; they assume they have no part in the creation and maintenance of the Idols they worship. Like the paranoid—very much like the paranoid, in fact—they devise baroque and ingenious Systems, and define them as "Given." They then carefully edit all impressions to conform to the System. There is no vanity, no vanity at all, in people who are so intensely creative and so unwilling to recognize their own cleverness.

One must love such saintly modesty.

I am not so modest myself, as the reader may have noticed. I take full responsibility for the reality-labyrinths presented in my novels, and in alleged works of non-fiction like this catalog of blasphemy and heresy. My business is intellectual comedy, or surrealism, and is offered as entertainment for those bold, bad folks who are not frightened out of their wits by such guerilla ontology. Since I am the artist who invented this emic reality, I cannot regard it as anything else but an extension of my hilarious good humor—or my madness—as you will—

The people who believe the stuff that gets into my books seem as amusing to me as the people who are terrified or thrown into fury by them. I am not asking anybody to *believe* anything. I am asking only that you play a neurosemantic game with me, and observe what sort of reports you can consider with humor or dispassion and what sort of reports trigger terror or rage. If this be subversion, then so are the Marx Brothers and Monty Python.

24 September 1981 *Nature*—under the headline "A Book for Burning"—

"This infuriating tract . . . The author, by training a biochemist and by demonstration a knowledgeable man, is, however, misguided. His book is the best candidate for burning there has been for many years . . . in no sense a scientific argument . . . pseudo-science . . . preposterous . . . intellectual abberations . . . "

You thought it only happened in backward nations like the United States, where they even elect Actors as President. But *Nature* is generally considered England's most prestigious scientific magazine.

The book that *Nature* wishes were burned is *A New Science of Life* by Dr. Rupert Sheldrake. Dr. Sheldrake's heresy is a theory of evolution different from fundamentalist Darwinism.

Of course, there *are* other evolutionary theories than the Darwinian orthodoxy. The New Inquisition insists that they have all been refuted absolutely, but—

Prince Peter Kroptokin, who was a trained naturalist and geographer before embarking on his more celebrated career as a Philosophical Anarchist, wrote a whole book proposing a non-Darwinian theory of evolution, called *Mutual Aid as a Factor in Evolution*. It stresses the survival-advantages of cooperation and argues that Darwin, influenced by Capitalist ideology, had outrageously over-stressed the role of competition. Kropotkin's model is still defended by many who haven't heard or don't believe it has been refuted. The American anthropologist, M. Asheley Montagu, defended Kropotkin's model against Darwin's in several books, most notably in his *The Direction of Human Development*.

Tielhard de Chardin's theory of evolution is also far, far from Darwinian orthodoxy, and even implies a creative intelligence of some sort. Dr. Julian Huxley, certainly a major biologist, insisted that de Chardin's model was at least as consistent with known facts, or appearances, as Darwin's.

Dr. James Lovelock's "Gaia hypothesis," which treats the Earth as an intelligent being, or a self-regulating computer, contradicts Darwin's mechanistic simplicity. To say that Lovelock has been "refuted" is as polemical and unfair as saying he has been verified. His theory is still a matter of heated controversy.

Even Lamarck, the most frequently "refuted" of non-Darwinian evolutionists—he posited the inheritance of acquired characteristics and thus allowed a kind of emergent intelligence—has not quite been "refuted" thorougly enough to end that argument once and for all. Darwin thought Lamarck might be partly right; Smuts and Driesch reformulated Lamarck in more up-to-date models; and Arthur Koestler was defending a neo-Lamarckian position until he died a few years ago.

Dr. Gregory Bateson, generally considered one of the greatest American anthropologists, presents a kind of neo-Lamarckian evolutionary theory in his *Mind and Nature*, using cybernetic metaphors to explain teleological behaviors that are extremely awkward to explain in purely Darwinian terms, and leading to the thought of Earth as a goal-seeking organism.

Henry Bergson's theory of evolution, positing a "life force," has never been refuted really; biologists have just rejected the "life force" on Occamite grounds as an "unnecessary hypothesis." But that which seems unnecessary at one time and in one context may appear necessary later, in a wider context of further knowledge[1]; and a great deal of Bateson, de Chardin and Lovelock amount to restating Bergson's philosophical claims in more scientific language.

Meanwhile, the philosophy Department doesn't know Bergson is unnecessary, and he is still studied there—along with Nietzsche, who rejected Darwinian mechanism as a "principle of least possible effort and greatest possible blunder" and stressed life's *unnecessary* and "exuberant" fecundity in a quite Bergsonian manner.

It is a sociological curiosity that the Darwinian theory alone is the model that best suits the blood-and-guts reality-tunnel of the Military-Industrial Empire that employs the Citadel.

That's another coincidence, no doubt.

In short, to claim that all these theories have been proven false appears more like a propagandistic assertion than a neutral factual observation. The issue is still open, except in the minds of those who wish it were not open.

And I wonder how many readers of this book, convinced that only Darwin has seen biology bare, could offer a detailed criticism of Kropotkin and de Chardin and Bergson and Bateson and Nietzsche and Smuts and Driesch, proving in specifics that all but Darwin were factually wrong? Or do most of us tend to lazily believe that, only because we have been told, so often and so authoritatively, that the case is now closed?

Fortean Times, issue 37, interview with Dr. Sheldrake:

He was educated as a strict fundamentalist Darwinian, he says. When he began to have doubts, or creative and heretical stirrings or independent mental activity, he decided to read Bergson and Driesch. He found their books in the university library "covered with dust." Nobody had looked into them for a long, long time.

Orthodoxies of all sorts are maintained by partly the intolerance I have been documenting and partly by—simple lack of curiosity. Heresy is not-tuned-in, if one already has certitude.

I, myself, have not gotten around to reading Driesch or Snuts; but I have read Bergson and Nietzsche and de Chardin and Kropotkin. I do not think any of them prove Darwin wrong, but I do not think Darwin's case has been proven right, either. The Darwinians simply have more missionary zeal and have made so much noise that most people do not even know that there are as many alternative evolutionary theories as there are alternative explanations of "the" "mind" in psychology and neurology.

Dr. Sheldrake's Heresy is that there are non-local fields in nature— somewhat like Dr. Reich's *verboten* orgone field but even more like the non-local fields in modern physics, which we will discuss in the next chapter. Dr. Sheldrake calls his fields "morphogenetic fields" and claims they allow certain kinds of transmission of information between organisms that are similar, so that, say, a rat in Australia might "know" not by material transmission but by "morphic resonance" something learned earlier by a rat in Massachusetts.

In fact, this theory was suggested to Sheldrake partly by a celebrated set of anamolous experiments in animal psychology in which just such an effect *seems* to have happened. Details can be found in Sheldrake's *New Science of Life*, Blond & Briggs, London, 1981, pp. 186-191. Briefly: Dr. William McDougall of Harvard University, in the 1920s, began a long-range test of the extent to which intelligence in rats was hereditary. He measured intelligence, in this case, by the ability to solve water-mazes. "Smart" rats, defined as those who solved the maze quickly, were bred with other "smart" rats and the slow learners were also bred with slow learners. 22 generations later, instead of only the "smart" rats getting smarter, all the rats were proportionally smarter, in the dimension of maze-solving. Even those rats bred from slow learners were solving the mazes nearly ten times faster than their ancestors. There is no explanation for this in orthodox genetics.

McDougall's experiment was later duplicated in both Scotland and Australia, with even more disconcerting results. By then even the *first generation* of rats was solving the maze faster than McDougall's last-generation fastest learners.

On the face of it—if one does not accuse Dr. McDougall *et al* of being Mad Scientists or remarkably incompetent—this seems consistent with a non-local field theory like Dr. Sheldrake's. It is hard to see how, with the most brutal hammering, it can be forced into a shape consistent with materialist orthodoxy.

February 1984 *New Age* magazine (Boston)—Interview with Dr. Sheldrake. He cites two attempts, since his book was published, to verify or refute his theory. One was sponsored by *New Scientist* (London) and the other by *Brain/Mind Bulletin* (Los Angeles). Both *seem* to confirm him. He does not claim he is vindicated. He merely says the results are encouraging and should inspire further research.

In the *New Scientist* experiment people in various parts of the world were given one minute to find the hidden faces in an abstract drawing. Averages were then taken. Later, the solution was broadcast on BBC-TV when about a million viewers were expected to be looking. Then, elsewhere, in places where BBC-TV was *not* received, immediately after the broadcast, the tests were given again. Those who found the hidden faces in a minute were a higher percentage—by 76 percent—than before. Dr. Sheldrake estimated—and *New Scientist* accepted his estimate—that the odds were 100 to one against getting this result by chance.

It *seems* that non-local fields *might* have carried the information to the people who hadn't received it by television.

In the *Brain/Mind Bulletin* test, various groups were asked to memorize three rhymes. One was a traditional Japanese nursery rhyme, the second was by a modern Japanese poet, and the third was gibberish. As the non-local field theory predicts, the traditional rhyme, having been learned by millions of Japanese children over the centuries, was memorized more quickly than the two alternatives.

Sheldrake has hardly been proven right in all respects. Darwin has hardly been overthrown. But—at this point—the issue is certainly open, even if the minds of the materialists are closed.

And if the alleged evidence for alleged "ESP" is not all spurious—if it was not concocted, every bit of it, by malign and derranged GSs and MSs deliberately or half-consciously "cooking" their data just to annoy the materialists—if there is "one just man in a hundred" among the parapsychological heretics, and they are not all liars—this so-called "ESP" is just one flavor of the non-local information field Sheldrake posits.

For instance:

Carl Jung, *Synchronicity*, Routledge and Kegan Paul, London, 1977, p. 38-39—the engineer, J.W. Dunne, had a vivid nightmare, in 1902, about a volcanic eruption. In dream-logic, this hadn't happened, but Dunne knew it would happen, and the nightmare consisted of the usual elements of hurrying, rushing, getting lost, etc. in the effort to arrive in time to warn people. The threatened island in the dream was French-speaking and Dunne "knew" that 4,000 would be killed in the disaster.

Two days after the nightmare, a volcano on French-speaking Martinique erupted, a town was swept away, and 40,000 people perished.

The materialist, or course, says "coincidence," although some of us may be haunted by the inconsistent consistency of the coincidence—in which 40,000 gets mis-read as 4,000 in the manner of errors in many communication channels—

One might manage to call it "ESP" if one assumes that some people near the volcano were noting, or almost-noting, abnormal pre-volcanic symptoms and worrying or repressing worry.

Jung, or course, prefers to regard it as synchronicity—his own label for an alleged resonance in nature, or between nature and its various parts, including us—a resonance which creates seeming "coincidences" so startling that most of us, fundamentalists excluded, sense deeply that they require an explanation.

Dunne himself, who had the dream, preferred the label of "precognition." He had not read Prof. Munge's pontifical announcement that precognition is forbidden by "basic physical laws"—i.e. by those personal prejudices which Munge fervently believes are laws—and so he devised his own mathematical theory by which precognition *is* consistent with physical laws. Dunne's theory is in his books, *An Experiment with Time* and *The Serial Universe*, and is elegant enough to have favorably impressed the astronomer, Sir Arthur Eddington, who said that it did not contradict any of the basic physical laws he knew and was worthy of consideration.

But this dream could also be a case of Sheldrake's non-local field, if all the animals in and around the crater were sensing the mounting turbulence and starting to move away from it.

Or the seeming connection between Dunne's dream and the subsequent tragedy could be just coincidence, after all.

Or—Dunne's dream and sombunall of our other Weird Tales might be explained next week or in fifty years by Kerflooey's Proof in topological geometry or von Hanfkopf's Law in general systems theory.

I don't know. But I suspect that dogmatism is a bit premature.

I also feel strongly, as a libertarian philosopher, that burning Sheldrake's book is not the best way to seek an answer to such questions; and as a psychologist, I think I detect the familiar odor of primate panic behavior in the suggestion that it should be burned.

Some of the most interesting evidence for a neo-Lamarckian or quasi-Sheldrakean model came from psychedelic drug research in the 1960s, as mentioned in a footnote. It is extremely curious that *"memories" of past human lives and even of pre-human states of evolution* were frequently reported by LSD subjects. This happened so often, indeed, that it led Dr. Leary in Boston to posit a "neurogenetic circuit" and Dr. Grof, independently in Czechoslovakia to posit a "phylogenetic unconscious." Both researchers recognized that this contradicts Darwin, but reported their conclusions anyway.

Since biologists seem to have good evidence that such "memory" cannot be carried by the genes, then these cases are either more "hallucination" and "incompetent research" or else they fit snugly into Sheldrake's non-local field theory.

Some heretics might like to see more research, to clarify the matter.

Such research is *illegal*. Since about 1965 or 1966, in various countries, there have been laws prohibiting other psychologists from experimenting in this area. This is because such research is regarded as "dangerous"—by governments who, oddly, do not think nuclear testing is at all dangerous.

It is Dr. Leary's model that psychedelics create *shock* and *stress* which break down old imprints and conditioning. He says that, in "normal" consciousness we are imprinted and conditioned to tune in only to (1) bio-survival needs, (2) emotional games that give us status, (3) conditioned Game Rules of our culture and (4) sexual gratification, and to remain *not-tuned-in* to other, potentially-available signals. We thus stay in one reality-tunnel all our lives. By breaking our imprints, he suggests, psychedelics allow us to tune in to other reality-tunnels, including the "neurogenetic" or "phylogenetic" or "morphogenetic" field-or-circuit in which such pre-birth "memories" are stored.

Dr. Leary, like Dr. Reich, went to prison.[2] And now other researchers are forbidden by law to check or test his models.

Meanwhile, meditation is still legal, even if the Fundamentalists will ridicule you for trying it. In intense meditation, under strict yogic rules, one undergoes a *stress* created by social and sensory deprivation. This stress may also break imprints.

Most intense meditators eventually "remember" past lives," and guided by the metaphors of India, decide that such memories are best described in the *reincarnation* model.

This is an odd effect of the New Inquisition:

Where scientists are legally or otherwise coerced away from certain areas of investigation, people do not all uniformly stop having experiences that such investigation might scientifically explain; people merely resort, *by default*, to pre-scientific models to explain the experiences.

Archetypes, by Anthony Stevens, Quill, New York, 1983, page 48:

It has been shown in many tests that new-born chicks, before any chance of learning from older birds, will exhibit alarm when a cut-out shaped like a hawk is flown above them. The cut-out, usually of cardboard, does not *smell* like a hawk; the chicks are reacting to the *image* of a hawk.

In 1939, the ornithologist David Lack tried a related experiment with finches captured in the Galapagos Islands, where there have been no predator birds for hundreds of thousands of years. (Darwin used the large variety of different species of finches on the Galapagos as an example of Natural Selection, by the way.) Lack captured over 30 finches from 4 different Galapagos species and sent them to a friend in California.

The birds showed the alarm reflex, and tried to crouch and hide, when a hawk or falcon flew above them.

This "image" and associated fear had continued for hundreds of thousands of years in an environment where it was unnecessary.

Jung's "collective unconscious," which is supposed to contain such *images* stored for aeons, is often rejected as unscientific, but the finches didn't know that, I guess. They had the information "hawk-image means danger," somehow.

This seems more Lamarckian than Darwinian, to me, and it even sounds, possibly, like the activity of Sheldrake's non-local field. If such acquired information cannot be transmitted genetically, and Lamarck is wrong, then the information was transmitted by some other means, and Sheldrake at least offers a model which might explain such transmission.

Two of our stories in this chapter involved people who were, it says, *"frightened to death."* Since people can, and do, die of depression, I assume they can die of fright, although I have never seen such a case.

Fundamentalism—whether it invokes Gods or Laws—is a way of reassuring the nervous, of *soothing* and *pacifying*. This was the role of the priests in a Theological Age. Since Science cannot provide certainty, for the nervous of our age the New Fundamentalists invent certitudes and attribute them to science.

Fundamentalists may be hostile to Freud and Jung not because Freudian and Jungian models are "unscientific" or "prescientific"— everybody knows we must "make do" with such models until a scientific psychology (or neurology) arises—but because Freud and Jung boldly call attention to such fears and repressions.

1   Neo-Lamarckian ideas infest psychology—e.g. Freud's "racial memory," Jung's "collective unconscious," Grof's "phylogenetic unconscious," Leary's "neurogenetic circuit of the brain." This is not because psychologists are necessarily less scientific than biologists, but because they encounter a different class of data. Specifically, all these neo-Lamarckian models are based on cases of patients, or experimental subjects, who *seem* to "remember" events in past history or earlier stages of evolution. As we shall see, Sheldrake's model explains such data without positing Lamarck's notion that the "memory" is carried by the genes.

2   Dr. Leary was convicted of possession of one cannabis cigarette. He claimed he was framed by the arresting officer. Be that as it may, he was sentenced to 37 years imprisonment, even though the normal sentence for that crime at the time in that state was six months imprisonment. The judge also described Leary's ideas as "dangerous," which is why the Swiss government later accepted Leary as a political refugee. After being re-captured, Leary served 5½ years, and now prudently devotes himself to designing computer software.

CHAPTER FOUR

THE DANCE OF
SHIVA

(with comments on Bell's Theorem, Po and mysterious fires)

Belief is an obsolete Aristotelian category.
> **Dr. Jack Sarfatti, physicist, in conversation**

**In addition to a "yes" and a "no," the universe contains a
"maybe"**
> **Dr. David Finkelstein, physicist
> Lecture, UC-Monterey, March 31, 1979**

A physical anthropologist, after conducting many examinations of Canadians, concluded that the average Canadian has one testicle. There was no mistake in the statistical techniques used. How is this possible?

Readers who are stumped by this riddle should notice that the same problem might arise with Americans or Australians but not with citizens of the British Isles. If one speaks of the average Englishperson or the average Welshperson, the avoidance of sexist terminology makes obvious that "the average" is not, as males tend to think, a male abstraction but an androgynous abstraction.

Language structures demark our reality-tunnels. I mentioned that earlier, but it needs repeating.

A bear leaves her cave and goes in search of food. She walks one mile south nibbling this and that, and then walks one mile due east still nibbling. Finally, she walks one mile due north and is back at her cave. What color is the bear?

This stumps many people a lot longer than the first riddle. If *you* are stumped, try to figure out what there is in your reality-tunnel that defines the question as impossible.

We tend to separate subjects or "areas of knowledge" in our heads, whereas in Universe everything is synergetically (holistically) related. In this case, we have separated *geometry* from *evolution*, if we are blocked, and that is why we cannot see a rather obvious answer.

However, if we think about both geometry and evolution, an answer quickly dawns. One then thinks: the only place a bear can start from on a sphere like Earth and still arrive back where she started after making two right-angle turns is the North Pole. For obvious evolutionary reasons, all bears up there have developed white fur, so our bear is white.

(Another problem may be that, while most of us have accepted the scientific *model* that the Earth is spherical, we retain neurosemantic reflexes from the Flat Earth reality-tunnel. In that case, we think the bear *cannot* arrive back at the same point after two right-angle turns and we grow so confused we cannot even consider the color of the bear. . .)

Or so it seems, when one has made one's first breakthrough with this problem. Most people never get any further. Actually, there are many, many other places the bear can start from and still arrive back home following the above conditons; but working this out still yields the answer that the bear is white.

I leave it to the reader's own ingenuity to deduce the other places on the globe that fit this geometrical peculiarity.[1]

A man is shown an object he has never seen before and immediately recites over a dozen facts about the place the object came from and the people who live there. No "ESP" is involved, and the man was never in the place where the object came from. How was this done?

Well, this is comparatively easy to explain in the abstract, even though most of us would find it hard to duplicate the feat described.

The man, of course, was an anthropologist who had already done decades of field work. His name was Leo Frobenius. Even though he had never been where the object—a pot for carrying water—had been found, Frobenius had developed a high "intuitive" feel for the laws that govern reality-tunnels—"cultural configurations"—and synergetically recognized the pot's environment the way a musicologist can quickly identify a composition as early 18th Century Italian and not late 19th Century Russian.

The late President Franklin Delano Roosevelt, as an experiment, once spoke the same sentence to every guest who shook his hand at a White House party. None of the guests actually "heard" the sentence even though FDR had one of the greatest speaking voices in American politics. Can you explain this?

Some of you may be uneasy about the expression "high 'intuitive' feel" which I used in discussing Frobenius's sense of what he called *Kulturmorphologie* and others call "cultural configuration" or emic reality. Nonetheless, every reality-tunnel has its own consistencies which are more visible from outside than from inside. (It is hard, for instance, for Fundamentalist Materialists to recognize the extent to which their reality-tunnel is a white male ruling-class construct.) Art forgeries which have escaped detection for as long as half a century often become obvious thereafter because the forger, while consciously imitating the style of, say, 1450 has unconsciously included some of the style of his own epoch (say, 1930). This unconscious style was "invisible" in the 1930s but around 1980 it becomes increasingly "visible" to professionals, because we are no longer "embedded" in the 1930s.

Ponder this one: Dr. Brown is Chief Surgeon at X hospital. Dr. Jones says that Dr. Brown is sometimes short-tempered. Dr. Smith says that Dr. Brown makes unreasonable demands on the staff. Dr. Black says that on the day of his divorce Dr. Brown made a serious mistake in surgery. Now, two weeks after the divorce, a nurse reports seeing Dr. Brown, dressed in a pink blouse and red skirt with high heels, trying to force the door of the lady's toilet in a nearby park.

If you think Dr. Brown is perhaps getting a bit weird, you have imposed your own reality-tunnel on this without noticing what you were doing. All employees sometimes complain that the boss is short-tempered or makes unreasonable demands. All surgeons make some serious mistakes. In an ambiguous sentence you guessed who is indicated by the "his" in "his divorce" and then forgot that that was only a guess. You also didn't reflect that the doors on public toilets often seem to be stuck and need some forcing. Most of all, you didn't suspect that Dr. Brown is a woman who happens to look well in pink and red. If you didn't consider that, you were in what I just called a white male reality-tunnel.

By the way, the words President Roosevelt spoke which no guest heard were "I strangled my wife this morning."

I assume the guests thought they heard something like "It's good to see you this evening."

The principle illustrated by Roosevelt's experiment—if this widely-published anecdote really happened—will surprise no psychologist. The perception process always includes both addition and subtraction. The reason for this appears to be concretely neurological and not just abstractly "psychological," as we tried to show in Chapter One. To give one more illustration of this *neurological* process: In a well-known experiment—cited, for instance, in Colin Wilson's *Criminal History of Mankind*, Putnam, New York, 1984 p. 93—Dr. Jerome Bruner measured the nervous path of sound traveling from a cat's ear-drum to the brain. A clicking noise was used as the stimulus to be traced along the nerve-paths. Two mice were later placed where the cat could see them but not get at them. When the click sounded again, there was *no electrical impulse recorded at the ear-drum.*

The cat was not just "concentrating" on the mice and "ignoring" the sound; it was literally *shutting off the nerve impulse at the ear.* There is nothing "occult" about this. The function of the synapse is to act as an off/on switch: when *off* it does not transmit a signal, and when *on* it does transmit. The senses pick up about 10,000 bits of information *per second,* and the synapses automatically turn on and off—passing the information to the brain, or suppressing it—according to habitual (imprinted and conditioned) programs. Estimates differ about how much information gets through to the brain, but it is safe to generalize that at least 90 percent is cut off or not-tuned-in. When one says in exasperation, "It was as if they couldn't even hear me," one may well be neurologically accurate. If—as is likely—"they" were already rehearsing their brilliant and crushing rebuttal, then they were not hearing a great deal of what you said, for a different "psychological" reason but by the same *neurological* process by which the White House guests die not *hear* Roosevelt confess to murder.

And:

A stone, eight feet long, with designs on it, fell from the sky onto Yacqui Valley, Mexico, in 1910. Onto Yacqui Valley, Mexico, from the sky there fell, with designs on it, a stone eight feet long. I did not get that yarn out of the *Brighton Yodel* or the *West Buggery Express*; I got it out of the *Scientific American*, and recounted it only about 20 pages back. I wonder how much our world-view, our emic reality, would have to change if we took that report seriously—but I wonder also how many readers have "forgotten" it already or "failed to notice" that it came from *Scientific American*—

And several objects *moving in alignment* across the sun in 1886— did that come from some damned tabloid or from a more respectable source? If you can't remember, why did you edit that bit of information out of your reality-tunnel? (The answer is only about 20 pages back in this case also.)

Have any of you started classifying our yarns as "true," "false" and "indeterminate" yet, or do you still make a quick "true" or "false" judgment on them?

From *Critics' Gaffes* by Ronald Duncan, Macdonald & Company, London, 1983, pp. 112-116:

Galileo's discoveries were not only rejected by the Old Inquisition, but by the English astronomer Martin Horsley, who decided the telescope was accurate on Earth "but represents celestial bodies falsely."

Prof. Ludwig Gilbert rejected Sertermeur's discovery of morphine in 1810, claiming such a drug was "unscientific and unchemical."

The surgeon Alfred Velpeau denounced the search for anesthesia as "chimerical" in 1832, on the grounds that surgery *must* cause pain. (Don't laugh too quickly. Surgery always had caused pain at the time Velpeau wrote. It required an agnostic, almost surrealist, imagination to separate the ideas of "surgery" and "pain" at that time.)

Prof. John Henry Pepper pronounced that Edison's electric light had no future, and Edison refused to believe Tesla's alternating current generators were safe. Lord Kelvin, one of the great physicists of the time, agreed with Edison and sent a telegram to the Niagara Falls Power Company saying TRUST YOU AVOID GIGANTIC MISTAKE OF ADOPTION OF ALTERNATING CURRENT. Frank Sprague, a pioneer in electrical railways, calculated that alternating current systems could not carry electricity more than 20 miles. (They presently extend as far as 1,500 miles in some cases.)

Quarterly Review in March 1825 heaped scorn on the idea that locomotives could travel *"twice as fast as stage coaches!"* (their italics and exclamation point).

Simon Newcomb, discoverer of the planet Neptune and Director of the US Naval Observatory, calculated in 1894 that artificial flight is impossible; he recalculated in 1901 that an airplane might carry something no heavier than *an insect*.

In retrospect all this is amusing, but—

Critical Path, by R. Buckminster Fuller, St. Martin's Press, 1981, p. 29-30:

Fuller, a recognized genius with documented achievements in many fields of engineering and mathematics, proposes that porpoises are descended from human beings.

I don't know whether this is another case of a first-rate mind making a World Class blunder, or if—as happened in several engineering disputes earlier in his career—this is another case of Bucky being right and the other experts being wrong.

I suspect strongly that here Bucky was overly imaginative. I march in step with orthodoxy; my agnosticism falters. Bucky Fuller, I conclude, was no more infallible than the Pope, or the Ayatollah, or Prof. Munge, or myself. I can't imagine porpoises are descended from humans.

In 50 years will this page be cited as an example of common sense breaking through in an otherwise deliberately outrageous book, or as a Case History showing that even a would-be heretic is hypnotized by some of the orthodoxies of his time?

When a parachutist has reached a constant velocity in falling toward Earth (a) the downward force on him is greater than the upward force (b) the upward force is greater than the downward force (c) both forces are equal. Which answer is correct?

The answer appears later on, but for a while I will consider a different kind of problem—or a problem that appears different—

Alleged "ESP" is absurd, in one common reality-tunnel, because "ESP" acts as if "space" is somewhat unreal. Precognition (also alleged) is equally, or more absurd, because it acts as if "time" is somewhat unreal. Jungian synchronicity (meaningful resonance) is even more absurd than "ESP" or precognition because it acts as if both space and time were unreal.

What happens to our own reality-tunnel if we consider that the words "space" and "time" might be, as suggested in Chapter One, human-invented metaphors?

Dr. John S. Bell of CERN, the center for nuclear research in Switzerland, published a mathematical demonstration in *Physics* 1-195 (1964). It is known as Bell's Theorem. It argues, in effect, that while separation in space and time are "real" in some contexts, such separation is "unreal" or unimportant in quantum mechanics.

Michael Talbot in *Mysticism and the New Physics* is keen on Bell's Theorem because he thinks it is scientific vindication of the monism of those mystics who have been telling us "All is One" for the last few thousand years. Dr. Fritjof Capra, himself a physicist, is equally delighted with Bell and in his *The Tao of Physics* virtually invites us to convert to Taoism on the basis of Bell's math. Gary Zarov in *The Dancing Wu Li Masters* joins this chorus of affirmation and celebration. Another physicist, however, Dr. Heinz Paigels, in *The Cosmic Code*, insists that, even if sound mathematically, Bell's Theorem is physically meaningless.

This is what Bell argues in simple terms:

INSTRUMENT   SOURCE   INSTRUMENT

Imagine a source that emits two photon streams (two "rays of light" in lay language) which are intercepted by two instruments, A and B. These instruments may be as far apart as you like, *even at opposite ends of the universe.* By a simple deduction from accepted laws of quantum mechanics, Bell shows that whatever property you measure at instrument A, a simultaneous measurement at instrument B will be mathematically complimentary. That is, the reading at instrument B will not only correlate with the reading at A but with the *type* of reading—which "property" of the photons you measured.

How startling this is only becomes evident when one reflects that the result is "as if" each photon *knows* what measurement is being carried out at the other photon, and knows it instantaneously.

Bell also showed that this kind of non-local correlation, as it is called, should happen with *separation in time* as well as with *separation in space*; but we will come to that later.

Bell's Theorem has attracted a lot of attention among physicists because it is mathematically elegant, but it was not entirely a surprise. That quantum mechanics seems to imply such non-local (or non-causal) connectedness had been pointed out by various physicists previously. Curiously, the first to point it out was Einstein, in 1935, who said such a non-local connection was "spooky" (which maybe it is) and that it "implied telepathy" (which maybe it does). Einstein concluded that there was something radically wrong with quantum mechanics, if it seemed to lead to such conclusions. Dr. Erwin Schrodinger—he of the dead-and-alive cat—noted a similar "monist" implication in quantum mechanics and even said (in his *What Is Life?*, Chapter 23) that the monist or holistic philosophy of the *Upanishads* might be more consistent with quantum math than any Western reality-tunnel is. Dr. David Bohm made the same point in a celebrated 1952 paper, which was widely discussed. Bell's mathematics, then, only brought to the surface what quite a few had suspected already.

It must be stressed that photons are either "particles" of light or "waves" of light—both models are useful—but, anyway, they are the thingamajigs by which light travels. There is, therefore, no way any signal can get instantaneously from the photon at instrument A to the photon at instrument B, or vice versa, since signals are defined as energy packets and energy packets move at the speed of light, or at a velocity less than the speed of light, but never *faster* than the speed of light, according to the best generalizations or "laws" now known.

This is why the non-local connection seemed "spooky" to Einstein and why it seems to imply monism. The photons behave *as if* some energy is causing them to be correlated, but there is no energy in physics that moves fast enough to do that job.

There is a way around such mathematical monstrosities, of course; it is known as the doctrine of "accidents of the formalism."

An "accident of the formalism" is something that is mathematically useful, even necessary perhaps to the elegance of the equations, but has no measurable consequence in the experimental world. Thus, the most popular way of disposing of Schrodinger's damned cat is to say that this remarkable feline is both dead and alive *in the formalism*, but there are no cats in the *experimental* world who will be found in that mixed state. A photon or an electron or any other quantum thingamajig "is" a wave sometimes and "is" a particle sometimes, similarly, because we use wave equations sometimes and use particle equations other times. (In the celebrated two-hole experiment, photons act like both waves and particles experimentally, but at different moments. That is a different problem.) The multiple-worlds interpretation of the Schrodinger wave equations, similarly, is an "accident of formalism" and to take it literally—as some physicists do—is the mathematical equivalent of an optical illusion, according to this line of thought.

Thus, those who found Bell's mathematical demonstration simply incredible decided it must be an "accident of the formalism" with no experimental meaning.

Berkeley, California, 1974—Dr. John Clauser tested Bell's Theorem experimentally. See Capra, previously cited, for details.

The damned photons behaved as Bell's math had predicted.

Every possible objection was raised, of course. Clauser repeated the experiment with more rigorous controls, and got the same result. Aspect in France repeated it. Others repeated it. Within a few years, there were six experiments, of which four supported Bell and two did not and all were being criticized on various technical grounds.

U.S. Patent Disclosure 771165 (May 12, 1978) by Dr. Jack Sarfatti, Physics/Consciousness Research Group—prototype of a proposed faster-than-light communication system, based on Dr. Sarfatti's model that, even if *energy* can't get around faster than light, Bell's math indicates that *information* is somehow getting around faster than light.

Dr. Carl Sagan of CSICOP, informed of this, remarked or pontificated that Dr. Sarfatti's prototype was "at best, a playful notion."

Meanwhile, letters flowed back and forth between Dr. Sarfatti and Dr. Nick Herbert. I have been privileged to examine them. Dr. Herbert, another physicist, argues that even if Bell's math is correct and even if it is meaningful (he thinks it is), Dr. Sarfatti's system won't fly. He has good arguments, as far as I can judge. Dr. Sarfatti replies. He also has good arguments, as far as I can judge.

Foundations of Physics Vol. 12 No. 12 (1982)—a *second* faster-than-light communication system proposed, this time by Dr. Herbert.

14 December 1982, letter from Dr. Herbert to me—his faster-than-light system was inspired, he says, by the debate with Sarfatti. He thinks it is more plausible than Sarfatti's system, but is becomingly agnostic. He says the main purpose of his paper is to provoke debate that will "clarify fundamental issues."

Dr. Herbert says also that he has heard of "about a dozen" alternative FTL systems—faster than light systems—being argued about in physics departments or seeking publication in the journals.

6 January 1983 *New Scientist* (London)—two new sets of experiments by Dr. Alain Aspect of the Institut d'Optique Theorique et Aliquee in Orsay, near Paris, are regarded as conclusively vindicating Bell's Theorem.

Aspect's experimental set-up was as follows:

PHOTON   POLARIZER   SWITCH   SOURCE   SWITCH   POLARIZER   PHOTON
COUNTER   COUNTER

The source is either a mercury atom or a calcium atom, because these emit photons easily. The jagged lines on each side of the source indicate that the diagram is condensed to fit the page—the photons travel a long distance (three meters) before encountering the rest of the apparatus. First they pass through specially-designed switches (which act in 10 nanoseconds, i.e. 10 billionths of a second) and then are polarized and arrive at photon counters activated by the switches. The switches are important, because the photon counters thus register only what happens *after* the photons have passed the switches—i.e. in the last 10 billionths of a second. Since the instruments are six meters apart, no energy-signal can travel in that time from one photon to the other "causing" each to adjust to the other. (That would require exactly 20 billionths of a second.) Nonetheless, the photons remain correlated in the way Bell predicts. It is like two ballet dancers at opposite ends of the stage who take up the same positions in the finale without looking at each other (i.e. with no signal passing between them).

We know how ballet dancers create such "synchronicities," of course. The information is "already in them." It has been fed in by a choreographer. But what sort of choreographer feeds the information to these photons? The question is far from trivial.

New Scientist (or their Mr. Basil Riley actually) sums up:

> I should emphasize that this result holds despite there being no
> interaction between the two separate particles . . . In other words, there
> appears to be some form of "non-local effect" . . . we must be prepared to
> consider radically new views of reality without placing locality in a
> central position.

Dr. John Gribbin points out in his *In Search of Schrodinger's Cat, op. cit.* p.
226 that this experiment is, in context, even stronger than it appears at
first sight. Out of seven experiments, five have vindicated Bell, while
the experiments themselves, under criticism, have successively been
more and more exquisitely subtle. A defect in the apparatus should
destroy evidence of correlation; it is very hard to imagine—try to imagine
it—what a series of incredible defects it would take to somehow
cumulatively produce a false correlation where there was none in
actuality.

Dr. Herbert has given me the following popular illustration of what
this sort of non-local effect means, adopted from a lecture from Dr. Bell
himself:

Imagine a man in Mexico City who always wears red socks, and
imagine a man in Belgrade who always wears blue socks. Imagine that,
in some way, we can "cause" the man in Mexico City to take off his red
socks and put on blue socks. If these men acted like Aspect's photons,
the man in Belgrade would then, instantaneously—before any news of
what happened in Mexico City could reach him—suddenly take off his
blue socks and put on red socks. Furthermore, if they were exactly like
Aspect's photons, every time we caused one of them to change in this
way, the other would still immediately change in the complimentary
way.

You can see why Einstein regarded such non-local effects as spooky.
Since no energy moves fast enough to cause them, they are *acausal*.

One technical point should be raised here. According to the
Copenhagen Interpretation—so-called because it was devised by Dr.
Niels Bohr and his colleagues at the University of Copenhagen, 1926-
28—there is a difference between science and "reality." Unfortunately,
the Copenhagen Interpretation is so subtle in its ramifications that no
two physicists seem to understand it in exactly the same way. Dr. Bohr
once stated it in the words, "It used to be thought that physics refers to
the universe, but we now know that it refers to *what we can say* about

that universe." (Italics his.) That is, if I understand him, "*the* universe" is a philosophic concept—it generally implies "*the real* universe," with all the philosophical problems of "reality" thereby invoked. *What we can say about the universe,* however, refers to our math and our experiments—the current reality-tunnel that seems useful to us, in explaining the currently tuned-in, in my terminology. We should remember that we are referring to the latter—our semantic systems—and not confuse it with the former. The menu is not the meal.

Dr. Eugiene Wigner, on the other hand, has said, or has been misunderstood to have said, that the Copenhagen Interpretation means that the universe is being created by our thoughts and experiments. I suspect that he meant the *universe-experienced-by-us* is being created that way, and that "*the* universe" is something we can't know about.

Gribbin, in *In Search of Schrodinger's Cat,* op. cit. begins by declaring boldly (page 1) that the Copenhagen view means "nothing is real" but he quickly sobers himself and says more restrainedly (page 4) that " 'Reality' in the everyday sense is not a good way to think about (physics)."

Dr. Nick Herbert, in several conversations, has insisted that the Copenhagen Interpretation amounts to "Christian Science," since he takes it as denying that there *is* a real universe. But he doesn't like the Copenhagen Interpretation.

Dr. David Bohm, in a recent conversation with me, described the Copenhagen view as one that "denies that we can make statements about actuality." I think he was consciously avoiding, or trying to avoid, the philosophical problems of "reality," when he said "actuality" instead.

You might suspect that I am sympathetic to Copenhagenism, insofar as I understand it; in fact, that is why I have written about the correlation of Bell's Theorem with "*the experimental world*" and have not attempted to say anything about its correlation with "the real world," whatever that is, or "the real universe," whatever that is, or "ultimate reality," whatever *that* is.

I take it that "experimental reality" or "the experimental world" or "the experimental reality-tunnel" is part of "existential reality," i.e. what people *experience*; and that it is a large part of experience, for those who spend their lives as experimentalists; but a relatively small part for those who spend their time writing music or poetry.

I further take it that, whatever categories we use to organize our experience in speech or thought, these categories will contain metaphoric elements; and that to talk about this process of creating metaphors will necessarily create more metaphors—metaphors about metaphors, in fact. Therefore, I think it reasonable to assume that the conflicting versions of the Copenhagen Interpretation are "really" trying to say the same thing, but the various physicists create different metaphors in trying to say it.

Thus, when Bohr distinguishes so exquisitely between "the universe" and "what we can say about the universe," he fundamentally means the same thing as Gribbin means when he says "nothing is real." Both can be restated in a middle or compromise proposition, to wit: Nothing we can say about the universe *is* the "real" universe. Wigner, hopefully, also means that we are creating *what we can say about the universe, which is not the "real" universe. When Herbert says the Copenhagenists don't believe in the "real" universe, this is also, maybe, what Bohm means when he says the Copenhagenists deny that we can talk about "actuality." Mathematical physics provides the most useful* emic realities available to us, but no emic reality *is* etic (non-verbal) reality.

And I hope this collectively means that science should be considered as a set of models *for talking about experiments*, as art is a set of models *for communicating evaluations*, and that neither these kinds of models nor any other kind of models should be confused with ultimate "reality" or "all" of ultimate "reality," whatever that is. We can talk meaningfully about the tuned-in but not about the not-yet-tuned-in.

If by some miracle I have managed to make sense out of this issue, where physicists themselves seem to have trouble understanding one another, the basic point of Copenhagenism seems to be similar to my own Nietzschean-existentialist view that the nonverbal or preverbal world never contained "meters" or "kilograms" or "ergs of energy" or "photons" or "good" or "evil" or "beauty" or "meaning" until primate nervous systems ("human minds") put them there as systems of classification.

Now, since Bell's Theorem—or the non-local connection as a mathematical-experimental generalization—seemed to "imply telepathy" to Einstein as far back as 1935, you can be sure the damned parapsychological heretics have noticed this. This *implication* is discussed at length in the works by Capra, Zarov and Talbot previously cited, as studiously avoided by Gribbin, and is invoked by Drs. Puthoff and Targ—both physicists themselves, incidentally—in their *Mind-Reach* (Delacorte, New York, 1977), the book in which they report, among other things, those experiments with Uri Geller in which they *thought* they observed that which Fundamentalist Materialist dogma declares impossible.

The Fundamentalist counter-attack thusfar as I have perused it— see, for instance Steven N. Shore's "Quantum Theory and the Paranormal: The Misuse of Science" (*Skeptical Inquirer*, IX, 10, Fall 1984)—amounts to a restatement of the Copenhagen view in its most simplified form. In short, they tell us that the non-local connection as described in mathematics and experiments is a statement about *what we can say* and not a statement about absolute "reality." That is true enough, I think, but the Fundamentalists manage to forget that the Copenhagen view applies this "model agnosticism" (as it is sometimes called) to every kind of model in science (or outside science, sometimes) and this specifically includes the allegedly absolute "laws" on which their own dogmas are based.

This isn't *kosher*. You can't consistently invoke absolutes to prove that certain things are *a priori* impossible, out of one side of your mouth, and then invoke Copenhagenism to discount Bell's math and seven experiments, out of the other side of your mouth. The only logical application of Copenhagenism to the whole "paranormal" question is to be agnostic in the abstract and to make tentative judgments (admitting their tentativeness) on the basis of current experiments and current mathematics.

The Fundamentalists, it seems to me, are talking theologically (in absolutes) almost all the time, and resort to modern scientific epistemology (Copenhagenian agnosticism) only when a new model affronts their prejudices. They are, in effect, saying "The models we want to believe are 'basic physical laws' and hence absolutes" (see Prof. Munge) "but the models we don't want to believe are—only models."

I don't want to complain about this too much. Even such *selective* agnosticism is, after all, an advance out of the medieval dogmatism which the Fundamentalists have hitherto espoused.

A much more honest, if startling, way of rejecting non-locality has been espoused by the Columbia physicist Dr. N. David Mermin.

Dr. Mermin's position can be found in two articles, "Quantum Mysteries for Everyone," *Journal of Philosophy*, Vol. 78 (1981) and "Is the Moon There When Nobody Looks?", *Physics Today*, April 1985.

Dr. Mermin concludes that non-local connectedness is so absurd, that we must choose the most agnostic variety of Copenhagenism instead of accepting non-locality. He does not mince words or shy away from the implications of what he is saying. "The moon is demonstrably not there when nobody is looking," he states flatly in *Journal of Philosophy* article; he says the same a little less bluntly in the *Physics Today* article.

If that doesn't deserve to be called "solipsism" I don't understand the meaning of solipsism.

Nonetheless, I salute Dr. Mermin for being clear and unflinching, especially in comparison with Steven Shore's article in *Skeptical Inquirer*, which I think also leads to solipsism even if Shore won't admit that.

The parachutist who has reached constant velocity?—remember him?—At this point, the downward force on him and the upward force from the parachute are equal. But I assume you all figured that out by now.

At least I hope you did.

If the non-local connection can be considered a model in science, on the grounds that it contains correlations between experiments and mathematics, which is what scientific models are supposed to contain, then it implies something about the-universe-we-experience, or the tuned-in even if it does not solve philosophical problems about the not-tuned-in, which are questions outside science. That, I think—or I hope—is what Copenhagenism means.

If the non-local connections says something about the *experienced* (tuned-in) universe, then we can make inferences from it, and find implications. These inferences and implications may be, and should be, debated, of course.

Capra, Zarov and Talbot all think the non-local connection implies some kind of monism, or holism, or what Bucky Fuller called synergy; Schrodinger thought that, too, even earlier.

Paigels, if I understand him, interprets Copenhagenism to mean that the non-local connection implies that we are the kind of critters who, after these experiments and mathematical deductions, will necessarily create the model or metaphor or non-locality, as our way of organizing the experiments and deductions. That's true, I guess, but some may think it carries scientific parsimony to the point of anal retentiveness.

The Fundamentalist Materialists, again, seem to me to be saying the non-local connection implies nothing—which may be carrying retentiveness to the point of mental constipation.

John Gribbin, *In Search of Schrodinger's Cat*, op. cit. p. 254 decides after much musing that the non-local connection implies that "either everything is real or nothing is real." That is, Gribbin's own analysis leads to the conclusion that we *either* accept the EWG multi-universe model, in which everything that *can* happen *does* happen—"everything is real"—the model that many other physicists regard as mathematical surrealism—or else we must retreat to the flavor of Copenhagenism which the Fundamentalist Materialists want and which Gribbin, more honestly than they, admits is tantamount to solipsism—"nothing is real."

Dr. Jack Sarfatti, in conversations, says the non-local connection means that his proposed faster-than-light communication system can work, once he gets a few more bugs out of it.

Dr. Fred Wolfe, in *Making the Quantum Leap*, seems to me to accept the most solipsistic version of Gribbin's second choice—"Nothing is real."

Dr. Nick Herbert, in a work in progress, agrees with Capra, Schrodinger et al that the non-local connection implies some kind of monism or synergy and may imply paranormal consequences.

Once again: I am not asserting a dogma in contradiction to Fundamentalist Materialism. I am merely indicating that—when the experts cannot agree and even seem to misunderstand each other at times—agnosticism is not only scientifically more appropriate, and more in line with that virtue of humility which most sages and philosophers have urged, but a matter of simple honesty with oneself.

20 February 1983 London *Sunday Times*—interview with Dr. David Bohm, after the latest Aspect experiments. Since Dr. Bohm is considered the most distinguished physicist in London these days, the *Times* asked him what *he* thinks it implies.

"It may mean," says Dr. Bohm, "that everything in the universe is in a kind of total rapport, so that whatever happens is related to everything else; or it may mean that there is some kind of information that can travel faster than the speed of light; or it may mean that our concepts of space and time have to be modified in some way that we don't now understand."

For convenience, let us call these three choices the Philosophical Monist alternative, the Science Fiction alternative, and the Neo-Kantian alternative. Let us also try to remember that they are not the *only* three choices.

The Philosophical Monist alternative ("whatever happens is related to everything else") does seem, on the face of it, to imply the kind of cosmology usually associated with Oriental mysticism. Schrodinger noticed that, as early as 1944, when he wrote that quantum mechanics seems more consistent with Oriental monism than with previous Western, or Aristotelian, habits of dualism. Dr. Capra's *Tao of Physics*, whatever else it proves or fails to prove, documents in detail that many Buddhist and Taoist texts also sound remarkably like some modern books on quantum mechanics. This looks pretty threatening to Fundamentalist Materialism, already, but it is even more hair-raising to note that the Monist model also bears a striking and hardly accidental resemblance to both Jung's *synchronicity* (universal resonance) and Sheldrake's *morphogenetic field* discussed in the previous chapter—two ideas which the Fundamentalists have repeatedly denounced as "absurd" and "absolutely forbidden" by their Platonic Eternal Laws.

In fact, Dr. Bohm has explicitly acknowledged that this implication of quantum mechanics inclines him to suspect Sheldrake may be right, after all, despite the condemnations of the Fundamentalists. See "Conversation Between David Bohm and Rupert Sheldrake," *Revision*, Fall 1982.[2]

I fear me, I fear me, but—there is worse waiting us—

Any kind of non-local monism or interconnectedness does *somewhat* strengthen the case for the "paranormal" insofar as it makes thinkable or possible those trans-time and trans-space linkages which Fundamentalism has declared unthinkable and impossible.

This can be seen more clearly, and more alarmingly for some, by skipping over such notions as "ESP" and "precognition" and proceeding directly to the Damndest of the Damned—*magic* (or, as some prefer, magick). What is magic supposed to mean? According to Frazer's classic *Golden Bough*, magic is a "primitive science" or false science which incorrectly assumes a "law of contagion" whereby "things once in contact continue to influence each other." *But that is precisely what the non-local connection asserts*, if it asserts anything and is not just mathematical poetry.

Wait a minute, here. I am not asserting that the non-local connection proves the validity of magic. Magic not only asserts a non-local connection but *also* asserts that there are known ways by which some humans (shamans or magicians) can exploit this connection to change the world in ways they want. This second assertion can still be doubted and denied, even if the first assertion sounds like the modern quantum assertion of non-locality. Bell's Theorem tells us *nothing* about what happens to a man when a witch-doctor performs malign rituals over a lock of the man's hair.

Similarly, Jungian synchronicity is not *proven* by these quantum experiments, but it is put in a context where it seems possible at least, and, if one accepts the monist interpretation here being discussed, not only possible but rather plausible.

Before leaving the monist interpretation, it is amusing to note—or, for some, it is terrifying to note—that if one accepts as meaningful both Bell's Theorem and the currently fashionable "Big Bang" cosmology, the monism that results is of a Buddhist or Hegelian "hardness." If all particles were together in one place at the first nanosecond of the Big Bang, then, by Bell's Theorem they are all still non-locally connected. Dr. John Clauser, the first to test Bell, calls this the "super-determinist" flavor of the monist interpretation of the non-local model. I think this abolishes "free will" and I suspect it ultimately elevates *synchronicity*, or something like synchronicity, to a position where all other alleged laws are just sub-cases of the general law of resonance.

Super-determinism also, I think, reduces the quarrel between materialism and idealism (or mentalism) to meaninglessness. As some Buddhists noted long ago, both the propositions "all is matter" and "all is mind" become pointless if all is connected monistically. You can only say, then, that "all is ineffable," which is the dominant trend in Mahayana Buddhist philosophy. As the semanticist, Korzybski, often said, at the stage one cannot speak but only *point*—which is what Zen Buddhists often do.

Dr. Clauser did not endorse super-determinism; he just included it in a chart of possible interpretations of non-locality. The chart is in Zarov's *Dancing Wu Li Masters, op. cit.*

Onward to Dr. Bohm's second alternative—"Information that can travel faster than light"—the Science Fiction alternative, I have called it—

Well, if information can get around faster than light, and no energy can get around faster than light, then we either have to think of some ghostly kind of information that travels without an energy to carry it—and parapsychology rears its head again—or else we have to think that the information isn't exactly traveling but is somehow *already everywhere*.

The second choice is, in fact, the one Dr. Bohm has chosen to defend as his own favorite model. He defends it ably in *Wholeness and the Implicate Order, op. cit.* This model is based on the proposition that energy can either enfolded (implicate) or unfolded (explicate). The enfolded energy of the universe contains the information on which the system operates; the unfolded energy is programmed, as it were, by this enfolded, implicate energy.

If this is too abstract, try the following metaphor, given to me by Dr. Sarfatti, the man with the FTL prototype:

Imagine that the universe known to us is like a great big jumbo computer. Imagine that each lesser system is a somewhat smaller computer within the Big Computer. Work your way on down to the smallest system now accepted—the quark—and imagine that as tiny little mini-mini-mini-computer. Now the hardware of each computer (Bohm's unfolded, explicate order) is localized in space-time—each part is *here*, not there, and *now*, not then. But the software (Bohm's enfolded, implicate order) is nonlocally everywhere-everywhen, here *and* there, now *and* then. Now you understand non-locality, according to Dr. Sarfatti.

I fear that this gives a Sarfattian flavor to Bohm's model, but at least you can visualize it (I hope). It also explains, sort of, why Sarfatti hopes his non-local or faster-than-light communication system will someday get off the ground, after he works out a few more details.

Here is another metaphor, used by Dr. Bohm himself, to explain the implicate order:

I pick up the phone and call you. My speech is unfolded or explicate in the form of sound waves as it leaves my lips. The telephone transmitter enfolds the form into the implicate order of electrical impulses and they travel in that form to the receiver on your phone. The receiver then unfolds the implicate order of electrical impulses into the explicate order of sound waves again and you hear me speaking.

This metaphor may make "implicate" and "explicate" more clear than Sarfatti's metaphor, but as Bohm himself admits it still involves movement in space, and his concept of implicate order is that it does not move in space but is everywhere already.

If you can think of the implicate and explicate being enfolded and unfolded like speech on a phone, and also of the implicate as the nonlocal software of all local or unfolded hardware, you are fairly close to what the Bohm model means, I think.

At this point it is obvious that faster-than-light (FTL) communication is thinkable, even if most physicists still find it implausible. (In fact, I recently participated in a seminar at Esalen Institute with several physicists—I was the resident Science-Fiction writer—at which this matter was discussed for nearly a week. All the physicists found FTL implausible but thinkable and were eager to think, and talk, about it.)

IF FTL ever does get off the ground we will be in the position of the young lady in the celebrated limerick:

> There was a young lady named Bright
> Whose speed was much faster than light
> She departed one day
> In a relative way
> And returned on the previous night

That is, if Dr. Sarfatti or Dr. Herbert or somebody someday sends out a real faster-than-light message—or if one of the "dozen or more" FTL systems Dr. Herbert mentions turns out to work—we will shortly be living in the Grandfather Paradox of Science Fiction.

That paradox is: If I travel backward in time and murder my grandfather before he mates—never mind why I would want to do such a thing—then my father would never be here, and I would never be here—and then—and then?

And then we either see from this example that time-travel is a logical contradiction, or else we have to return to the multiple universes of the EWG model—Gribbin's "everything is real"—There is a universe in which I am here, and a universe in which I am not here, and by traveling back and doing the dirt to poor Grand-dad I have navigated from universe-1 to universe-2. Grand-dad, meanwhile, like Schrodinger's cat, is both dead and alive. But so am I. And so are you.

I don't see how the New Fundamentalism can survive that alternative. Ultimately, it leads to the possibility that we can travel far enough back to intervene at the Big Bang and create universes with different laws, including every chaotic and cock-eyed law that cannot exist in the Fundamentalist's universe.

Maybe we will do it, and therefore in a sense *have done it*. Maybe the present "universe" of experience is midway between the Ideal Platonic Universe of Eternal Laws the Fundamentalists posit and one of the cock-eyed universes created by our future meddling with the past. That may explain some of the weirder yarns in this book, if you think about it . . .

So much for the Science-Fiction alternative.

But before we leave information faster-than-light and information therefore going backwards-in-time—

If that is possible, then "precognition" is also possible.

Prof. Munge who told us that precognition is impossible because it contradicts "basic physical laws" also tells us in the same article—*Skeptical Inquirer*, op. cit. p. 42—that precognition is specifically impossible because it "violates the principle of antecedence ('causality') according to which the effect does not happen before the cause." But we have just seen that, in one line of interpretation of quantum mechanics, the effect can indeed happen before the cause.

So I repeat: the Eternal Laws of the Fundamentalists may exist in some other universe, but we have no grounds for certitude, yet, that they exist eternally in this universe.

Because any message that can get back to Grand-dad would have the same theoretical effect as if "I" went back physically and killed the old boy—it *might* cause him to act in such a way that I wouldn't be here—another "I" would have sent the messsage, from the universe next door—

And it would ultimately get back to the Big Bang and create a universe or many universes with laws we cannot guess.

Dr. Bohm's third alternative—which I have called neo-Kantian— "our concepts of space and time will have to be modified"—

This seems to lead back to the monist alternative, in which "space" and "time" are not quite real, or are *only* "appearances"—

Or it leads to even wilder alternatives, which nobody has thought out yet.

Because, as Kant pointed out, and as Einstein demonstrated even more tellingly, our ideas of "space" and "time" are interconnected with our ideas of "mass" and "matter"—connected both by definitions and by mathematical equations—

If our ideas of "space" and "time" change, then, our ideas of "matter" will also have to change, and the Fundamentalist Materialists will have to become Fundamentalist Somethingelseists.

In a sense, Bohm's three alternatives are interconvertible. That is, if all things are in harmony or resonance, then the universe will behave *as if* information is getting around faster than light, or is already everywhere; and if "space" and "time" are somewhat unreal, or only real in some contexts, then it will again be *as if* information is everywhere simultaneously; and if information is so ubiquitous, it will be *as if* space-time is somewhat unreal or is an aspect of a deeper implicate order; and if there is an implicate order, it will be *as if* space-time is somewhat unreal and/or *as if* information is dashing madly backwards-forwards-and-sideways in time instantaneously.

It appears again to be a question of which metaphors we prefer.

If we try to apply the Occamite principle of picking the simplest model, we grow more confused, because each group of physicists claims, and believes, its favorite model is the simplest. This looks like an artistic choice, almost.

Po?

I mentioned it in the sub-title to this chapter; some of you have been wondering when I will get around to discussing it.

Po is not another abominable bit of jargon I have invented like *sombunall.*

Po is an abominable bit of jargon, if you will, that was invented by the psychologist Edward de Bono. It is intended to denote a kind of thinking that goes beyond the Aristotelian true/false game we played in chapter one, into the alternatives implied in our multiple-choice game in chapter two. *Po* is simpler and more radical than our multiple-choice game: it takes us into the mode Dr. Finkelstein was suggesting when he said the universe contains a "maybe."

Dr. Finkelstein was paraphrasing another physicist, Dr. John von Neumann, who, back in the 1930s, proposed a non-Aristotelian system of his own called Quantum Logic. In place of our multiple choices, von Neumann extends Aristotle's two-valued logic to only three values— true, false and maybe.

In Aristotelian logic, Schrodinger's cat is *either* dead or alive. (That is equivalent to saying the statement "The cat is alive" is *either* true or false.) Since quantum equations do not obey the Aristotelian game, von Neumann proposes a mathematics in which the cat is in three possible states: that is, "The cat is alive" may be true, false or in the "maybe" state.

Some physicists find this formalism more helpful than saying the cat is dead and alive in different universes or that the Schrodinger equations which give rise to this problem are only formalisms that yield accurate results in the laboratory for reasons we cannot fathom. Other physicists think von Neumann has explained the obscure by the more obscure and consider Quantum Logic a "stunt" rather than a meaningful model.

Be that as it may, *Po* has some of the functions of von Neumann's "maybe" in taking us beyond Aristotelian true/false or either/or games. Po also has some amusing and entertaining functions of its own. For instance, where linear Aristotelian logic works with familiar associations or generalizations (called "laws of thought," of course, by those who have made Aristotle their Idol), Po thinking moves *laterally* with unfamiliar associations.

Dr. de Bono claims that Po thinking unleashes creativity and measurably improves students' ability to solve *unfamiliar* problems.

In the case of the bear riddle at the beginning of this chapter, a strict and unimaginative Aristotelian would start from geometry and move in linear fashion along familiar mathematical associations. Unless interrupted by a burst of "intuition" this would proceed indefnitely into an infinite regress of more-or-less geometrical thinking. In the Po mode, recognizing that the problem is intended to be tricky, one proceeds laterally into the unfamiliar and the deliberately bizarre, almost in the manner of Freudian free-association. Any concept can be attached to "geometry" just by placing the symbol *Po* in between. Thus, one might consider geometry *Po* Charlie Chaplin, geometry *Po* sexual desire, geometry *Po* Chinese painting, etc. If one looks back at the problem for clues, one tries, say, geometry *Po* color. It is not long before one comes to geometry *Po* evolution, and the solution begins to dawn.

De Bono asserts that this process underlies creative breakthroughs in the sciences. He may be right. It seems that, somewhere along the path that led to Special Relativity, Einstein must have been thinking something like photons Po humans. In Aristotelian logic, this is a very, very unlikely connection. *Photons*, in Aristotelian logic, lead to physics and thus to mathematics and cosmology etc., while *humans* leads to psychology and thus to sociology and evolution etc. Einstein probably did think something like photons Po humans, however, because he tells us somewhere that David Hume impressed him more than any other philosopher and Hume's method was always to relate philosophical concepts to human beings—that is, to how humans invented the concepts and why they continue to find them useful (if they do). But once you think photons Po humans, you are halfway to Relativity already, and maybe on your way to Copenhagenism as well. Photons Po humans leads to how humans came to think of photons, which leads to questions of measurement, which leads to "length" and "time" as human grids: *presto*, Relativity dawns!

Similarly, the formula for Darwin's breakthrough was species Po change. We all see change around us constantly, but we do not *see* species change, because the rate of change is so slow there. Ergo, nobody put species and change together before—(or, rather, the few who did, were either too timid or too prudent to follow the thought very far)—But, once you follow the chain species Po change for a while the "unthinkable" concept of evolution becomes thinkable.

Part of the creation of psychoanalysis probably included Freud pondering sexuality Po forgetting or sexuality Po dreaming or something equally "unconnected"—before he connected them.

Of course, some Po thinking may lead to poetry or great surrealist paintings, instead of science. There is no guarantee as to where Po will land you, which is part of the justification for thinking it relates to that mystery we call "creativity."

Try some of the following and see where you go:

> UFOs Po National Debt
> Mother Po History
> Death Po Ecology
> Houses Po Relativity
> Astrology Po Genetics
> Revenge Po Cigars
> Photons Po Post Offices
> Pornography Po Bell's Theorem
> Evolution Po Werewolves
> UFOs Po Rabbits

Those couplings were assembled at random, from covers of magazines around my house, but some interesting possibilities leap out. Houses Po relativity, for instance, is probably something like what was going on in Buckminster Fuller's brain before he created the geodesic dome. Fuller was interested in Einstein's geometry (Reimannian) and also in cheaper housing; something like houses Po relativity led to the link "geodesics" and now we have 300,000 very efficient geodesic buildings that looked "peculiar" at first but now look increasingly beautiful as people get accustomed to them.

Evolution Po werewolves led me to a plot for a possible science fiction story. Genetic engineering of werewolves is adopted to colonize a new planet. Later, some of the man-beasts come home to Earth and confront the usual prejudice and discrimination. Lycanthrope Liberation rallies. Court cases: how human do you have to be to possess "human rights"? "Maybe the government says they can move into my neighborhood, but I'm gonna keep my silver bullets handy."

Freud's "heresy"—it *was* heresy, then, and still is to some (e.g. Prof.

Munge)—might have derived, we said, from sexuality Po dreaming. Reich's heresy began from sexuality Po politics, which led him to theories about the political function of sexual repression which offended both orthodox Freudians and orthodox Marxists.

Reich went on to the "worse" heresy of sexuality Po physics, which led to thoughts of an Erotic force in all things—the "orgone"—

The Citadel burned his books that time.

Obviously, if the Po process is part of creativity, and if the Po process also arouses anxiety in the blocked or repressed mind, then we can see easily why so many creative people have been so viciously persecuted in their life-times.

We perhaps begin to understand Fundamentalisms of all sorts.

Oh, yes, by the way—in passing—if you were at all astonished to be told that the upward force equals the downward force when a parachutist has constant velocity, you should not reject Materialist models too quickly, or laugh at them too smugly. Any Materialist would tell you that in the Newtonian reality-tunnel, the reality-tunnel that best meshes with this sort of falling body problem,

$$F \text{ equals } m \times a$$
$$F \text{ equals mass times acceleration}$$

I even reminded you of that equation, back in Chapter One, in case you had forgotten the Elementary Physics of school days.

If acceleration equals 0, as it does at constant velocity, then mass times acceleration equals 0, since anything multiplied by 0 still equals 0. Ergo, force equals 0. The upward force and the downward force are in balance, in such a case.

If you thought the downward force must be greater than the upward force, then nobody ever explained the Newtonian meaning of *the metaphor of force* to you, and you were probably thinking of a theological or demonological kind of force. The mental image/concept was something like: the downward demons pull down, the upward demons pull up, he's going down, ergo the downward demons are pulling harder than the upward demons.

Don't feel too badly about it. We all relapse occasionally. Think of those brilliant technicians at Houston asking "How are things *up* there?" as if they never heard of Copernicus.

The superiority of the materialist reality-tunnel in this case, and many other cases, explains, I think, why it has displaced theological and demonological reality-tunnels in educated circles, outside Ireland and Iran.

Nowhere does this book intend to deny the superior virtues of many materialist models in many areas of experience.

I am merely suggesting, playfully at times, maybe seriously at other times, that Universe is a bit more complicated than anybody's models; and that using several reality-tunnels—as in Po or quantum mechanics— *may* show a great many interesting correlations and details and exciting and beautiful aspects that we will never see if we look always and only through one monotonous reality-tunnel which we have made into an Idol.

You walk through an art museum, one which is quite large and cosmopolitan. Assuming you have some esthetic sense (are not "picture-blind"), some paintings move you deeply and others move you considerably less. You look at Chinese art, without Western perspective. You look at African art, assembled according to space-time games even more alien to "us" than Chinese art. (I am assuming we haven't spent so many years specializing in Chinese art that it is as familiar to us as Western art.) You look at a da Vinci, a Rembrandt, a Van Gogh, a Mondrian, a Hopper, etc. Each painting is a window to another reality-tunnel. Art critics, using various specialized jargons—there are as many schools of art criticism as there are of physics—try to explain why each reality-tunnel is *important* in some sense.

In terms of mathematical information theory, each great painting is important because it contains information. In this theory, information is, roughly, that which you haven't encountered before. A painting you have encountered often contains new information again if you suddenly *see* it in a new way. Norbert Weiner, one of the inventors of information theory, expressed this thought by saying great poetry contains more information than political speeches. In a great poem, as in a great painting, you encounter a new and different emic reality, a new way of perceiving/experiencing humanity-in-Universe. A political speech, typically, merely regurgitates old reality-tunnels. Great art, in terms of this metaphor, is merely the opposite of cliche—it takes us to a new window, instead of gazing through a habitual window. That is why the greatest art, notoriously, is always denounced as "bizarre" and "barbarous" when it first appears. The best books are called "unreadable" because people at first do not know how to read them.

The perspective of anthropology and of ethnomethodology, and of this book, is like the perspective of a cosmopolitan art critic. It asks us to try many reality-windows instead of standing hypnotized at our habitual window all our lives.

6 August 1982 Chicago *Sun Times*—see also Chicago *Tribune*, same date—a man named Winfield Cattlin, 45, of Marrillville, Indiana, thought he saw a woman burst into flames on the street in front of him. According to Mr. Gattlin's surrealist perceptions, the woman was walking across the road in front of 4052 South Wells Street, and was not smokey or burning in any way until suddenly she was enveloped in flame. She fell to the street and Gattlin rushed to help her, but found her scorched and disintegrating. He called the police.

Detective Dan Fitzgerald of the Violent Crimes Unit told the press "She was completely scorched. It was obviously not just a case of her clothing catching fire."

The next day—see *Sun Times* and *Tribune* for 7 August—the medical examiner gave his reoprt. He said the woman had been dead at least 12 hours before being burned.

Then how was she walking across the street?

The medical examiner, Dr. Robert Stein, says the witness, Gattlin, simply did not perceive correctly. Somebody must have carried the dead woman's burning body onto the street and then threw it into the road.

The medical examiner does not explain how this somebody was invisible to Gattlin or how he made his escape after dumping the flaming cadaver.

16 August 1982 London *Daily Mirror*—see also 11 September 1979 London *Daily Mail*—90 mystery fires in a French farmhouse. It began 6 August 1979 and was still continuing in 1982. 20 gendarmes and hordes of psychologists, as well as those accursed parapsychologists who are always hallucinating, were among the witnesses. Maybe the cops and the ordinary psychologists began hallucinating *by contagion* because the parapsychologists were there?

The farmhouse belonged to the Lahore family in the village of Seron. Each fire began in the same way: first there was a smell of smoke, then an object would be noticed with a circular charred spot, then the object would burst into flame and be rushed out doors to be doused in a bucket. One day there were as many as 32 of these mystery fires while 20 gendarmes were on the scene investigating. Towels, sheets, clothes and furniture were all equally susceptible. On one occasion the clothes of a family member burst into flame while she was wearing them.

Or that's what witnesses thought they saw. That is, it's as much of whatever was going on as they were able to tune in.

I don't know what else to say about this. As usual, I wonder a bit. The trouble with being an agnostic is that you are always wondering, a bit. That's what *a-gnosis* means: you lack the Inner Certainty of those Fully Enlightened Beings like the Pope or the Ayatollah or some Marxists we have all encountered.

But if I make a wild stab at Po thinking, if I dare to look for a connection, like, say

Fire Po Bell's Theorem

Oh, no. That's the way the Damned parapsychologists think. That is *verboten*. CSICOP would hang me in effigy, if they're not already planning to do that.

Or suppose I think

Fire Po Roosevelt

If Gattlin, in the Chicago story, misperceived—if somebody carried the woman onto the street and dumped her—and if misperception is ordinary and commonplace, as our neurological data suggests—if all perception involves both addition *and subtraction*—editing things out the way the cat in the sound experiment tuned out the sound when fascinated by the mice—as people edited out Roosevelt's confession of wife-killing—

Then events "worse" than these two—truly "monstrous" and "incredible" things—could be happening all around us all the time, and we simply wouldn't notice them. We would "look the other way," so to speak. Or we would come out of the experience with confused or jumbled memories, or holes in our memory—Maybe the so-called "paranormal" is perceived, not because everybody outside CSICOP is prone to hallucination, but because the "paranormal" is a more convenient reality-tunnel than the truly *unthinkable* things that our brain edits out.

9 September 1982 London *Daily Record*—and 10 September and 11 September also, for further details—Carole Compton, age 20, of Aberdeen, Scotland, was arrested and held in jail in Livorno, Italy. She

was charged with setting two fires in the home of the Cecchine family, for whom she had been working as a nanny.

The evidence indicated that in at least one of the cases Ms. Compton could not have physically set the fire, since she was having breakfast in another room when it broke out. The Cecchine family did not care about that. They had a non-local explanation, in terms of Italian folk-beliefs. They said Ms. Compton set the fires with the "Evil Eye," i.e. witchcraft.

Despite the absurdity of this, the police arrested the young Scotswoman anyway. Maybe the police in Livorno are as superstitious as the general population.

Ms. Compton denies having, or using, the "Evil Eye," but states that "something strange" was happening in the house where the fires started. She says that a bowl jumped off a table and a glass fell for no reason, before the fires.

Maybe "something strange" was happening, or maybe the superstitious Italians caused the young Scotswoman to share their hallucinations?

But if one were to reason without bias—assuming such an act were possible among domesticated primates—one might think that something that is reported in Chicago and in France and in Italy, and that leaves results as tangible as a corpse in one case and circumstantial enough to involve 20 gendarmes in another and to lead to arrest in a third, might be deserving of a more thoughtful response than the quick label of "mass hallucination" or "superstition."

23 March 1981 Wolverhampton *Express and Star* (England)—mystery fire in a broomcloset at Leasowes Sports Center. A mop caught fire inexplicably.

The caretaker, Victor Webber, is quoted: "It looks like one of those cases of spontaneous combustion."

The head of the fire brigade says "It's a mystery. There were no electrics or anything around it which could have set it off."

14 November 1978 Reading *Chronicle* (England)—and follow-up 17 November 1978, same paper—Mrs. Lucy Gmiterek found burned to death in her basement apartment. "Police and fire experts are known to be puzzled why Mrs. Gmiterek should have burned to death while the rest of the room was only barely damaged."

And I think of the woman in Blyth in 1905 who burned to death—see back to page 77—while her room was completely undamaged. And I wonder, again, if these monstrosities might be fairly common, but are always quickly *edited out*, forgotten . . .

In Chicago, a woman who seems (to a witness) to burst into flames but seems to a medical examiner to have been dead 12 hours when the witness "saw" her corpse walking and flaming; in France, 90 mystery fires that baffle police and other investigators; in Italy, jumping furniture followed by more inexplicable fires; in Wolverhampton, a mop ignites with no known cause; in Reading, a woman is burned to death but her room is barely damaged. The appearance, to me, is not of occult "violation of natural law," but of violation of our pre-Bell and pre-Aspect metaphors of "space" and "separation" and linear *causality*.

6 April 1919 Dartford *Chronicle* (Kent, England)—J. Temple Thurston found dead in his home, Hawley Manor, near Dartford. He was burned to death—"scorched" the paper says—but his clothes were on him and they were not burned.

STTUE, Persinger and Lafreniere, p. 106—1856 Bedford, England: 40 unexplained fires in a short period; 1878 Bridgewater, England: mystery fires accompanied by *"poltergeist"* sounds; 1929 Antigua, West Indies: a girl's clothes burn, but no burns found on her body; 1939 Borely Rectory, England: mysterious fires culminating in one that burns the building down; 1953 Silver Springs Md.: accordion bursts into flame while being played; 1957 Stephenville, Newfoundland: mysterious fires in closets and drawers.

Ibid. p. 107—1773 Coventry, England: "spontaneous" combustion of a woman, no known cause; 1890 Ayer, Mass.: woman burned to death, clothes not scorched; 1904 London: woman burned to death, clothes not burned; 1952 New Orleans, La.: man bursts into flames spontaneously; 1964 Dallas: woman burned in car, car not burned.

And I think of Eddington, the astronomer, who wrote in his *Space, Time and Gravitation*, 1932: "We have certain preconceived notions about location in space which have come down to us from ape-like ancestors." Notions which may be only the result of our ape-like perceptor organs?

Dr. Reich sets out to make a rain storm with his non-existent orgone, and the rainstorm happens. Maybe we need to consider that the *verboten* orgone really does exist, or maybe, as Carl Jung insisted for so long, we need to re-examine the whole idea of "coincidence."

A boy in Malaysia radiates abnormal heat, and so does a girl in Singapore. Maybe TUUR invented them out of whole cloth, or maybe they are sub-lethal cases of whatever we are examining here.

An asthma patient of Italian origin radiates a glow like the Catholic saints in the art she has presumably seen all her life. A blacksmith, who has to deal with fire all the time, develops an immunity to pain from fire, but not to other kinds of pain. Maybe TUUR invented these cases, too, or maybe we need to think more about "psychosomatic" (neurosomatic) *wholeness.*

Controlled immunity to fire—fire-walking—gets reported again and again, and in one case is observed by doctors from the University of London. Other fires reach out and incinerate people without damaging their clothing (in some cases) or the rooms they are in (in other cases). The "iron laws" of biology are flexible enough to produce Siamese twins on occasion, and, perhaps, if our stories are not all hoaxes, maybe a two-headed girl, a two-headed goat, and a man with black blood. Perhaps we can credit the fertile mule, but can we credit the winged cats?

Do we *think* at all—about these allegations, or about anything else— or do we just respond mechanically with conditioned prejudices, as the Behaviorists assure us? If we laugh at the gross bigotries of the 13th Century, what do we think about the data that seems flatly impossible *to us?*

12 May 1906 London *Daily Mail*—at Furnace Mill, Lambhurst, Kent, England, a man named J.C. Playfair went to his stable to feed his horses. He found surrealism. All but one of the horses were turned around in their stables and the one not turned around was totally missing from its stable. Mr. Playfair looked here and there for the horse, and then became a surrealist himself. He looked in the hayroom, even though the door was too small for the horse.

He found the horse there. I imagine they looked at each other with a wild surmise.

The story says that Mr. Playfair had to knock the wall down to get the horse *out* of the hayroom.

I know, I know—that's going too far even for a book like this. It sounds like the damned horse either passed through a solid wall or shrunk down to get through the door and then expanded again.

As if some of the strange properties of objects in Relativity and quantum mechanics occasionally manifest in our everyday world?

Critics Gaffes by Ronald Duncan, *op. cit.* p. 118-126:

January 1906 *Scientific American* rejected reports of the Wright Brothers' first flight as a hoax.

Professor Poggendorf in 1860 announced that it was impossible to transmit speech electrically and called the telephone "as mythical as the Unicorn."

The millionaire J.P. Morgan, after seeing the telephone demonstrated, wrote to Bell, the inventor, that the device "had no commercial applications."

Lord Rutherford, a very brilliant physicist, announced in 1933 that the release of nuclear power was "moonshine."

Admiral Leahy declared in June 1945 that the Manhattan Project was "the biggest fool thing we have ever done. The bomb will never go off, and I speak as an expert in explosives." The first nuclear bomb was exploded by the Manhattan Project one month later.

Dr. Vannevar Bush pronounced in 1945 that no rocket could go further than 3000 miles, and Dr. Richard Woolsey, then Astronomer Royal, assured us in 1960 that space travel was "bilge." In 1957 Sir Harold Spencer Jones wrote in *New Scientist* that "generations will pass before man ever lands on the moon." Neal Armstrong landed on the moon twelve years later.

Pablo Picasso was once present at a dinner where one guest loudly denounced modern art. Picasso ate quietly, saying nothing. Later, the same guest showed a wallet photo of his wife, and Picasso asked to look at it more closely. When it was handed over, Pablo stared at it intently and then asked innocently, "My God, is she really that small?"

The great Soviet film director, Sergei Eisenstein, once wrote an essay claiming "the camera is a liar." What did he mean by that?

An old Zen Buddhist riddle asks "Who is the Master who makes the grass green?"

If you are puzzled by the Zen riddle, or if Picasso's joke and Eisenstein's paradox seem a bit fey to you, perhaps you will find it enlightening to look back at the optical diagram in chapter one, showing how we create the visual part of our reality-tunnel.

In introducing that diagram I said everybody *thinks* they understand it at once, but when we really understand it we will shout "Eureka!" (or something equally expressive).

Everytime we Fundamentalize or Absolutize, we have forgotten what we thought we understood in looking at that diagram.

Everytime we treat the tuned-in as *all* of "reality," we have again forgotten that diagram.

Everytime we sneer at those people and cultures that are tuned-in to different reality-tunnels than our own, we have forgotten again what we thought we learned in elementary physics.

But:

If the space-time event in the optical diagram is what we call "grass," is the *green* "in" the synergetic eye-brain system, or "in" the higher-order holism of eye-brain-grass?

Comptes Rendus 5-549—a strange rain at Geneva on 9 August 1837; the drops were far apart and they were *warm.*

Comptes Rendus 1839-262—another fall of warm rain on Geneva on 11 May 1842.

And *Yearbook of Facts* 1839-262 lists another warm rain, in between these, on Geneva, on 31 May 1838. This peculiar warm rain seems to have come back to Geneva three times, in 1837, 1838 and 1842.

Report of the British Association 1854-112—*hot* rain fell on Inverness, Scotland, 30 June 1817.

STTUe, Persinger and Lafreniere, *op. cit.*—

Page 81—1790: sudden pitch-blackness at noon in New England area; associated green lights (UFOs?) reported; end-of-the-world panic—1819, Massachusetts area: another sudden darkness in the daytime, with falls of normal rain and particles of matter—1839 Brussels: another sudden darkness, with falls of ice—1904 Memphis, Tenn.: sudden daytime darkness lasting 15 minutes.

Occultists would "explain" some of this stuff by talking wisely of "water elementals" and "fire elementals." I don't believe that—partly because it sounds too much like Moliere's physician who explained sleep-producing drugs by saying they had a sleep-producing property—and partly because I agree with Dr. Sarfatti that *belief* itself is an obsolete habit.

The disciples of Charles Fort would say that Universe behaves according to our models part of the time and just does what it damned pleases part of the time.

The Fundamentalist Materialists repeat in chorus that It Never Happened or If It Did It Was Trickery.

The parapsychological heretics talk, vaguely, *too vaguely* for my taste, about "psychokinetic forces" or about "emotional energies" that, like Reich's orgone, are not contained or stopped at the skin surface—or, lately, they speculate that the non-local connection exists not only in quantum mechanics but in other aspects of Universe—

And I think: according to Fundamentalist Materialism, I cannot have a thought that does not use energy in my brain—the moving energy in the brain *is* the thought, Dr. Carl Sagan insists—And then—if the damned non-local connection means *something* and is not just a mixture of mathematical poetry and "coincidental" hallucinations in various physics laboratories—

Universe will respond non-locally to my thought. Maybe it will average out to a microscopic or invisible response most of the time, but occasionally things may wobble and jump visibly.

And pranksters who seem to be very, very clever—or people who, against Authoritative fiat, experiment on their own—trying to project energies—trying to heal, I hope, and also, I fear, in some cases, trying to harm—

And Universe averages it all out most of the time—but occasionally— wobbles and jumps—fires and mutations—fluctuations—and, one case in a billion maybe, the energy is fired precisely as a weapon—

8 December 1931 New York *Times*—on the steamship *Brechsee* a deckhand was seen, by the captain and other crewmembers, to suddenly display a four-inch-long bloody gash on his forehead. The appearance was as if he had been struck by an invisible weapon or an invisible asailant, and he fell unconscious. No projectile was found in the wound.

No. No. No. We Must Not Think That. It Is Forbidden.

Besides, as Nietzsche says, we don't really want fearful thoughts. We want comfortable, *soothing* explanations.

So it is best to say, then, that TUUR somehow managed to infiltrate the usually scrupulous New York *Times* again.

And then we can conveniently forget the matter.

But that Picasso joke, a few pages back—We know, of course, that the guest's wife wasn't "really" as small as the photo—she was "really" the size she looks *to our eyes*—

But Bishop Berkeley argues that the leg of a cheese-mite, invisible to us, is just as "big" relative to the cheese-mite as our legs are relative to us—and the same thought appears in General Relativity—

And we are back to the thought that "space" is only a metaphor.

One Zen student, who pondered long on "The Master who makes the grass green" ran to his *roshi* (teacher) in excitement and announced, "I've got it! I've got it! That rock over there is inside my head."

"You must have a big head," the *roshi* said, "to hold a rock that size."

Try the following multiple choice test:

	TRUE	FALSE	GAME RULE	STRANGE LOOP	INDETER- MINATE
A. Space is real	□	□	□	□	□
B. Space is a metaphor	□	□	□	□	□

1   It is necessary to warn the reader that no bears actually live at the places suggested here, but they would be white for evolutionary reasons if they did live there. Incidentally, I owe this delightful puzzle to Martin Gardner, whose mathematical games have delighted me almost as much as his dogmatism frightens me.

2   In the same conversation Dr. Bohm also raises the possibility that the "laws" of the universe are not *absolute* but are, like everything else, *evolving* in time. When I first suggested this, I thought I was being whimsical, but Dr. Bohm is serious, and he is considered one of the most brilliant physicists of our time.

CHAPTER FIVE

CHAOS
AND THE ABYSS

(with comments on phantom kangaroos and blasphemies against Reason)

I don't *believe* **anything.**

John Gribbin, *In Search of Schrodinger's Cat*

The Old Agnosticism defined itself chiefly by its opposition to the dogmas of religious Fundamentalism.

The New Agnosticism of this book seems to define itself by its opposition to the dogmas of materialist/rationalist Fundamentalism.

Yet the agnostic attitude—which I keep gently hinting is also the creative attitude, the Po attitude—remains similar. The agnostic does not want to be bulldozed into joining a stampede of any sort, or bowing to any Idol.

Even if the reader has some affinity for one Fundamentalism or another, you might, if you think about it, agree with this: If you were on trial for a serious crime, you would be glad to have at least a few agnostics on the jury; a few who have what Nietzsche called *the habit of caution.*

For instance, Mr. Robert Sheaffer of CSICOP has recently written a book called *The UFO Verdict.* I have not yet read it and therefore do not presume to criticize it, but I cannot help noticing the classic Fundamentalism of the title. A muddle-head like myself cannot even put together a plausible UFO *theory* yet (not even to my own satisfaction) but Mr. Schaeffer has *a verdict.*

No. He is even more wonderful than that. He hasn't merely got himself *a* verdict; he has *the* verdict.

As the reader knows by now, I am a simple, ignorant man (with a gaudy vocabulary). You would want me on a jury, I think, if you were charged with a major felony. I don't think you would really want Mr. Schaeffer on the jury if you were even charged with a misdemeanor traffic violation. His Verdict would be quick and certain.

For some reason at this point I think of what has been called the Right Man syndrome.

This is not a concept from clinical or experimental psychology. It is a mere empirical generalization by the writer A.E. Van Vogt, in a pamphlet *Report on the Violent Male,* cited by Wilson in *Criminal History,* op. cit. p. 64-71. Van Vogt was inspired to investigate this personality type when writing a novel about concentration camps. Investigating war criminals, he went on to investigate other types of criminals. He thought he saw a pattern. The Violent Male—and almost all violence is committed by males—seems to be a man who literally cannot, *ever,* admit he might be wrong. He *knows* he is right; he is the total psychological opposite of the agnostic, in claiming absolute *gnosis,* total certitude, about all things. Van Vogt found that an astonishing amount of violence is committed by these males, and he calls the type *The Right Man*, because this man always insists he is Right. Colin Wilson, in the pages cited and throughout the *Criminal History*, points out again and again how much of the violence of history is committed by these Right Men, whether they are identified at the time as "criminals" or are in such high positions of power that their behavior is only called "criminal" long after their deaths—e.g. the more murderous politicians and theologians.

Not all Right Men become criminals, however. Van Vogt found considerable records of them in divorce cases, too. He claims that in every such case it was the wife who was seeking divorce. The Right Man not only knew he was Right, but also knew the wife had a duty to remain with him. Sometimes, Von Vogt noted, the transition from Being Right All The Time to violence only occurs while such a divorce is being sought by the wife.

In some respects, the Right Man seems to me like a chronic case of what clinical psychologists call the Authoritarian Personality and Freudians call the anal retentive. In these milder versions of the syndrome the same dogmatism appears but not the close link to violent behavior. Still, the Authoritarian Personality is Always Right and tends to seek positions of power. They are obsessed with facts and figures, frequently, and are rather "cold" toward human beings (because of traumatic toilet training, according to unscientific Freudian speculation). They also have a statistical inclination toward being unwilling to experiment with "foreign" or "exotic" foods, and they regard philosophical speculation with extreme hostility. I think it was men of this type who killed Socrates, and I suspect they filled the top offices in the Old Inquisition.

Thank God there are none of them around today.

Once, many years ago, I was an engineering aide in the electrical engineering department of a large consulting engineering firm. I conducted many tests, in the field, relevant to Ohm's Law which holds that

$$E \text{ equals } I \times R$$

voltage equals current times resistance

According to the Law, if the current is 5 amperes and the resistance is 2 ohms, then the voltage should be 5 x 2 or 10 volts.

It very seldom was, in my experience. It was usually something like 10.1 volts or 9.9 volts, or even 10.2 volts or 9.8 volts, or even on occasion as bad as 8.9 volts.

There is an explanation for this, of course. Ohm's Law, like other scientific laws, is only "obeyed" exactly if there is no extraneous factor that interfered with the instrument reading. In the field, such extraneous interference always gets into the system.

But then "under laboratory conditions"—at University—the same wobbles would sometimes appear. Ohm would be vindicated many times, indeed, but then—the damned meter would once again say 9.8 or 9.7 when it *should* say exactly 10.

This didn't just happen with Ohm's Law. It happened with every damned law that I ever personally investigated in the field or in the laboratory.

The explanation, of course, is instrument error. "No instrument is perfect," etc.

But then the Eternal Laws invoked by all Fundamentalists do not apply to the sensory-sensual world—the existential world, the world of ordinary experience—but to some sort of Platonic Ideal World that somehow *underlies* this messy experienced world?

Well, not exactly. If both we and our instruments were perfect, then—*lo!*—we would actually see all the laws actually "obeyed" and "obeyed" precisely.

Really? And how would one go about proving such a proposition, when all we have to work with is our imperfect senses and our imperfect instruments, and what they tune in?

It seems that to believe in that Ideal World requires another "leap of faith" and I, as an agnostic, won't jump. I'll just stand here and wonder. Maybe there *is* such a world, but since we can't tun it in or experience it, we can't talk meaningfully about it—as the Copenhagenists say—I think that's why they gave up the word "reality"—

Back in the sub-Platonic and messy world of what people experience or think they experience:

31 August 1982 *Irish Times* (Dublin)—two inexplicable critters recently seen. First, in Lough Stanford, Ireland, was found a tern of a species normally seen only on the Pacific coast of Mexico. Then, two days later, a penguin was found swimming near one of the Western islands of Scotland.

Maybe TUUR has landed a job in Dublin, where the best Guinness is served, and we can expect even more spectacular efforts from him in the future.

Or maybe the tern got caught in a whirlwind or lost its directional sense—and that penguins, since penguins don't fly and are normally found only in the Southern Hemisphere—well, maybe some "prankster" brought it to Scotland—

Maybe. And maybe this world is not only sub-Platonic but wobbly— maybe somebody will be (and has been) messing with the Big Bang from somewhere in the future, as suggested in the last chapter, so this damned world is just a blurry remnant of the real world they started from—or is that just the Platonic metaphor in a quantum disguise?

October 1984 *Science Digest*—"Turning Einstein Upside Down," by John Gliedman, an article about the current theorizing of Dr. John Archibald Wheeler, one of the top men in quantum physics. You remember Dr. Wheeler. He was one of the co-creators of the EWG model, in which the state vector never collapses and everything that *can* happen *does* happen. He repudiated that model later, but now he's back to it, or something like it.

Dr. Wheeler proposes that since the non-local connection in space has been experimentally verified by Drs. Clauser and Aspect and others, we should think about the other side of Bell's Theorem, which also proposes non-local connections in time. (A non-local effect is everywhere and *everywhen*, as we have said.) Dr. Wheeler argues that our experiments today can "reach back billions of years" to literally *create* the past, including the Big Bang. He says "we are wrong to think of the past as having a definite existence 'out there,' " and that the Big Bang has been/is being created by our "acts of measurement" now.

The only way this backward-in-time causality is thinkable to me, or to any physicist I've discussed it with—and it is unthinkable for Prof. Munge, remember—is if out of the Big Bang are coming many universes, not one universe. Otherwise, we run into the Grandfather Paradox again. (See page 122.)

So maybe I wasn't joking when I suggested we happen to be in one of the more wobbly universes.

February 1965 *Fortean Times*—Mrs. Lawrence Loeb of Calumet, Ok., saw another of our Damned Things. This one had the body of a wolf but the head of a deer.

It was only an appearance, of course, but we begin to fear that in this wobbly and imperfect world appearances are all we've got.

Same article in same *Fortean Times*—another Damned Thing. This appearance was seen by two men, D.B. Clarke and H.H. Christianson in Canby, Minn. It appeared to be half-deer and half-horse. Worse: when Clarke tried to see if this walking blasphemy against Eternal Law would run like a deer by making a noise to frighten it, it appeared unimpressed. When he fired a shot in the air, it appeared still unimpressed. Worst of all: when Clarke fired a shot near its legs, it appeared to walk off *slowly*, unlike normal deer, or normal horses, for that matter.

Clarke and Christianson signed affadavits, saying they thought they saw what they thought they saw.

21 May 1921 London *Evening Standard*—thousands of frogs allegedly fell out of the sky at Gibralter. They allegedly were alive and allegedly hopped about in agitation, as you or I might hop if we arrived in Gibralter that way.

TUUR strikes again.

Or else the ever-faithful Segregating Whirlwind, maybe. It ignored everything else and only picked up frogs.

The *Standard* adds that a similar shower of frogs had fallen or appeared to have fallen on Gibralter seven years earlier, in 1914.

Two segregating whirlwinds then, and "just by coincidence" they hit the same town seven years apart. As the warm rains came back to Geneva three times "just by coincidence." As the parapsychological loonies "just by coincidence" obtain "runs of coincidences" that seem to them in their ignorance to imply the existence of the type of non-local connectedness they call "ESP."

Maybe.

21 July 1979 *Soviet Weekly*—in the village of Dargan-Ata in Soviet Turkemni, another shower of frogs. Alive and hopping.

The segregating whirlwind again, with its usual delicacy, depositing the frogs without harming them? Or another Damned Commie Lie, as Mr. Reagan would say?

31 May 1981 London *Sunday Express*—another shower of frogs in Narplion, Greece. Thousands of them, alive and hopping. Scientists (gullible, no doubt) at the Meteorological Institute in Athens are quoted. It was the Segregating Whirlwind, they say, but one of them adds that it was "remarkable" that the frogs escaped injury in being picked up by a whirlwind, hurled across the landscape and then plunked down again.

Remarkable indeed.

Some of you recall that Charles Fort collected over 300 cases of these falls of segregated living organisms. Motivated by the same desire to liberate humanity from dogma as I am—or motivated by the same blasphemous desire to subvert and corrupt, the Citadel will tell you—Fort published these cases in four huge books that annoyed Martin Gardner so severely that he decided that Fort was "sinister." I predict that Mr. Gardner will say the same about me.

Whatever motivated Fort, he had a wicked sense of humor. He said we should seriously examine the possibility that "God" is heaving these frogs around, and then indicated other oddities that suggested that "God" might be a mental case.

The *other* Fundamentalists don't like Fort, either.

Personally, I'm more conservative than Fort was; I don't want to blame any of this madness on "God." For the time being at least, if I must come out of my agnostic relativism, I prefer to guess that somebody has been monkeying around with the Big Bang and we are in one of the Imperfect Universes.

Here are some of the frogfalls collected by Fort:

Comptes Rendus 3-54—letter from Prof. Pontus who alleges that frogs fell from the sky near Toulouse in August 1804.

Notes and Queries 8-7-437—a downpour of frogs in heavily populated London on July 30, 1838.

Canadian Naturalist 2-1-308—frogs embedded in *ice* fell on Pontiac, Canada, July 11, 1864.

The segregating whirlwind also does refrigeration on the side?

12 July 1873 *Scientific American*—frogs fell during a rainstorm in Kansas City, Missouri.

Monthly Weather Review June 1882—on June 16, 1882, a rain of frogs and ice had fallen on Dubuque, Iowa.

L'Astronomie 1889-353—a fall of frogs in Savoy on August 2, 1889.

Notes and Queries 8-6-190—a fall of frogs in Wigan, England, during August 1894 and, in the same month, a fall of mysterious jellyish substance, identified by one investigator as frog-spawn, in Bath, England.

One whirlwind that month selected only frogs and another whirlwind, equally fastidious, selected only the spawn?

I turn again to the paradoxical symbiosis of skepticism and blind faith. Is it easier to believe in segregating whirlwinds that pick and choose until they have frogs and only frogs in their grip, or to believe that the fundamentalist materialist reality-tunnel is, like the Thomist reality-tunnel and the Methodist reality-tunnel and the Lesbian Vegetarian reality-tunnel, a human construct, containing its own self-referential subjectivity and group Game Rules?

That depends on temperament, I think. Those who have an emotional need for the materialist reality-tunnel will cling to it at all odds, even if that requires them to hypothesize unscrupulous reporters *ad. lib.*, gullible scientists *ad. naus.* and even gentle and segregating whirlwinds *ad. infinitum.* Great is the faith of such "skeptics," as I shall continue to demonstrate as we go along.

11 November 1979 Manchester *Guardian*—a more persnicketty whirlwind perhaps. This one didn't bother with frogs, or penguins, or even terns. It evacuated black puddings, eggs, bacon and tomatoes on four houses in Castleton, Derbyshire.

The pattern of segregation or seemingly conscious choice continues. The materials for a North Country English breakfast were selected by this anthropomorphic whirlwind.

But there is worse: it came back several times. Like the personalized whirlwind that dumped frogs on Gibralter in 1914 and then came back to do it again in 1921.

Maybe it wasn't a whirlwind. Maybe it was an aerial prankster.

The police considered that. They started a nightly patrol. The edibles fell again, and again, and again. Tons of them. Nobody was caught dumping them.

The police investigated thefts, or unusually large purchases, from local foodstores. They found none.

A very, very clever prankster then? He went as far away as France, maybe, to secure all the produce for these bombardments.

Yes, that must be it. It does get a bit thin to invoke the ubiquitous unscrupulous reporter over and over, again and again. Besides, the *Guardian* has a good, solid reputation for scrupulous reporters. It must have been a diabolically clever prankster then. The police never even saw his airplane.

19 September 1980, Essex *Evening Echo*—a block of ice "two feet square" fell on the local golfcourse and was seen by several players. Ray Wood, one of the golfers, said "There wasn't any explanation. The sky was blue, without a cloud in sight, and there were no planes about."

Maybe it was the prankster of Derbyshire with his wonderful *soundless* and *invisible* airplane?

Or maybe the universe has wobbles and weirdness indeed. Maybe belief in any *system* is maintained by "forgetting" all data that does not fit the system?

4 June 1981 Stockport *Express* (England)—a rain of *coins* in Reddish, between Stockport and Manchester. The coins varied between one pence pieces and 50 pence pieces.

The whirlwinds have given up on frogs—taken the pledge, sworn off—and now spew food on Derbyshire, ice on Essex and coins on Reddish. They must have rummaged through somebody's bureau drawers to select only coins, for the Reddish escapade. Most whimsical whirlwids indeed.

Or that pernicious reporter, still without a scruple to his name, is now working in Stockport?

Fortean Times Winter 1982—they contacted a witness in Reddish, a Rev. Graham Marshall, who confirmed the rain of coins. He also said there were no buildings nearby high enough to serve as a perch for a practical joker.

Then it must have been the hoaxter of Castleton again, with his ingenious *soundless* and *invisible* airplane?

Rev. Marshall added that the strangest part of the coinstorm was that the coins landed so that they were embedded in the ground by their edges. He tried to duplicate this, he says, or he alleges, and he found that hurling coins at the ground did not embed them in that sidewise fashion.

Now a UC (unscrupulous clergyman) enters the cast of villains. Well, I don't trust clergymen much, myself. Some of them are as dogmatic as some scientists.

Charles Fort, *The Book of the Damned*:

A block of ice fell out of the sky at Seringpatam, India, in 1800. It was the size of an elephant.

There were no airplanes back then for the hypothetical practical joker. It must have been the marvelous segregating whirlwind then?

Fort's source is the *Report of the Smithsonian Institute* 1870-479, by the way.

30 December 1956 London *People*—a fall of coins in Hanham, Bristol.

5 August 1940 London *Daily Express*—a fall of coins all over the city of Mesherera, Russia, during a rainstorm.

10 December 1968 London *Daily Mirror*—rain of coins lasting fifteen minutes in Gateshead, County Durham. Worse yet, they were all *bent* in the middle as if to invoke the supreme demoniac horror of Fundamentalist Materialism, Uri Geller himself.

C. Blinkenberg's *Thunderweapons*, 1911, gives a long—*quite* long—list of "arrows" and "axes" said to have fallen from the sky in China, Burma and Japan, from ancient times to modern. Many of these are preserved in temples and shrines.

Of course, Dr. Jacob Bronowski assures us in *Science and Human Values* that the Orientals know nothing of science and are therefore untrustworthy and can't distinguish fact from fancy. Leaving aside the curious taint of chauvinism and mental imperialism in Bronowski's view—it is, after all, basic to the New Fundamentalism that no other philosophy but the scientific materialism invented by white people in the last 300 years has anything to offer at all—there is the dissenting view of Joseph Needham in *Science and Civilization in China*, Vol. II. He claims that the Chinese not only invented scientific method before the West but were ahead of the West in basic discoveries throughout almost all history. He lists hundreds of basic inventions that appeared in China before they came to the West and argues that people capable of such mechanical genius were also capable of careful observation and rational thought.

Still, if such ideas become accepted, Fundamentalist Materialism begins to crumble and only a liberal materialism, willing to learn from other cultures and other reality-tunnels, can survive. It is that liberalization and cosmopolitinization that the fundamentalist most dreads, I suspect; just as the Right Man fears the "foreign" and "exotic."

Report of the British Association, 1860, lists a pillar-like *carved* stone that fell, or allegedly fell, in Constantinople in 416 A.D. *Phenomena* by Michell and Rickard, *op. cit.* lists many similar worked or seemingly worked objects that have allegedly fallen from the sky, and includes a photo of a 12-inch marble cylinder, looking as if crafted by intelligence, that fell in Ohio in August 1910.

Proc. Canadian Institute 3-7-8: one of the members, J.A. Livingston, exhibited an object which he asserted had fallen from the sky.

It was globular. It was quartz. It was *hollow.*

Tallius, writing in 1649, explained such anamolies, which have been seen, or hallucinated, to fall from the sky since the dawn of time, as the result of "fulgurous exhalation conglobed in a cloud by the circumfused humour." While I don't totally buy that theory, since I don't understand it, it makes a little more sense than the segregating whirlwind of fundamentalism.

American Journal of Science 2-34-298—a brick, or something mighty like a brick, fell out of the sky on Richland, South Carolina.

Edinborough New Philosophical Journal 2-32-298—another Damned Thing, described as a brick, fell onto Padua, Italy, August 1834.

Monthly Weather Review May 1884-134—on May 22 that year, a fall of non-meteoric (cold) stones upon Bismarck, North Dakota. 15 hours later, upon the same town, another fall of inexplicable stones.

The prankster with the soundless and invisible airplane could not have done it, in 1884, before there were airplanes.

Maybe he had a balloon.

Sure, that must be it. There's always a sane, rational explanation of these things, if you think about it.

1 May 1932 *Reynold's Illustrated Newspaper* (London)—the sky turned blood red over Annuncion, Paraguay, and stayed bloodshot for several days.

There was no volcanic eruption recorded in that area at that time.

Well, then, it was another fulgurous exhalation conglobed in a cloud by the circumfused humour?

There were continuous earthquakes of minor level throughout the weeks of the bloody sky. Earth tremors do not dye the sky, according to conventional theory—but then red skies do not produce earthquakes either, according to said theory. Then this was just "coincidence"—like the segregating whirlwinds that visited Gibralter twice, or like the one that dumped stones on Bismarck twice—or like a lot of our data—

STTUE, Persinger and Lafreniere, op. cit. p. 90—during the great Illinois-Missouri earthquake of 1857, UFOs were seen and fish fell out of the sky—page 93: there is an area in Devonshire, England, where drivers feel a compulsion to leave the road—an area near Santa Cruz, CA. where abnormal gravity readings and abnormal magnetic readings are frequent—another gravitational and magnetic anomaly in Odd Acres, Missouri—in 1954 in Barrie, Ontario, Canada drivers experienced a force trying to pull them off the road—near Philadelphia, Pa., an area of "singing" rocks where people experience altered states of consciousness—in Trenton, New Jersey, in 1958, rumbling noises in a sink, and then blue flames shot out—

And maybe there is a Beautiful Eternal World where these things never happen, a world known only to Platonists and other Fundamentalists—and maybe our world, the world of experience, is only an imperfect copy of that—Maybe the voltmeters give the right readings there, not *sometimes* but *always*, and fish and frogs do not fall out of the sky, and an animal is a deer *or* a horse but not both—

If you believe in it, you can almost see it. Or, at least, you can convince yourself that anything else is mere appearance or hallucination.

But then again, maybe Nietzsche was right. Maybe we created that world, by the process discussed earlier—turning $leaf_1$ and $leaf_2$ and $leaf_3$ etc. into "the leaf" and man_1 and man_2 and man_3 into "mankind" (leaving out the women) and experienced $measurement_1$ and experienced $measurement_2$ etc. into "the" "average" "real" "measurement" which should exist somewhere—and dropping out the other wobbles and bumps as we went along, devising a lovely abstraction of a world that exists nowhere but in our heads.

If we follow this subversive notion far enough, as Nietzsche did, we come to Chaos and the Abyss, as he did. Maybe that is why we prefer not to follow this notion very far.

Of course, Chaos and the Abyss are metaphors, of the special kind that we have called metaphors about metaphors. They attempt to describe what is left when abstractions like "the leaf" and "the" "average"—linguistic reality-tunnels—are dropped from our minds.

Nietzsche was a linguist and philologist before he became a philosopher, and his philosophy starts from linguistic analysis. He was one of the first—after the enigmatic Giambattista Vico—to observe that linguistic grids mold perception and constrain thought. His scandalous, hilarious and *dangerous* (he loved the concept, criticism of conventional morals grew directly out of this and was largely a criticism of neurosemantic habits, of how words hypnotize us and predetermine hasty Verdicts. Eventually, he asked himself: what if linguistic grids are only in our heads and not "out there"? What if etic experience, existence itself, not edited by the brain's emic card-index system, is formless, or multi-form, or perpetually evolving—too fluid and "dancing" to be captured in one model or one linguistic reality-tunnel?

Well—and this is what drove Nietzsche to flights of poetry and sarcasm unequalled in the history of philosophy—if that is the case every *standard of judgment* must eventually collapse.

A standard is only a way of judging whether something fits a pre-existing system. If systems are like people, mortal and mutable, then—

He who believes a system, any system, wears a blindfold.

Curved space did not fit the 19th Century system, anymore than quantum backwards-in-time causality fits Prof. Munge's system, or rains of frogs fit into any system I know.

If Nietzsche's existential relativism be accepted, then there will always be true things that do not fit any existing reality-tunnel, just as in mathematics Godel demonstrated that *there will always be true theorems not deducible from any set of axioms.* (See page 44.)

We are, of course, here trying to speak about the unspeakable—an oxymoronic task. Buddhists, trying to indicate this pre- (or post-) verbal etic awareness, noncommittally call it the Void—which is supposed to make you realize you can't say anything about it. (Chaos, to Nietzsche, who knew ancient Greek, also meant *void,* along with its modern meanings.) Mostly, the Buddhists prefer not to speak about the unspeakable, and just tell you to experience it by sitting, for instance, staring at a wall and trying to remove verbal systems from your brain. Others have tried to speak about this and given philosophy such memorable if meaningless terms as "Being," "Pure Being," "Absolute Being," etc.

Prof. F.S.C. Northrop deserves a medal of some sort for trying to describe this indescribability as "the undifferentiated esthetic contiuum." I wish I'd said that.

To go a bit further in naming the unnameable and eff-ing the ineffable—etic reality is the state, recorded in Dr. John Lilly's *Simulations of God,* of those who have been in an isolation tank, cut off from human reality-grids, for several hours. It is also, as Lilly notes, the frequently reported state of sailors who have been alone after a ship-wreck, drifting in a small boat, or explorers who have been isolated for prolonged periods. It may even be the original meaning of the Indo-European root from which we get our verb-form "to be"—to be lost, to be separated from tribal reality-tunnels. (See page 47.) It is also the *whereof* of which Wittgenstein speaks in the famous last sentence of *Tractatus Logico-Philosophicus:* "Whereof one cannot speak, thereof one must remain silent."

In short, it is that old-fashioned "reality" which the Copenhagen Interpretation wisely informs us cannot be contained in scientific models.

It cannot be contained in any models.

So we are back, by linguistic analysis, or analysis of what is *not* linguistic, to Gribbin's position about quantum mechanics: Everything is real or nothing is real. Every reality-tunnel is real to those who experience it, and none are "real" in the old sense of existing apart from us in a platonic Absoluteness.

Chaos and the Abyss.

And—to complete Nietzsche's analysis—it is the fear of that Chaos, that "transvaluation of all values," which may be the emotional motor behind all Fundamentalisms.

Sociobiologically:

Domesticated primates do not want their territorial marks erased.

Onward into the Abyss—

September 1982 *Omni*—a giant "UFO" seen over Moscow in June 1980. Tens of thousands of people allegedly running through the streets, fearing nuclear attack—reports of extraterrestrial "humanoids" seen—aliens allegedly chasing cars and boring holes through windows.

James Oberg, who is in the business of explaining UFOs for *Omni*, explains this one.

It was only a satellite launching, he says.

But hundreds of satellites have been launched, and people don't usually mistake them for nuclear attacks.

Oberg explains. This was a *great big* satellite.

Oh. But what about the "humanoids" seen in Moscow?

Oberg explains. "The KGB," he writes, "eager to muddy the waters and cover up public recognition of the military space center at Pietsk, is only too happy to promote scintillating stories about aliens chasing cars and boring nasty holes in windows."

Just another Damned Communist Lie, you see. I knew we would eventually hear one type of Fundamentalist sounding remarkably like the other type of Fundamentalist.

But, according to a widely-published Gallup Poll, over 15,000,000 U.S. citizens have seen a UFO, or think they have. Could all that be the work of the demoniac KGB?

Oh, no, that's "mass hallucination."

Of course, how could I forget?

23 September 1973 London *Times*—in Brignoles, France, "tens of thousands" of toads falling out of the sky.

Must have been more "mass hallucination." Sure is a lot of it going around these days. Seems almost as common as amnesia in the old radio soap operas.

Or maybe it was the Wonderful Segregating Whirlwind again. Or another fulgurous exhalation conglobed in a cloud by the circumfusing humour. Or maybe French Military Intelligence were "eager to muddy the waters" and "cover up public recognition" of their own military secrets and are "only too happy to promote scintillating stories" about toads falling out of the sky?

Or maybe existence is Chaotic in Nietzsche's sense—too vast and abyssmal and wobbly to be contained in any one reality-tunnel?

Michigan Anomaly Research, MAR Report no. 7, 1979, "Phantom Kangaroos: A Catalog," by Loren Coleman and David Fideler:

Several *dozen* newspaper reports are listed, describing kangaroos inexplicably seen hopping around the suburbs of Chicago, Illinois. The earliest report comes from 1940 and the latest from 1978. In no case did a newspaper locate a zoo keeper who averred that he had lost some kangaroos from his zoo.

Some segregating whirlwinds select for frogs, some for coins, some for individual penguins and some—but only around Chicago—for kangaroos? But if they don't get them from zoos, do they pick them up in Australia, zoom them across 8000 miles and then, very gently, drop them near Chicago without harming them?

Perhaps before these temperamental whirlwinds grow as spooky as poor Dr. Reich's "orgone" or the hypothetical "teleportive force" of the damned parapsychological heretics, we had better assume a huge migration of unscrupulous reporters to Chicago c. 1940-1978.

But worse is yet to come.

The kangaroos are still hopping. And not just around Chicago.

Fortean Times, London, Winter 1982—an update by Loren Coleman, co-author of the 1978 MAR report. The damned kangaroos are now being reported from Wisconsin, Utah, Oklahoma, North Carolina and Ontario and New Brunswick, Canada. No zoo-keepers have even yet come forth to claim them.

A typical cluster of cases:

April 5, 1979, Waukesha, Wisconsin—two men named Wilcox and Kroske saw a kangaroo bouncing along Highway A at 6:45 in the morning.

April 12, 1979—seven days later—a family named Haeslick saw the same damned kangaroo, or another damned kangaroo, a few miles away in Pewaukee township. It hopped around their backyard.

April 13, next day—William Busch of Waukesha saw it, or its brother or sister or cousin, still hopping.

April 23—Brooksfield township, near Waukesha, *two* kangaroos seen by members of the Nero family. Tracks were left and were photographed by Loren Coleman. Photo on page 27 of issue cited.

Another fake photo? Or mass hallucinations leave tracks? Or fulgurous exhalation conglobed in a cloud by the circumfused humour?

April 24—a photo of the kangaroo, or one of the kangaroos, taken by a young man who gave it to Mr. Coleman but refused permission to print his name "For fear of ridicule." Photo on page 26. Looks like a bloody kangaroo to me, guvnor.

Another fake photo, of course.

May 1978 (still citing Coleman, *Fortean News*)—a kangaroo, or several kangaroos, reported in and around Toronto. Witnesses, or hallucinators, include a policeman, a guard at a factory, a taxi driver, the taxi passenger, and others over the border in Maine.

1981—kangaroo sightings in Utah, Oklahoma and North Carolina.

Phenomena, Michell and Rickard, op. cit. p. 12, citing the *Deipnosophists* of Athenaus—in the fourth century A.D. there was a three day shower of fishes and frogs in Chersonesus, Greece. The roads were blocked and people were unable to open their doors, so great was the deluge.

The town stank for weeks afterwards, or at least there was an appearance of stench.

Ancient Greek intelligence agents "eager to muddy the waters" and "cover up public recognition" etc.?

19 September 1918, *Nature*—thousands of toads fell on Chelmsford, Massachusetts. A Mrs. Lillian Farnham collected a tub full of them.

STTUE, Persinger and Lafreniere, p. 23-36—fall of stones with "explosions" in the sky (1866 Hungary)—fall of a block of limestone (1888 Florida)—fall of large chunks of ice, approximately two pounds each (1888 Illinois)—fall of a seventy pound chunk of ice (1958 New Jersey)—fall of a jelly-like substance (1833 Virginia)—falls of seeds in Germany 1822, Persia 1913, Georgia (U.S.A.) 1958—fall of hay 1971 New York—fall of a five-pound ball of steel, Washington State 1951—

But perhaps all this rollicking about in Chaos and the Abyss has gotten a bit *thick*. Perhaps we should seek a little light, or at least the appearance of light—

If we are not to be too literal about all that Nietzschean Chaos—if we admit that, after all, some generalizations are a *little* bit better than others—if we are not to become, oxymoronically, Absolute Agnostics or solipsists—

Here is a model that may help, a little. It is from STTUE—*Space-Time Transients and Unusual Events*, so often *op. cit.* here in recent chapters.

Persinger and Lafreniere are "behavioral scientists"; that is, they don't like the old word, "psychologists." They collected 6,060 of the sort of reports that we have been concerned with here. They did extensive computer analyses of the data, looking for various possible patterns and correlations. They think they have found some.

What they propose is, briefly, that physical laws are not Platonic absolutes, contrary to Prof. Munge, but statistical generalizations.

Sounds familiar, that.

Persinger and Lafreniere propose further that when there are wild statistical fluctuations in various *known* physical fields—the geomagnetic field, the gravitational field, etc.—they do not propose new and innovative things, like Reich's orgone or Sheldrake's morphic resonances —but if there are fluctuations in known fields, then—

Abnormal things will really happen; but also humans near such fluctuations will have *abnormal brain waves*, and will hallucinate.

To some, this will seem to lead us further into Chaos and Old Night. It is easier, and more traditonal, to think of the Aristotelian choice—the phenomena "is" "real" *or* it "is" "hallucinatory"—than to consider the non-Aristotelian model that the Damned Thing might be a little bit of both. Nonetheless, even without Persinger's-Lafreniere's field fluctuations, neurology already indicates that we should regard all perception as involving addition (projection) and subtraction (abstraction), which is a good working definition of partly real/partly hallucinatory.

It seems to me that there is a *topology* to UFO stories that is quite consistent with this fluctuation model. That is, if energy fields fluctuate, then those at the perimeter will only report "strange lights" in the sky or on the ground—ball lightning and other, unnamed electro-magnetic effects. Those a little closer in will report the wilder electro-magnetic effects, and possible gravitational effects, that are so often described—auto engines malfunctioning, lights turning off and on, jumping furniture of the *"poltergeist"* type.

And those misfortunate persons who wander into the epicenter, where gravity and brain-waves both go mad—

They will come back talking of extraterrestrials in Nazi uniforms, like Betty and Barney Hill—or they will tell us they went up in a spaceship with Jesus Christ, as in many cases—or sexual fantasy will surface, as in those who claim to have been raped by malign midgets or seduced by sexy Venusian ladies.

Persinger and Lafreniere suggest also that sombunall of our strange falling Things or "teleportations" may be *extreme* gravity fluctuations.

Then even some of our genetic monstrosities may be fluctuations caused by energy waves that impinge on the DNA?

I think this model may very well fit a lot of our data. At least it saves us from the Fundamentalist absurdity of dismissing *all* inconvenient reports as "mass hallucination," and then, when there is too much supporting evidence, explaining that hoaxters mixed with the hallucinators and *manufactured* the evidence, so to speak, on the spot.

There is even some statistical support for this model in Persinger-Lafreniere's computer analyses, which reveal seemingly significant increases in these Monstrosities around earthquake faults and in the weeks preceeding major tremors.

Some readers will think I have just explained the mysteries that have annoyed or amused us thusfar. I have not. I have just offered one possible model. Not *the* verdict or even *a* verdict. A model or theory only.

Try to think, just for a moment,

Persinger-Lafreniere Po Bell's Theorem

Try. Thoughts are the one phenomena still private in this world; they won't come around and arrest you at once. You have nothing to lose but mental chains. You might have a world of psychological freedom— "creativity"—to gain.

The enigmatic Chinese seals, or coins, of Ireland:

They were first reported by Joseph Hubbard Smith, to the Royal Irish Academy, in 1839. Charles Fort, the master of mischief, has a lot of fun with them in his *Books*; see his index under "Ireland." Arthur Clarke, inventor of the communication satellites now circling the globe, but unfortunately also the author of novels crazy as my own, takes them seriously enough to give them elbow room in his *Mysterious World* (Clarke, Welfare, Fawley, A&E Visual Library, New York, 1980) on pages 43-44 of which the following account is given.

These seals or coins are found all over Ireland. Some of them are on the surface, but some have been found under the surface, by people digging for something else. There is no conventional explanation of how they got there. The segregating whirlwind is a bit absurd in this case.

Persinger-Lafreniere gravitational disturbances, long ago? Or— maybe the early Irish were better and braver navigators than we think.

5 August 1837 *Niles Weekly Register*—more fish falling, this time in Kentucky. Reported by "Dr. Woods, a naturalist."

21 December 1923 *Science*—fish fall in Siberia; natives claim it happens regularly.

So maybe we should stretch our reality-tunnel at least wide enough to consider the Persinger-Lafreniere model, or something like it.

6 January 1881 *Nature* (23:223)—remarkable hailstones that fell in Bavaria. The correspondent says some had studs or "handles" on them, and some were shaped like tadpoles, and some looked like a lady's looking-glass.

Chaos lurches forward again. I don't see how even Persinger-Lafreniere and their geophysical wobbles can accommodate that.

September 1967 *Fate*—article, "The Night The Sky Turned On," by John Keel—on 16 August 1966, the most spectacular UFO story ever to happen in the U.S. UFOs in Flandreau, South Dakota, followed by similar odd lights in dozens of parts of the midwest. A small light (two to three feet wide) hopping along treetops in Walker, Minnesota. Multi-colored lights of all sorts seen by 1500 persons in Port Smith, Arkansas. And so on, and on. The key fact that emerges is that every damn place that had these *appearances* had them in different colors and different sizes.

Sounds more like a Persinger-Lafreniere geophysical fluctuation than anything else.

You see? *Even a new and unfamiliar model sometimes feels better than no model at all.*

29 November 1913 *Literary Digest*—quoting *Cosmos*, Paris, 16 October same year—somebody anticipated Persinger-Lafreniere. A Prof. Ignazio Galli examined 148 unexplained lights in the sky from 89 B.C. to his own time, and found that they correlated with earthquakes very well. His statistics are not quoted, alas.

February 1959 *Monthly Weather Review*—odd lights that are seen during tornadoes are discussed. Some appear to be ordinary lightning, and some appear to be the little-understood ball lightning, and some are classified as "other kinds of electrical discharges."

Looks better and better for Persinger and Lafreniere.

Science 201: 748-750 (1978)—David Phillips presents statistics suggesting strongly that airplane crashes increase after widely-publicized murders and suicides. He offers the hypothesis that *some* of the airplane crashes are murders or suicides—"copycat killings" as the police call it when such a chain of destruction exfoliates from one violent death.

That's plausible. But I feel the stirrings of heresy again. I think of Persinger-Lafreniere Po Bell's Theorem and even of Persinger-Lafreniere Po synchronicity.

20 July 1980 *Sunday Times* (South Africa)—mysterious falling rocks again—a whirlwind more whimsical than any we have encountered yet—it came back again and again to torment one man.

The man was a tennis player, Okkie Kellerman. The first rock was unaccompanied. It just landed on Mr. Kellerman's foot. The whirlwind then went away, without dumping anything else or leaving any other calling cards, without even being noticed by anyone else. Minutes later, it came back and hurled a bigger stone at Kellerman. Later, it was back again, and hurled barrages of stones. All this on a tennis court in broad day light.

Maybe it was a prankster hiding in the bushes?

Unfortunately, the whirlwind or prankster continued to harass Kellerman even when he was indoors. The stones kept on flying at intervals for nearly a week. Another tennis player, Andre Wulfse, says he saw them repeatedly flying around the rooms he shared with Kellerman. The landlord, Peter Dove, says the rocks were flying from the time Kellerman checked in until he left town.

Kellerman says it all began the day *after* he insulted a witch-doctor.

Oh, damn. I feel more Heresy coming on, maybe a full chapterfull of it.

The Persinger and Lafreniere model, like all models, may cover only part of the universe, not all the universe.

CHAPTER SIX

"MIND," "MATTER"
AND MONISM

(with comments on coincidence and the Damndest Heresy of all)

Anyone who is not shocked by quantum theory has not understood it.

Niels Bohr, quoted by Gribbin
In Search of Schrodinger's Cat

The sum total of all minds is one.

Erwin Schrodinger, *Mind and Matter*

Mr. Kellerman insulted a witch-doctor, and then for a week he was attacked by mysterious stones of unknown origin.

Some people will think a rather obvious thought at this point. Other people will absolutely refuse to think it.

A crewman on the *Brechsee*, hit by a "projectile" from nowhere, which goes back to nowhere after it hits him—stones falling *slowly* at certain places but not elsewhere—

Some persons (e.g. in Africa, where Mr. Kellerman was afflicted) believe in magic, and others, closer to home, do not necessarily believe, but wonder—and try experiments. They concentrate, they try to project "mental" energies, they think of spectacular effects and visualize them vividly—they hope, they strain—

And there are, findable by me, four and only four theories in philosophy about the relationship of "mind" and "matter":

1. "Mind" is an epiphenomenon of "matter."
2. "Matter is an epiphenomenon of "mind."
3. "Mind and "matter" are both equally real, but separate, and work in predetermined harmony with each other.
4. "Mind" and "matter" are human metaphors.

The first is the theory of the most Fundamentalistic of Fundamentalist Materialists. Of course, they never admit it is a theory; they insist it is a "proven fact." It is or appears a "proven fact" only to those who avoid reflection on such issues as the uncertainty of all inferences, Godel's demonstration of the infinite regress that can enter a non-trivial argument at any point, and the Copenhagenist-Pragmatist argument that no theory can be proven true, but at best can be shown to be useful for a while.

Liberal materialists, of course, know this. They justify regarding "matter" as primary and "mind" as a by-product on the Occamite principle that this is simpler than the alternatives. There is a great deal to be said for this position, and it is one that I use as a *working hypothesis* much of the time myself, but it does not close the question forever. As we have seen abundantly, there is no longer any consensus in physics about which model is "simpler" than another, and this increasingly looks like a non-scientific, almost esthetic judgment. Is the EWG (multiple universe) model "simpler" than the Copenhagen Interpretation —that is, is it more economical to take the equations at face value and accept approximately 10^{100} alternative universes, or to ignore the clear meaning of the equations and just regard them as tools which "coincidentally" mesh with laboratory results?

Is Euclidean space simpler than the Reimannian space of relativity?

Is Fuller's synergetic space simpler than Hilbert's n-dimensional space?

Is the Persinger-Lafreniere energy-wobble model simpler or more complex than segregating whirlwinds or an endless stream of hoaxters *ad hoc*?

It seems to depend partly on one's intuitive sense of "simplicity," which varies from person to person. It also seems to depend on the context or field in which one is working.

The second theory ("mind" is primary) is that of Christian Science and of Idealist philosophers.

A major criticism of both the first and second theories is that no experiment has ever verified them precisely, and that it is likely that no experiment *can* verify them. That is, they are, as usually stated, so "philosophical" or abstract that they lack the *crispness* to be either proven or disproven experimentally. They refer to an assumed "reality" that is outside the area of what can be discussed at all in experimental contexts. (The materialists usually raise this issue only to criticize the idealists, but it refers to both—which is why Copenhagenists have given up trying to talk about that kind of "reality" at all, at all.)

To be pedantic about it, no experiment or series of experiments entitles us to make absolute statements about "mind" and "matter." Experiments only entitle us to say, *at a date,* that one kind of model seems more useful than another kind of model. To go beyond that and *believe* in a model remains an act of faith; the Christian Scientists recognize their own act of faith, but the Fundamentalist Materialists do not.

The third theory—"mind"-"matter" parallelism—was invented by Descartes and there is no current thinker, findable by me, who seems to take it seriously. It is extremely unwieldy and *ad hoc*, and there is a lingering suspicion that Descartes invented it only to apply some mechanistic principles to the analysis of behavior without explicitly saying anything that would offend the Old Inquisition.

The fourth theory—"mind" and "matter" as metaphors—is, nobody will be surprised to learn, the one that seems most sensible to me. To paraphrase Hume, I never observe "my mind"—much less "the mind" or "mind" in general. All I ever observe or experience is mental state$_1$, mental state$_2$, mental state$_3$ etc. And we never observe "matter" either, but only sense datum$_1$, sense datum$_2$ etc. (Historically, as noted earlier, measurement$_1$, measurement$_2$ etc. led to the concept of "that which is measured" which seems to be what "matter" means etymologically. The metaphoric nature of this is seen when we remember how Plato derived from chicken coop$_1$, chicken coop$_2$ etc. the Eternal Chicken Coop.)

Of course, some metaphors appear to be more useful than other metaphors; and "mind" and "matter" have seemed to be useful for a long time, and still seem useful to many.

Nevertheless, just as the old metaphors of "space" and "time" seemed unprofitable after Einstein and had to give way to the modern metaphor of "space-time," there are many signs on the horizon that "mind" and "matter" may have to give way to—something new.

Psychosomatic metaphors seem more and more useful to physicians, psychiatrists and social scientists. Evidence accumulates that what people think and feel can make them ill, and that thinking/feeling in different modalities can make them well again. This is "explained" by invoking a vague "psychosomatic unity" or, increasingly, by bluntly admitting that the old models of "mind" and "matter" cannot explain the data and calling for a new holistic model in which "mind" and "matter" will be integrated as neatly as Einstein integrated "space" and "time" into "space-time." Behavioral scientists note also that there seems to be a great utility (pragmatic value) in models that regard "my" "mind" and "your" "mind" as aspects of a social field and not as isolated, block-like entities of the Aristotelian sort. Every version of the Copenhagen Interpretation either says explicitly or at least implies that "experimental reality" is a synergy *including the experimenter* and not the old philosophical "reality" "outside" and "apart from" us. One school of psychologists observes that, just as "mind" influences "body" in psychosomatic effects, so, too, "body" effects "mind" in many cases where, for instance, chronic tension of the muscles produces habitual negative "mental states" of worry or anger, etc. and relaxing the muscles eases the "mental" tension. Another school of psychologists observes that there is no "neurotic" or "psychotic" individual who does not appear to be part of a social field of habitual anxieties or evasions. Thus, "mind" merges into "matter" in some models, "matter" merges into "mind" in others, and "mind" becomes more and more a thing that cannot be adequately modelled at all without including the social field around it. And what sort of thing—"mental" or "material"—is a *social field*, by the way?

If "mind" and "matter" are metaphors that are losing their usefulness—if we need a new, synergetic (or holistic) model—

An elephant in Bay Ridge, Brooklyn—a centaur in St. Louis—a wolf-deer and a wolf-horse and a two-headed goat—fish and frogs from nowhere—oh, I can feel it: the Heresy is welling up inside, I cannot hold it in—I may actually utter it—

Or maybe we should ease our way gradually, and tentatively, into this one.

We don't want the gent at CSICOP, who is reading at least part of this before writing his predictable review, to have apoplexy.

The "miracles" or "hallucinations" or appearances at Fatima in 1919: I take my details from *The Invisible College*, by Jacques Vallee, Dutton, New York, 1973—

The first "hallucination" was seen by three peasant girls in May 1919. The second, by fifty additional witnesses. The third by 4500 witnesses. The fourth drew 18,000 witnesses. The fifth and last in October 1919 was witnessed or hallucinated by 30,000 at the scene and an estimated 70,000 more saw some of the effects for hundreds of miles around.

"Mass hallucination" again. Some will wonder about the mechanism by which such "hallucinations" propagate and even ask if such propagation is any less "occult" than the alleged propogation of alleged ESP. Some, who are really around the bend, will even speculate that probably far, far fewer than 100,000 ever saw "George Washington" and ask if we should consider seriously that the Colonists needed a man like George, *wanted* a man like George, *dreamed* of a man like George, and thus finally manifested the "mass hallucination" of George himself.

Among the mass hallucinations at and around Fatima were explosions, puffs of smoke, unexplained humming and buzzing in the sky, bright flashes of multi-colored lights on the clouds, etc. and finally a gigantic "UFO" or Whatzit "brighter than the sun"—the last being seen (pardon, hallucinated) by the aforementioned 100,000 all over that part of Portugal.

I think of Persinger-Lafreniere's electromagnetic fluctuations and energy wobbles, and, of course, of disturbed brain waves.

I think also of 100,000 "minds" or 100,000 *aspects of a social field* inflamed by Catholic teaching—this was in Portugal—inflamed by Catholic art, inflamed by the Catholic reality-tunnel which is as existentially "real" from inside as the experience of Beethoven is from inside the Western Musical reality-tunnel—

And I think it *may* be as Aristotelian and old-fashioned to think of these "minds" in isolation from energy fields as it is to think of them in isolation from the social field.

Phenomena, Michell and Rickard, op. cit. p. 124-125:

The so-called "Surrey puma" was first sighted on 4 September 1964 at Munstead, Surrey, England. He or she—or they?—has or have appeared regularly ever since, to hundreds of witnesses or hallucinators. Track marks, found by local police, were identified by them as puma tracks, not tracks of a big dog which people were mistaking for a puma. A photo of the beast was taken, and appeared in London *People* 14 August 1966. The curious may examine it in *Phenomena*, p. 125; it looks like a very big cat indeed, and there is a house behind the beast to give you a sense of scale. In January 1965 police were so convinced they were dealing with a real puma that they warned people to stay out of the wooded areas of Surrey. Hunters, farmers, reporters and policemen have all shared this hallucination.

Although no pumas were reported missing from English zoos, one can regard this case as non-hallucinatory if one assumes some eccentric had a pet puma which escaped. Such a person might keep his mouth shut to avoid persecution for the damage a big cat might do.

Sure. That makes sense.

Unfortunately, the Surrey puma has not done any damage. It has not attacked either cattle or people. It hasn't even taken a nip at any pet Fido or Tabby, according to Michell and Rickard.

According to BBC's "Tomorrow's World" TV show for 21 May 1986, there are three possible cases of animals that might have been killed by the Surrey puma. All three, however, are ambiguous. Some Surrey residents on the show suggested they thought a dog might be responsible for these killings.

Real pumas eat about 300 pounds of meat a week. Pumas are predators. They attack and kill cattle and other animals to survive.

The Surrey puma has at best eaten 2 deer and a sheep in 22 years.

So, then, logically, there is no puma in Surrey, or a very peculiar Puma indeed. The witnesses, like the poor Papist dingbats at Fatima, must have been all hallucinating after all.

The tracks found by the police? Some hoaxter could have done that. The photo? Another fake; people are forever faking photos. Some morning *you* may wake up with a strange, uncontrollable desire to rush out and wallow in some juicy photograph-fakery—it can happen to anyone, if we believe the Citadel. Claw marks were found on a fence and identified by the RSPCA as those of a feline weighing over 100 pounds—but that must be the work of another of the hoaxters who are so malignantly determined to undermine the Faith.

Unless, in a "mind-matter" continuum, or a continuum in which "mind" and "matter" sometimes act separately and sometimes act synergetically—some things we tune in are more "mental" than "material," and some more "material" than "mental"—and—and—

20 October 1879 London *Times*—there had been a severe drought in Spain all during the summer. Public prayers were offered. Down came the rain.

"The materialists are refuted," some of the devout, of the Old Idol, must have thought—for the first few minutes.

Down came the rain. And came. And came. And came.

Five villages were destroyed and 1500 persons perished.

No: despite Charles Fort's cynicism, I don't care to attribute these appearances to a particularly tricky "God"—especially when an appearance has apparently killed 1500 people. But I do think, heretically and "dangerously," of non-local effects, of the "maybe" in between "yes" and "no" in Quantum Logic, of "solid" "objects" that are superimpositions of waves, according to one quantum model, and of "minds" that are superimpositions of waves if the "minds" are transactions involving brains and the brains are made of cells which are made of atoms which are made of electrons which are superimpositions of waves.

21 March 1913 Wellington *Evening Post* (Australia)—another drought, and more public prayers for rain.

"The greatest disaster in the history of the colony" says the *Post*, describing the subsequent flooding.

If "God" is not mad, as Fort claimed, then maybe "God" is, as Buckminster Fuller once wrote, not a noun but a *verb*. That is, "God" is what religious people *do*, as, in some models, an electron is an *operation* performed by people (physicists)—"God" as the *act* of praying, the energy raised—

4 June 1913 *Homeward Mail* (China)—another drought, and more prayers, this time to the Chinese "gods." Thunder and—

Sixteen persons killed in the floods. Canton was a month in digging out and rebuilding.

Well, anyway, some may be relieved that it isn't only the Christian "God" who sometimes malfunctions.

16 September 1905 *Times of India*—another drought, and prayers to the Hindu "gods," who were also out to lunch.

An earthquake followed and smashed the town of Lahore.

We can all be glad that the word "coincidence" exists. Otherwise the Materialist Fundamentalists would find these stories just as puzzling and frightening as the Religious Fundamentalists will find them.

Good old "coincidence"—once we think of it, we can banish the puzzlement and the fear at once, and forget these stories. Mention "coincidence" a few more times and you can forget most of the disturbing side of most of our stories. Just keep thinking "coincidence, coincidence, coincidence"; you'll find it wonderfully *soothing*, as Nietzsche would say.

Unless you stop to ask what "coincidence" means. I think it means two incidents are associated: co-incidence: coordination of incidents. So, then, to explain two associated incidents (prayers for rain followed by rain) by saying "coincidence" is to say that the two incidents were associated because the two incidents were associated. That may be soothing enough, but it is hardly analytical.

23 August 1981 London *Sunday Express*—Mr. G.L. Tomlinson of Kent was playing golf when a ball came to rest next to a *red fox*, who picked it up and ran off with it.

Nothing odd about that one.

The golf ball was made by R. Fox and Sons and had a *red fox* logo on it.

Oh, that's another "coincidence" then.

And looking at it again I note the date: 23 August. That's the birthday of my younger daughter.

It is pure superstition to think *at all* about such a thing. All the experts tell us that. So, of course—this is one of the effects of militant orthodoxy, as all Inquisitors, old and new, never realize—some of us, perversely, will insist upon thinking about it.

September 1982 *Science Digest* p. 88—the smallest unit now scientifically recognized is 10^{-23} seconds.

There's that damned 23 again.

And this time it sneaked its way into *Science Digest*, of all places.

The context—for those of us deranged enough to continue at this point—is even more interesting. *Science Digest*, op. cit. still p. 88—"The Delta-1232, for example, created when a photon and a pi-meson collide, exists for only 0.66×10^{-23} seconds. Is it only a coincidence that the lifetimes of such particles are nearly always close multiples of the chronon?" (The chronon is the above-mentioned 10^{-23} seconds.)

Is it only a coincidence that they ask "is it only a coincidence?" when I am thinking "is it only a coincidence?"

That's the kind of question that got Carl Jung thinking about *synchronicity* (universal resonance) which is a little bit like Sheldrake's morphogenetic field and also, coincidentally, a little bit like the non-local effect in quantum mechanics.

I've been collecting mysterious 23s for a number of years—and not to annoy the Fundamentalists, but to *annoy myself*, which is how I provoke myself into thought, or at least ito neurological reactions which sometimes are not totally mechanical and predictable.

In 1981, I was writing an article for the above-mentioned *Science Digest* and wanted a quote from Dr. Schrodinger. I thought it was in his *What Is Life?* but found I didn't have a copy of that anymore. I called a physicist I knew who I assumed would have his own copy, Saul Paul Sirag. I quoted, from memory, the sentence I wanted and asked him to find it and give me the exact words.

Saul Paul, who knows about my collection of 23s, was in high good humor when he called back. "You'll love this," he said. "It's the first sentence of Chapter 23."

Indeed it is. It says, "Mind, I submit, simply does not exist in the plural," which is the kernel of the Heresy we keep circling in this book. It introduces Schrodinger's argument for mind-matter monism, or synergy.

When my article (not mentioning this "synchronicity") appeared in *Science Digest*, the editors prudently accompanied it with a rebuttal by somebody using the pen-name "Dr. Crypton." Whoever he was, he said I was "groveling in awe before inscrutible gods." He said coincidence is just coincidence and that's all it is, period. Then he gave an example of a coincidence and "proved" to his own satisfaction that it was only a coincidence. It involved 23 people at a party, of whom two had the same birthday—17/5 European style, 5/17 American style, or plain 17 May.

One of my Immortal Novels, *The Eye in the Pyramid*, has a series of 5/23 coincidences and a related series of 17/23 coincidences. Now mine enemy, uttering fierce oaths and grimacing with outrage, had just handed me a beautiful 5/17/23 coincidence.

For a moment, I almost believed my own theories, despite my chronic agnosticism.

See any genetics text—in conception, the father and mother each contribute 23 chromosomes.

Coincidence.

Euclid's *Geometry* begis with 23 definitions.

Coincidence.

26 March 1919 London *Daily Mail*—story told by soldiers returned from World War I. Every time their battery received a book by H. Rader Haggard, they shortly received an S.O.S. Eventually, they all became so convinced that this "coincidence" was repeating that they requested that no more Haggard books be sent to them. The number of S.O.S.s then declined.

Arthur Koestler, Aleister Hardy and Robert Harvie, *The Challenge of Chance*—Hardy, a biologist, and Harvie, a psychologist, performed one of the most massive tests of so-called ESP ever accomplished. The subjects scored well above chance, which often happens and means that *something* is being measured, according to the testers, or else that the testers are incompetent or worse, according to the Fundamentalists. But this time, before the Fundamentalists could criticize the data, Harvie and Hardy shuffled the response cards at random, to see if results that far above chance could be obtained "by accident" (aleotorically). They found correlations so far above chance that they were stunned, as was Koestler, the philosopher, when they showed him the data.

All three of them interpret this result as very damaging to previous "ESP" research—as I do also—but they further argue that it also casts doubt on our traditional ideas of *causality*. They suggest that some sort of "formative" or "organizing" principle is at work in such appearances of order out of chaos (randomness).

In short, they are suggesting something like unto Jung's synchronicity and/or Sheldrake's morphic resonance and/or Bell's non-local connectedness.

Recently (e.g. *ReVision, op. cit.*) Dr. David Bohm has suggested that the non-local connection has "mind-like" aspects. I presume he is following the tendency, common among physicists since Relativity, to speak of "space-like separations" and "time-like separations," rather than assuming the old Aristotelian "separations *in* space" and "separations *in* time." In a recent conversation, I asked Dr. Bohm if he thought "matter-like" might be useful to supplement "mind-like" and he agreed that it might be useful, yes.

So: if we think of non-local connections that are unitary, monistic or synergetic, and if we think that these do not act "in" "space" and "time" and "on" "mind" and "matter" but, rather, have appearances or aspects which may be called "space-like," "time-like," "mind-like" and "matter-like"—

18 October 1946 London *Daily Dispatch*—Scotland Yard figures reveal that day after day, year after year, the number of mysterious disappearances remained approximately the same: it averages out to 23 a day.

There's that damned 23 again.

In a letter from Robert Rickard, co-author of *Phenomena* and co-editor of *Fortean Times*—William Blake, the first great critic of Fundamentalist Materialism, lived at 23 Hercules Street, Lambert; the Turin shroud, which allegedly contains the image of Jesus, is kept at a constant 23º Centigrade.

Look back to page 21 and note where Schrodinger's dead-and-alive cat first saw print. Flip over the pages of this Infamous Text at random and notice how many other 23s pop up in our data—or our yarns and hoaxes, if you prefer.

It is quite safe to expect, on the basis of past experience, that you will notice some peculiar 23s in the next few days. Such is the contagion of this phenomenon—or, as the Fundamentalist would say, such is the power of suggestion and the sinister ability of the forces of Unreason to seduce us.

19 March 1982 London *Daily Star*—Ann Hill, 39, had put a message in a bottle and thrown it into the sea back in 1959, to see if it would ever come back to her. In 1982, it was washed ashore at the same spot in Winterton, Norfolk, and was returned to her by a fisherman.

It had been afloat 23 years.

"Coincidence, coincidence, coincidence"—it's a lovely word. If you repeat it over and over, and over, and over, it will work exactly like a Hindu *mantra*: it will quiet anxieties and suppress doubts; it will relax and soothe you; and it will finally stop thought entirely.

On a recent tour I was approached, after a lecture in St. Louis, by a fan who told me he had figured out how the "23 gimmick" works— why so many readers of my books encounter dramatic 23s while reading them.

"It's a neurological grid," he said. "You set up the expectation, and then we *notice* the 23s more than ordinary numbers."

I congratulated him on his perceptivity. Indeed, that is one of my major messages, in everything I write—our emic realities are programmed by our expectations. *You* are the "Master who makes the grass green."

Then this chap invited me out to dinner with himself and his wife. I was in no mood for a real dinner; after a lecture, I want junk food and beer. We went to a fast-food Pizza joint, of the sort that gives you a ticket with a number to hold and then calls the number when your pizza is ready.

Our number, of course, was 23.

"How do you do it?" asked my friend, confused again.

And—"My God," asked Picasso, "is she really that small?"

More recently I was giving a seminar in Amsterdam and took the opportunity to visit the Van Gogh museum. Walking past one astounding "psychedelic" canvas after another, I marveled again at the marvelous reality-labyrinth Van Gogh offers us—his multiple vision, his poetry, his creative acts of *seeing*. I realized again that, just as Van Gogh "is" great precisely because he did *not* copy Rembrandt's reality-tunnels, and Picasso "is" great because he did *not* copy Van Gogh, and Mondrian "is" great because he did *not* copy Picasso, etc., all "greatness" in art is a new synergy, a new transaction between "observer" and "observed."

I suddenly remembered that Adolph Hitler once said that "anybody who paints the sky green should be sterilized at once."

I thought I understood the Right Man more deeply. The Right Man stays in one reality-tunnel because wandering into the reality-labyrinth of the creative mind terrifies him.

But we shall continue to wander that labyrinth for a while . . .

Dr. Evan Harris Walker and Dr. Nick Herbert—in the anthology, *Future Science*, ed. by Dr. Stanley Krippner and John White, Doubleday, New York, 1976—propose a variation on Dr. David Bohm's theory of the implicate order—the enfolded order which Bohm proposed might underlie the explicate, unfolded order of "space," "time" and "matter." Bohm sometimes calls the implicate order a "hidden variable" which programs the explicate order. Drs. Herbert and Walker propose a "hidden variable" theory of what parapsychologists have hitherto vaguely called "psychokinesis."

I have discussed this model with Dr. Herbert—I haven't met Dr. Walker yet—and I think I understand what this model implies. The best way to introduce the subject, however, seems to be through a digression about two other friends and a further digression about Dr. Carl Sagan and Fundamentalist Materialism.

The two friends mentioned are Saul Paul Sirag, physicist, and Dr. Paul Segall, biologist. They have had a friendly argument going on for about twenty years about whether physics or biology is the more important science. Not unexpectedly, Sirag, the physicist, votes for physics, and Segall, the biologist, casts his ballot for biology. The essence of the argument is more or less this:

The brain, according to Dr. Segall, produces all our ideas, including our best scientific models. When we understand the brain *fully*, we will understand how ideas, including scientific models, are produced, and even how to produce such models more efficiently and creatively. Biology is the science most likely to achieve this; *ergo*, biology is the most important science.

Sirag argues that the brain, which does these wonderful things, is made of cells, which are made of molecules, which are made of atoms, which are made of the fascinating thingamajigs ("particles" and/or "waves") that are studied in quantum mechanics. *Ergo*, to understand the brain *fully*, we must first understand quantum physics fully, and therefore physics is the most important science, even for a biologist.

Segall replies, Copenhagenishly, that the "waves" and "particles" etc. are still models generated by the brain, and so we must understand the brain as an entity before we can understand its models . . .

And the argument, like Godel's Proof, vanishes into an infinite regress.

The Fundamentalist Materialist position has most recently been restated in elegant but popular form by Dr. Carl Sagan of CSICOP in his famous *Dragons of Eden*. The argument avoids the infinite regress by *assuming* that the brain can be understood entirely in terms of molecular chemistry. *If* this assumption is granted, then, obviously, "mind" is an epiphenomenon of "matter" (the molecules) and Fundamentalist Materialism is the sound philosophy for a scientist.

Of course, the heresy—or *one* of the heresies—of the present book is that Fundamentalist Materialism "is" pre-Einsteinian as well as pre-Quantum, in the sense that the technicians at Houston "are" temporarily relapsing into pre-Copernicanism every time they talk about "up there." The Houston chaps, however, only relapse temporarily and (despite Fuller's warnings) remain post-Copernican most of the time (although I wonder about Challenger . . .). Fundamentalist Materialism, on the other hand, does appear, from our point of view, not a temporary lapse but a chronic neuro-semantic distemper. From a post-Einsteinian and post-Quantum perspective, "molecules" appear as—insofar as they "are" more useful scientific models than "ghosts" or "psychokinetic forces" or great lines of poetry—models that are to be *understood* within the larger models of bio-physics, including quantum mechanics. That is, they *should be considered as* containing atoms, and electrons, and quarks, and the other entities of quantum mechanics.

As such, "molecules" do not explain consciousness *fully*, since they themselves need to be explained by their sub-units on the atomic and sub-atomic levels.

When we get down to sub-atomic or quantum level we encounter the "model agnosticism" I have been presenting. We have not one model but several; and we have also a widespread opinion that having more than one model may not be a fault or defect but a useful procedure in "freeing up creative energies." We arrive—at least temporarily, and *maybe* permanently—at multi-model agnosticism rather than one-model Fundamentalism.

And if we consider the various quantum models, we find that the materialist proposition, "consciousness 'reduces to' molecules" now appears not only Aristotelian and pre-Einsteinian but definitely incomplete. Consciousness now "reduces to" those thingamajigs ("waves" and/or "particles") which are either

—models created by us for something so basic that we cannot speak meaningfully about it (Copenhagenism)
                              and/or
—aspects of a "state vector" which mathematically produces every possible result, so that any manifestation as "matter" or "mind" here is balanced by the opposite manifestations in parallel universes (the EWG model)

                              and/or
—locally tuned-in aspects of a non-locally connected Whole which does not fit into Aristotelian either/or models and may need to be described in metaphors similar to those of Oriental Monism (various interpretations of Bell's Theorem)
                              and/or
—being created, along with their own "past" by our acts of measurement (Wheeler's model)
                              and/or

—the local explicate unfolding of a non-local implicate order (Bohm's model)

In any of these cases, "consciousness" seems to "reduce to" something not describable or containable in Fundamentalist Materialist models

To quote Drs. Walker and Herbert:

> The hidden variable theory of consciousness asserts (1) there is a subquantal level beneath the observational/theoretical structure of ordinary quantum mechanics; (2) events occurring on this subquantal level are the elements of sentient being.

In other words, *in this model*, consciousness "is" a function of the subquantal implicate order of Bohm, functioning non-locally.

Consciousness, *in this model*, is not *"in"* our heads. Our brains are merely local receivers; consciousness "is" *an aspect of the non-local field*. The "ego" then is the locally tuned-in aspect of this usually not-tuned-in non-local field. This sounds like Schrodinger's notion that if you add up all the "minds" around the total you will arrive at is one. It also sounds like Sheldrake's morphogenetic field, the "formative principle" of Harvie-Hardy-Koestler, and—perhaps?—the necessary result of taking some of our data seriously, or considering that, in addition to hoaxters and liars, the world contains some more-or-less accurate observers, or that even the worst of us can occasionally note what is happening around us and report it in ways that are not always as muddled as dreams or nightmares.

If this model has any value—*if* it is sensible to talk of "consciousness" as non-local "software" rather than local "hardware"—then it is permissible to ask *to what extent* a local receiver, or "ego," can tune in or influence the non-local field. Walker and Herbert do ask, and they deduce a set of *predictions* in answer.

The predictions, they claim, are confirmed by the longest-running "paranormal" experiments on record, a series of experiments on "psychokinesis" conducted by Hakoon Forwald, a retired electrical engineer, between 1949 and 1970. Forwald's subjects got results better than chance—the Fundamentalist "knows" they were cheating, or course, but those of us who do not "know" may still go on thinking at this point—and just *as far above chance* as they should have got, according to Walker and Herbert's predictions, based on their model of how Bohm's implicate order should function.

In other, simpler words, the results are "as if" any local mind "is" an aspect of a non-local "mind" in something like the way a "personality" is an aspect of an environment in sociology.

Herbert and Walker conclude:

> . . . we find that our consciousness controls physical events through the laws of quantum mechanics.

This is only one model; it is not *the* model. Nonetheless, despite the Fundamentalists, it is neither illegal, immoral nor fattening to think about it.

For those who want to think in specific detail—i.e. to design, maybe, a large experiment—more technical details of this model, and Forwald's experiments, will be found in Dr. Walker's "The Compleat Quantum Anthropologist," *Proceedings of the American Anthropological Association,* Mexico City, 1974.

It may surprise some readers when I repeat that this book is not intended as a refutation of materialism *per se*. On the contrary, I am convinced that it is impossible to refute materialism—or idealism, or mentalism—or Theism—or pantheism—or any of the other hardy perennials of philosophy. All of these reality-tunnels or models have had advocates in every age, and still have advocates, and will almost certainly continue to have advocates, because none of them can be conclusively proven or disproven. My objection to Fundamentalist Materialism—and Fundamentalist Idealism, and Fundamentalist Theism, and Fundamentalist Pantheism—is that Fundamentalism *stops thought and perception*, whereas model-agnosticism encourages us to think further and look more deeply.

It is traditional—I fear it is even predictable—to quote William Blake somewhere in every polemic against Fundamentalist Materialism. It is even traditional or predictable to quote, from Blake, the following lines:

> Now I a fourfold vision see,
> And a fourfold vision is given to me;
> 'Tis fourfold in my supreme delight
> And threefold in soft Beulah's night
> And twofold always. May God keep
> From single vision & Newton's sleep!

While I don't claim to understand Blake's visions any more than any other critic does, I think that, possibly, he is in at least partial agreement with the multi-model approach. He may even be saying, in our modern jargon, that he has four models usually, and a minimum of two models always, and that one model seems to him a type of trance of hypnosis. Of course, this is very hard for one-model people—*modeltheists*—to understand. It is especially perplexing to Aristotelians, for whom "a model is either true or false," and once you find "the correct model," all other models are *by definition* false. Perhaps we need to remember that that kind of modeltheism underlies the *intolerance* which perpetuates most of the violence and wars on this backward planet and creates the violent Right Man personality.

An example, again from quantum mechanics, of the kind of minimum twofoldness that Blake, perhaps, was trying to convey:

The famous or infamous two-hole experiments, also called the double-slit experiments.

Here I mostly follow Gribbin, *In Search . . . op.cit.* p. 164-170.

Take a screen with two holes in it, some distance apart, and place the screen at a good distance in front of a wall with another screen on it that will register patterns of light. Then, from in front of the first screen, flash a light toward the two holes.

This has been done many times, starting in the 19th Century. The pattern on the second screen—the pattern made by the light after passing through the two holes—will be consistent with the wave model of light. That is, it will look like what you would expect if two waves came out of the two holes and made an *interference pattern* when they hit the second screen. They will also be consistent with the mathematical equations for such interference of waves. According to the experiment in this form, both vision and mathematical analysis indicate that light "really is" waves and that each hole had its own separate waves coming through it. It is very much of a muchness with what is observed near a beach when water waves pass through a fence with two holes in it.

On the other hand, if you open only one hole, and keep the other closed—this experiment has also been performed many times—the results are consistent with the particle model. The pattern on the second screen is now mathematically what it should be if light was not waves but particles—little tiny "bullets," so to speak.

If you open one hole and then the other, the total result is still consistent with the particle model. That is, adding up the number of assumed particles that should have passed each hole to create the observed pattern gives the result it should give if the particles "really are" particles and behave like separate bullets would behave. There is no *interference pattern*, such as we found in the two-hole experiment. However, if we open both holes again—the two-hole experiment repeated—the wave pattern again appears, with its associated interference; an interference consistent with the wave model but mathematically inconsistent with the particle model.

It is "as if" light traveled in waves when it "knew" we were going to open both holes, but then decided to travel in particles when it "knew" we were going to open one hole or the other, or both successively, but not both simultaneously.

It has been tried experimentally to find out what the damned light would do if we tried to "trick" it by starting with two holes open and then quickly closing one of them when the light is in motion but has not yet reached the screen. It behaves in accord with the proper model consistent with the conditions *at the instant when it arrives at the screen.* That is, if one thinks of it "really" starting out as waves, to be consistent with the wave model, it "discovers" *en route* that we are "cheating" by changing from two holes to one, and it immediately changes itself to fit the particle model. But that is absurd (I hope).

In Bucky Fuller's metaphor, one experimental set-up tunes in the wave aspect and the other tunes in the particle aspect; but the not-tuned-in is not non-existent—it is merely not-tuned-in.

These experiments have been duplicated continually, first because physicists themselves could hardly believe the results, and latterly to demonstrate to physics students that quantum mechanics does indeed violate traditional Aristotelian either/or logic or traditional notions of "reality."

This is why physicists, following Bohr's Principle of Complimentarity, no longer believe in either the wave model or the particle model but say both models are equally useful. (Which is more useful at a time depends on the context.)

The same experiments have been performed with so-called electrons, which are the thingamajigs of which "matter" is composed, as photons are the thingamajigs of which "light" is composed. The same complimentarity appears. Electrons "are" both waves and particles, or—and by now you can see that this is not pedantry—can be described by both wave models and particle models.

Thus, the minimum twofoldness: when physics gets to basics, we need, as Blake may have foreseen, two models at least. One will not serve.

As for the *four*foldness—I'm only guessing, but—

1. We can say "it is waves."

2. We can say "it is particles."

3. We can say "it is both waves and particles," i.e. either of the first two will serve, at different times.

4. We can say "It is neither waves nor particles," i.e. the models are our metaphors; the Etic non-verbal event remains—*unspeakable*.

This, of course, is the traditional Buddhist logic—*It is X, it is not-X, it is both X and not-X, it is neither X nor not-X*—which Capra *(Tao of Physics)*, and others here and there, have argued is more consistent with quantum mechanics than is the traditional Aristotelian logic of *It is either X or not-X*. If it's too much of a mind-boggler, the reader can retreat to the Quantum Logic of von Neumman which has only three choices—"Yes, no and maybe." That may seem now, however it seemed at first, comparatively conservative.

The Mysterious Case of Garry Owen and the Three Quarks:

Garry Owen "was" a "real dog." That is, if we *assume* we possess accurate records—if we do not worry about the carping of possible Revisionist Historians—Garry Owen was born in 1888. He was a pedigreed Irish Setter. He was owned by a Mr. J.J. Giltrap, a breeder of pedigreed dogs.

Garry Owen appears twice in James Joyce's *Ulysses*. The first time, Garry is seen-or-hallucinated by the anonymous and drunken narrator of the "Cyclops" chapter and appears as an ugly, mangy, evil-tempered and dangerous hound. The second time, Garry is seen-or-hallucinated by the adolescent, sentimental Gerty McDowell and appears as a dear, sweet dog "so human he almost talked."

Which is the real Garry Owen?

Joyce's text sayeth not—which may be one reason *Ulysses* increasingly appears as *the* archetypal 20th Century novel. We can believe the drunk, or we can believe the sentimentalist, or we can believe a little of both, or we can believe neither.

Garry Owen is X and not-X and both X and not-X and neither X nor not-X.

Now the Objectivists hate me as much as the Fundamentalist Materialists do.

The three quarks in *Finnegan's Wake*, which have gotten into quantum mechanics via Dr. Murray Gell-Mann:

Joyce symbolizes them, in his notebooks, as ∧ , ⌐ and ⁄⌐ , which is obviously a synthesis of ∧ and ⌐ . Sometimes ∧ and ⌐ are Abel and Cain and then ⁄⌐ is "cainapple" which combines both and includes the Forbidden Fruit. Sometimes ∧ and ⌐ are Brown and Nolan, a bookstore in Dublin in Joyce's youth, and then ⁄⌐ is Bruno of Nola, who was both "brown" and "nolan"—and who, incidentally, said all things are a coincidence of opposites. Sometimes ∧ and ⌐ are Shaun and Shem, two deaf-mute twins in Dublin in Joyce's youth, and ⁄⌐ is "Shimar Shin," a sinister Hindu. Sometimes ∧ and ⌐ are "offender" and "defender" and ⁄⌐ is a composite "fender" who is guilty and innocent at the same time. Sometimes ∧ is Mick (the archangel Michael) and ⌐ is Nick (the devil) and ⁄⌐ is "Micholas de Cuzack"—who combines Nicholas of Cusa, medieval mystic, and Michael Cuzack, founder of the Gaelic Athletic Association, or Mick-and-Nick combined.

Many of the word-coinages in *Finnegan's Wake* are ⁄⌐ s. For instance "chaosmos" is a ⁄⌐ combining cosmos (∧) and chaos (⌐).

I think the idea behind Joyce's literary experiments was that we are all too quick in pronouncing things "real" or "unreal" (∧ or ⌐) or "right" or "wrong" (∧ or ⌐) and that much of experience should be considered in the ⁄⌐ mode.

Quantum Logic (von Neumann) easily converts into this symbolism. Schrodinger's cat is alive (∧) and dead (⌐) and in-between (⁄⌐).

Transactional Psychology, similarly, says we cannot understand observer (∧) alone or observed (⌐) alone but can only understand the synergetic transaction (⁄⌐).

Somebody does something that *seems* offensive *to me*. The Right Man approach—the modeltheist approach—is to decide "He *is* offensive," and to counterattack accordingly (or to slink away and day-dream of revenge, as Nietzsche would add).

The Principle of Complimentarity (Bohr) applied to this situation would be "He is offensive and he is not offensive." That is, he is offensive, in one way of looking at it, but he is not offensive in a relativist model which suggests that maybe he doesn't know the local "rules" of courtesy. If he is a visitor from elsewhere, this is worth thinking about.

In Buddhist Logic one would think, "He is offensive and he is not offensive and he is both offensive and not-offensive and he is neither offensive nor not-offensive," which reminds us of the FourFold Vision, including the model in which all our evaluations are *not* the non-verbal event "out there" being evaluated.

"Social fields" are "real" enough that, as psychologists have demonstrated, people react visibly when you come within their "personal" space: they become defensive or nervous.

"Social fields" are not "real" enough to remain constant, as physical fields do, or usually do. They vary from culture to culture. An American reacts nervously when you get within one foot of him, but a Mexican wants you that close and becomes nervous if you stay further away.

In Buddhist Logic, then:

Social fields are real. Social fields are not real. Social fields are both real and not-real. Social fields are neither real nor not-real.

This may have important implications for many *necessary* models in social studies, including the alleged "unconscious" and the "collective unconscious."

A field that depends on *what people believe* is "unthinkable" to a Fundamentalist Materialist, but social studies seems to "need" such fields.

13 August 1904 *Maui News* (Hawaii)—the British steamship *Mohican*, commanded by Capt. Urquhart, arrived in Maui with a strange yarn, even by the standards of this book. Some damned thing or other— which Capt. Urquhart thought might be "magnetic"—had stopped the motors and brought the ship to a complete halt in mid-Ocean.

Maybe Capt. Urquhart and the good ship *Mohican* never existed, for all I know. Maybe TUUR had managed to find himself a job in sunny Hawaii that year, to enjoy the world's greatest climate and relax after the strain of inventing so many of the stories in this book.

Maybe.

And then again maybe the captain and the ship and the story were all real, in whatever sense you and I are "real," or photons or quarks or the Gross National Product may be "real." At this point, some readers at least may be seduced into thinking about the Captain's description of what he and his crew thought they had experienced.

Capt. Urquhart said that during the "magnetic" disturbance there were strange lights radiating from the crew members. They didn't burst into flame like some of our cases, and their temperatures didn't stay at high levels for many years like Fireboy's, but they definitely had a glow on. Everybody seemed to have a halo, as it were. And while the ship was stalled and the motors wouldn't move and everybody glowed like that, all metal objects stuck to the decks and could not be lifted.

That was what was tuned-in. I don't know what remained not-tuned-in.

Sounds like some modern UFO stories, especially the UFO-related auto accidents mentioned on page 80. Sounds like a Persinger-Lafreniere field fluctuation, too, I think.

Phenomena, by Michell and Rickard, op. cit. p. 101—on 5 November 1975 a young logging camp worker named Travis Walton, together with five others, saw a strange, glowing something-or-other in the woods near Snowflake, Arizona. Having experience of mass media reality-tunnels and unaware of the venom of Fundamentalist Materialism, they called it a UFO.

Actually, it should be called at most a UO, since it never left the ground.

Walton allegedly had the courage to approach It, whatever the devil It was, while the other five stayed back. I don't know about you, but I think I would have stayed back, myself.

There was allegedly a flash of light and Walton was allegedly ingested or *schlurped* into the glowing body. The other five fled in a truck.

When a sheriff's possee was summoned, Walton could not be found. In fact, he was not found for five days. When found, he was either in a state of disorientation and anxiety, or was giving a good imitation of that state. His story was that he had been held captive by experimental extraterrestrials during that time.

Maybe extraterrestrial scientists *were* doing research on primate behavior that day.

Maybe what we have here is a "strong" Persinger-Lafreniere fluctuation with electromagnetic bogles (the glowing, flashing Whatzit) and brain-wave disturbances (hallucinations) in the person who got closest to the epicenter.

Or *maybe* Walton and his friends just made up a yarn, or hoax, and he hid out for five days to make it more convincing.

To the Fundamentalists, strict Aristotelians all, there was no maybe about it. You can imagine the kind of things they have said about

Walton and his five friends. I repeat: you would not want them on the jury if you were on trial for a serious, or even a minor, offense. They Are Never Wrong, or even uncertain.

Walton subsequently took two polygraph ("lie detector") tests. He passed one and failed one. At this point you should be able to guess which test is considered conclusive by Fundamentalist Materialists and which by Fundamentalist Believers in Space Brothers. If you can't guess, primate conditioning prevailed: the FMs all believed the test that said Walton lied. The FBISBs all believed the test that said he was telling the truth. Each side claimed the *other* test, the one they didn't like, had been bungled by an incompetent technician who should be sent back to plumbing school.

The other five men also took polygraph tests. Four passed and one failed. You will not be guessing wrong if you suspect the four passes will be stressed in books by those who *want* Space Brothers to come visit and the one fail will be stressed in books by those who *don't want* any Space Brothers in their reality-tunnel.

Of course, the polygraph is not a lie detector. It merely measures skin-potentials usually associated with anxiety. Assuming that the skin-potentials *were* associated with anxiety in this case, the ambiguous results—one pass and one fail for Walton, four passes and one fail for the others—may merely mean that what happened was so far outside any convenient reality-tunnel that everybody had the kind of anxiety associated with fear of going, or seeming, insane.

I think it might help to regard this UFO, not as an external event ($\wedge$) or a human "hallucination" ($\sqsubset$) but as the synergetic product ($\wedge\!\!\sqsubset$) of event-plus-human-interpretation.

The "angels" of Mons in World War I—glowing figures, which might remind some readers of certain other yarns in this book, who appeared amid the British troops. Aristotelians in some places are still arguing about whether these "really were" angels or "really were" hallucinations.

17 February 1930 London *Daily News*—the angels of Mons explained. Col. Friedrich Hozenwirth of the German General Staff confesses that they were projected with a film projector, from an airplane, in an attempt to frighten the British.

Perhaps we should not stampede in haste to pin the label of "mass hallucination" on all anamolies but should consider other explanations?

18 February 1930 London *Daily News* again—the "Colonel Horzenwirth" who had explained the angels of Mons was himself as an imposter.

There was no Col. Horzenwirth on the German General Staff either in 1914 at the time of the "miracle" or in 1930 when the imposter gave his interview.

Oh, well—back to "mass hallucination" again.

London Daily News again, same day and same page as above:

Some had attributed the "miracle" to our old friend TUUR. Private Robert Cleaval of the First Cheshire Regiment signed an affidavit that he had seen the glowing figures of Mons with his own eyes, and so had his mates. The story was not invented by the unscrupulous reporter back in London. Cleaval had his affidavit notarized.

One imagines that Pvt. Cleaval was rather sure about what he had seen, even though he carefully avoids the word "angels."

I think I can guess why many of the troops did use the word "angels." I think it is for the same reason that so many people recently have used the word "extraterrestrials" to account for odd things they saw.

"First principle: any explanation is better than none."

Most books that deal with this mystery—or this boldfaced lie—as you like—mention that Arthur Machen, the fantasy writer, described a precisely similar miracle in his story, "The Bowmen" published before the events or hallucinations at Mons.

Skeptics all claim that the story was published in time for reports of it to cross the channel, get circulated among the troops, and inspire the "mass hallucination." Those of occult bias are equally insistent that the first reports of the miracle came back from Mons hours before the story reached the newsstands. I deduce that everybody tends to believe the clock, or alleged clock, that fits his own reality-tunnel.

Just in passing, with no ulterior motive really, I mention that the Arthur Machen who either provoked or was "coincidentally" involved with the miracle or hallucination at Mons was himself a member of the Hermetic Order of the Golden Dawn. That was a society of "magicians," or would-be "magicians," or loonies who thought they were "magicians." Golden Dawn people—the members included actress Florence Farr, poet William Butler Yeats, engineer Alan Bennett and the egregious Aleister Crowley, among others—were always trying to project "mental energies" and produce "psychokinetic" effects.

On the other hand, maybe we had at Mons the same kind of magnetic disturbance as aboard the *Mohican*, and the glowing figures were just ordinary Tommies. Maybe everybody, in the heat of battle, didn't notice that he himself was also glowing.

Maybe, in a non-locally-connected Universe, Machen's poetic-magical imagination was not un-connected from such a magnetic fluctuation.

Think of the cock-eyed room designed by Dr. Ames where men "become" giants and midgets, because we cannot reprogram our brains fast enough to change perception accurately when confronted with dissonance, so we choose "the lesser of two evils," and accept congenial hallucination, rather than—Chaos and the Abyss.

Maybe the world is like a cock-eyed room, and when we cannot believe what we see, we see what we can believe, choosing among hallucinations.

We know that Copernicus has a better model than Ptolemy but we still speak of "sunset" and even *"see"* the sun "going down" at twilight, accepting the hallucination cheerfully because we're accustomed to it.

Buckminster Fuller often urged his audiences to try this simple experiment: stand, at "sunset," facing the sun for several minutes. As you watch the spectacular technicolor effects, keep reminding yourself, "The sun is not 'going down.' The earth is rotating on its axis." If you are statistically normal, you will feel, after a few minutes, that, even though you understand the Copernican model intellectually, part of you—a large part—never *felt* it before. Part of you, hypnotized by metaphor, has always *felt* the pre-Copernican model of a stationary Earth.

This experiment also might help some persons understand such terms as "existential reality," "emic reality," "reality-tunnel," etc. You might get a real insight into how "real" bizarre reality-tunnels are to those who "live" inside them. This effect can be multiplied by trying to feel/perceive a larger hunk of the Copernican model: on evenings when the Earth's moon and Venus are both visible at "sunset" find them and tell yourself, "That great *big* moon is actually only about 1/6 the size of that *little* pin-prick I call Venus. The moon *looks* relatively bigger, and Venus *looks* relatively smaller, because Venus is about 120 times further away than the moon." If you can *feel* you are seeing all this from a rotating ball, you might understand why you are not seeing it accurately, and why it is not extravagant to say Universe is like a cock-eyed room, and why Picasso wondered how big the woman "really" was.

Another interesting experience happens if you remind yourself of the laws of optics, and then go for a walk, trying to remember that everything you see is inside your head. If you are as dumb as me, you will relapse 100 times in a 10-minute stroll into "seeing" them outside you. Such is the power of perspective and metaphor.

It is even more amusing to remember that an orange "is" "really" sort of blue in the model accepted in optical physics. That is, the fruit has absorbed blue—blue is *conducted* through its skin. We see "orange" precisely because there is no orange in the fruit—because orange is being *reflected* off the skin, to our eyes. The "substance" or "isness" of the fruit contains the blue we do not see; our brains contain the orange we do see.

Who is the Master who makes an orange, orange?

20 February 1980, London *Daily Telegraph*—Tseng Shu-Sheng, Chinese mountaineer, alleges that he and his team found a woman's high heel shoe 25,700 feet up the north slope of Mount Everest. Mr. Tseng alleges that it was a fashionable, stylish shoe of fine brown leather. He offered a theory: "Maybe a climber carried it as a memento of his wife or girlfriend."

1 March 1980, *Daily Telegraph* follow-up story—Alpine Club of London finds Mr. Tseng's explanation "totally impractical." A spokesman says "At those altitudes no climber would take anything that was not absolutely vital to the expedition."

Lord Hunt, leader of the British 1952 expedition, concurs. Tseng's explanation, he says, "is not only incredible; it is impossible."

Then how did the shoe get there?

Lord Hunt says he has "doubts" about the "veracity" of the Chinese mountaineers.

Another damned communist lie, in other words. Like the "humanoids" seen in Moscow that year, chasing cars and drilling holes in windows.

Again: I'm sure there are damned communist liars (DCLs) just as there are TUURs, but one gets uneasy when all inconvenient data is disposed of by such rationalizations. Maybe it would be better to invoke the segregating whirlwind again, or another fulgurous exhalation conglobed in a cloud by the circumfused humour.

Or maybe the Abominable Snowmen are married to Abominable Snowwomen who wear the latest fashions in footwear?

10 July 1980 Berkeley *Independent and Gazette* (U.S.A.)—a sled belonging to the Rogers family of 2675 O'Hare Avenue, San Pablo, allegedly flew out of the Rogers' backyard. It allegedly rose 30 feet in the air. It soared over the next house, allegedly zoomed across the street and struck the

wires of the Pacific Gas and Electric Company where it became entangled and stopped flying.

The newspaper says there was no sound of an explosion and the rubber swimming pool next to the sled was undisturbed.

"I'm not sure we'll ever know what happened," said an alleged Captain Richard Traxler, allegedly of the local fire department.

I know the Berkeley-San Pablo area; I lived there for eight years. It is full of witches, or would-be witches, or loonies who think they are witches. They are constantly trying "psychic" experiments, such as thought-transference, or moving objects by the power of the mind. There are also parapsychology laboratories in Berkeley and nearby Palo Alto. Maybe somebody was concentrating—wishing—hoping—

No: It Is Forbidden To Think That Way. It Is Blasphemy. It must have been the finicky whirlwind again. It rejected the rubber swimming pool, rejected everything else in the yard, and in the whole neighborhood, and just picked up one sled.

I will only note in passing that the New Reformed Orthodox Order of the Golden Dawn has its headquarters in Berkeley. They trace their lineage back to the London Golden Dawn of Arthur Machen and William Butler Yeats and others interested in non-dualistic "mental" research, or research on "mind-like" behavior of the synergetic whole system.

But, of course, Berkeley is on a wellknown earthquake fault, which passes near San Fablo. Persinger and Lafreniere claim a statistical clustering of energy fluctuations on earthquake faults. A liberal materialist might be willing to think about that.

Quicksilver Messenger (Brighton) issue 7, 1982—interview with artist Paul Devereaux. While a student at Revensbourne College of Art in 1957 Mr. Devereux saw an AUFO (an *absolutely* unidentified flying object)—something that not even the most devout believer in "Space Brothers" could possibly consider a spaceship. This damned thing, when first sighted, was shaped like a rectangle and was a bright orange color. That is, it looked orange and was therefore "really" blue. Anyway, about a dozen people in the quad also saw it. The "object" or appearance or monstrosity or whatever it was hovered, or appeared to hover, about a hundred feet above the ground, or what appeared to be the ground, for about fifteen minues, or what was experienced as about fifteen minutes. It appeared to gradually change its shape. Devereaux was watching from a second-floor window, the other witnesses from the ground. Before the apparition faded completely, it looked like da Vinci's "Universal Man" to most of the groundlevel witnesses, but it looked like an angel in flowing robes to Deveraux. At the end of the apparent 15 minutes, the appearance appeared to fade away.

Of course, this one certainly sounds like "mass hallucination." Being a simple-minded person, I personally cannot imagine how such a "mass hallucination" can happen without a field somewhat like that suggested by Persinger-Lafreniere to propagate it. The ordinary materialist label of "mass hallucination," without such a model to explain it, sounds to me as if it implies the *verboten* "ESP." How does an image or idea get from one brain to another, without either "ESP" or some field fluctuation to transmit it?

One answer might be that there were verbal transmissions of the idea which, due to excitement, were forgotten afterwards. Somebody at Ravensbourne in 1957 shouted "Hey, look at the big orange rectangle in the sky"—and somebody in Snowflake said "Do you see that UFO?"—and somebody at Fatima remarked "I say, take a squint at that remarkable light brighter than the sun."

Try it. See if you can create a "mass hallucination" that way.

Maybe some have been seduced by my heresies by now and will apply Buddhist logic and/or Quantum Logic instead of the old Aristotelian logic:

It was mass hallucination. It was not mass hallucination. It was both mass hallucination and not mass hallucination. It was neither mass hallucination nor not mass hallucination.

By and large, I think that's a good description of our experience in general, and not just of one kind of experience. But Quantum Logic gets its turn:

Yes, it was mass hallucination. No, it was not mass hallucination. Maybe it was mass hallucination.

Somehow, to me at least, either of those logics seem to fit the enigmas of our existence, here in the cock-eyed room of primate perceptor organs, better than Aristotelian yes/no choices. Of course, if after long analysis, *some* experiences can finally be reduced to an Aristotelian choice, that is convenient. But *starting* from the Aristotelian either/or may be rather constricting or strangulating.

It is worth quoting Mr. Deveraux's subjective reactions to the Damned Thing that came to the art school that day:

"To see something disappear, man, you see it on T.V. but when you—and this is what non-witnesses don't understand—when you actually see a UFO and are not prepared for it . . . You cannot put it into a cosmology. It's not a film. It should be a film but it's not, and it leaves a trauma. It's conceptual rape; there's no doubt about that. It leaves a shock. . . . To be seeing it in ordinary waking consciousness with other people seeing it: it really makes you wonder about the nature of Reality."

Those who have had similar forbidden perceptions will have a certain sympathy for Mr. Devereux. I continue to maintain that Fundamentalist Materialism, like other Fundamentalisms, is, or appears within psychological models to be, a *defense mechanism*, and within neurological models, an *editing-out device*, to stave off the shock and sense of "conceptual rape" that causes the unsophisticated to panic when confronted with "wonder about the nature of Reality."

Part of the "mystical" teaching of all the Oriental systems I know anything about is that most people are hallucinating most of the time; that techniques exist for lessening the effect of this habit of hallucination; that these techniques *must* be taught slowly, because otherwise the pupils will go wild, hallucinate even more, and think the teacher is "attacking" them or trying to drive them insane. Some say the pupil, if this *panic-button* is accidentally pushed, will try to kill the teacher "in self-defense."

Sounds like an extreme view—something only a "mystic" would say.

Ask any psychiatrist or consulting psychologist. The ones I know—especially the ones who dare the more aggressive or "active" therapies—generally study martial arts on the side, to protect themselves in case this happens.

Phenomena, Michell and Rickard, op. cit. p. 94—citing Dr. Andrija Puharich—with "hundreds" of other witnesses, Dr. Puharich "saw" an Hindu fakir perform the celebrated Indian Rope Trick. The rope was thrown upward and appeared to stay that way "in violation of gravity." A boy climbed up the rope and appeared to vanish. The fakir then appeared to climb the apparent rope, with a knife, and what appeared to be screams were heard. A hideous assortment of what appeared to be parts of the human body then fell. The fakir descended, or appeared to descend, assembled the grisly organs, put them in an apparent box, and, after a few moments, the boy apparently emerged, appearing whole and healthy.

Of course, the Fundamentalists will tell you that this could all be accomplished by ordinary techniques of stage magic; as indeed it could.

But evidently it was not managed that way in this case. A film was taken during the performance by another psychologist. When the film was developed, it showed the fakir and the boy standing by the rope, which had never risen from the ground.

So, then, everything the hundreds of witnesses saw was "only" mass hallucination.

And again I say: try it. See if, by techniques imaginable by you, you can induce that kind of mass hallucination. (Remember: the camera did not see any stage magic tricks. It saw only the fakir and the boy standing still.)

You might, after this experiment, see some sense in Buddhist logic: It is mass hallucination. It is not mass hallucination. It is both mass hallucination and not mass hallucination. It is neither mass hallucination nor not mass hallucination.

At this point, some may find it easier and more soothing to simply decide it was another fulgurous exhalation conglobed in a cloud by the circumfused humour.

Ibid., still page 94:

The Hindu rope trick performed in London in 1934. Again, the witnesses "saw" the miracle. Again, there were hidden cameras. Again, the cameras saw no miracle.

In the two-hole experiment, the second screen "sees" light as waves in one design (both holes open) but "sees" light as particles in other designs (one or the other hole open). In the phenomenological models of sociology, "consciousness" is not merely a product of a brain but a synergy of the brain and the surrounding social field. In the Walker-Herbert quantum model, "consciousness" includes also the non-local connection described by Bell's Theorem in which "space" and "time" are either unreal or at least irrelevant.

And:

According to the super-determinist model, mentioned but not endorsed by Dr. Clauser of UC-Berkeley, I cannot think a thought without effecting the whole universe, including its past—just as in the Wheeler model, our current experiments are affecting the whole universe including its past—because the thought either "is," or "is connected with" an energy-event in my brain, and that energy-event is non-locally connected to everything, everywhere, everywhen.

But, of course, to say it that way is misleading, because it stresses one half of the non-local connection. To see non-locality correctly we have to add: I cannot think a thought unless the whole universe (past, present and future) collaborates in producing such an energy-event in my brain.

Dr. Capra in his *Tao of Physics* seems to me to be saying, or implying, that only if you see *both* of these sides of the non-local connection can you comprehend the real meaning of quantum mechanics.

But, of course, this is only two-fold vision. If we are to try, experimentally, to share in the Blakean or Buddhist fourfold vision, we would have to say: I am creating the universe. The universe is creating me. I am creating the universe and the universe is also creating me. I am neither creating the universe nor is the universe creating me.

The only way, thinkable by me, that this remotely makes any more sense than random gibberish, or at least as much sense as *Alice in Wonderland*, is if old Schrodinger was right all along. The appearance of separation between "minds" is, like the appearance of separation "in space" or separation "in time"—*only an appearance.*

The sum total of all minds is one.

In other words, the You who is making the grass green is non-local. The local You is, like the greenness of the grass, or the flatness of Earth, a social Game Rule or hallucination.

Did you get it that time?

CHAPTER SEVEN

THE OPEN
UNIVERSE

(with further comments on energy fluctuations and "spooks")

Against that positivism which stops before phenomena, saying "there are only *facts*," I should say: no, it is precisely facts that do not exist, only *interpretations*.

Nietzsche, *The Will to Power*

Since the publication of Packard's *The Hidden Persuaders*, McLuhan's *The Mechanical Bride*, and similar books, it has been realized that techniques of inducing "mass hallucination" or something like "mass hallucination" are well known to advertisers.

Almost all cigarette smokers, for instance, have a favorite brand and insist that they cannot be satisfied by any other brand. When blindfolded, however, they cannot distinguish this favorite brand from any other brand. They are not buying the cigarettes but buying the package. The same is true of most beer drinkers: they have a favorite brand, but cannot distinguish it from other brands when blindfolded.

This species of "mass hallucination" has been created by *conditioning* and *association*. Each advertiser tries to associate his product with something most domesticated primates desire, such as Sex or Status. The commercials carry the association, sometimes fairly blatantly, sometimes subliminally. The repetition of the association gradually produces the conditioned response. The victim is not exactly "buying the package" as we just said but buying the hope for Sex and Status.

Of course, the satisfaction of the smoker or drinker is just as "real," within that conditioned reality-tunnel, as the meanings of a Rembrandt are within the traditional Western Art tunnel, or the meanings of a Van Gogh within the Impressionist tunnel, or the meanings of an African mask within that tribal tunnel, or the meanings of a Picasso within the Modernist tunnel, etc. All are equally unreal, also (or equally meaningless, to say it otherwise) to those who haven't learned or conditioned themselves to enter these tunnels.

Existential or emic "reality"—the reality of daily life—the "reality" of experience, sensory-sensual "reality," as distinguished from the assumed "real" "reality" of various philosophers—appears then to be too interactive and synergetic to reduce to Aristotelian either/or choices. It fits more adequately into Buddhist logic:

It is real. It is not real. It is both real and unreal. It is neither real nor unreal.

Just like the smoker's satisfaction.

It is only a coincidence that with modern technology we find also that "experimental reality" on the sub-atomic (quantum) level—and the "reality" of *specially-designed* experience, sensory-sensual "reality" *magnified* by instruments—also appears less Aristotelian and more Buddhistic?

I have suggested in other books that Einstein's *physical relativity* is just a special case of a more general *neurological relativity*: the observer, with or without instruments, always remains co-creator of the observation. To quote Nietzsche again: "We are all greater artists than we realize."

Each *nervous system* creates a great art-work which it usually considers "the" "real" "reality" in the philosophical sense and projects outward. These reality-tunnels, assumed to be "realities" and experienced as "realities," are not only as varied and imaginative as the paintings of Rembrandt and Van Gogh and Picasso, etc.; they are as marvelously creative as the musics of Vivaldi and Beethoven and Wagner and Harry James and Rock and Indian *raga* and Polynesian chants; they are as miscellaneous as the novelistic styles or "frames" of Jane Austen and James Joyce and Raymond Chandler and Leo Tolstoy and Lewis Carroll and Samuel Beckett.

And every social reality-tunnel perpetuates itself by basically the same techniques as advertising, of which the chief is repetition. This is maintained half-consciously, by group reinforcement. "Birds of a feather flock together." You do not see many Roman Catholics in Methodist churches, nor do a large number of Marxists sit in the cabinets of Mrs. Thatcher and Mr. Reagan. The *signals* (speech units) that maintain the group-reality are repeated endlessly and quite cheerfully, while others are edited out by selection of *who* gets in. As Dr. Timothy Leary once remarked, most domesticated primate conversation consists of variations on "I'm still here. Are you still there?" and "Business as usual. Nothing has changed."

For instance, most of us are annoyed frequently by the daily newspaper. "News" or alleged news that we don't want to read gets printed; heathenish and heretical opinions appear on the letters page, and sometimes in the columnists; politicians (of the opposite camp, of course) tell the most outrageous lies, which also get printed. With modern computer technology, all of this can soon be avoided. Just fill out a simple questionaire and mail it in. The computer will print a slightly different version of that day's paper for each reader, and your Personalized copy will come to you in the morning containing absolutely nothing but what you want to know. After a year, or maybe five years, you will have forgotten entirely all the "alien" and uncomfortable signals that once got through to you and caused you distress.

This great breakthrough in computer technology has not *yet* occurred, but, meanwhile, most people do the best they can, and manage fairly well to edit out what they don't want to know. When they get together in groups, this is aided by the aforementioned group reinforcement. Everybody tells everybody how reasonable the group-reality is, and how wicked and perverse are all the alien groups with alternative group-realities.

At this point, you and I can repeat the Pharisee's prayer—"Thank God I am not as other men"—and congratulate ourselves on not being so mechanical.

Or can we?

Of course, we *all* hallucinate frequently—and not just in the sense revealed by the Ames' cockeyed room or similar "tricks"—and not just in "seeing" the moon as bigger than Venus because of the ilusions of distance—

This happens to everybody occasionally:

You are walking down the street. Half a block ahead of you, in the crowd, you "see" a friend. Maybe it's a small surprise (you thought he or she was in another city, or another country) or maybe it's no great surprise at all (he or she lives near this part of town), but in either case you feel happy because it is always good to see a familiar face in a crowd of strangers.

You walk closer and the features of the person you "recognized" become clearer. It is not a friend at all. It is a complete stranger.

In "seeing" the friend who wasn't there, you selected—at a guess—30% to 50% of the gross features of the figure approaching, and then out of a blur, superimposed or added the remaining 50% or more of the features necessary to create a face you could recognize.

Of course, we do not like to think of ourselves as hallucinators. We prefer the more soothing term, "misperception," for cases like this. Only the mentally "ill" are hallucinating, we think.

Still—the difference is only a matter of *degree* . . .

December 1932 *Popular Science Monthly* (England)—a shower of *eels* on 4 August that year in Hendon, Sunderland, England. They landed on roads, in gardens, and on the roofs of houses. A physician, Dr. Harrison, had the impression that he saved a few specimens and showed them to the correspondent from *Popular Science*, who had the impression he saw them.

4 September 1866 Charleston *News and Courier* (U.S.A.)— a fall of warm stones at 7:30 a.m. followed later by a second fall of warm stones

at 1:30 p.m. The editor says he himself witnessed this.

The Unscrupulous Reporter, in that case, was so clever he got promoted to Unscrupulous Editor?

Scientific American 36-86 (1877)—on 15 January 1877 "thousands" of snakes fell on Memphis, Tenn. during a rainstorm. The fall was localized, within about two blocks of houses; the snakes were all less than two feet long.

And I think: Part of what we see seems more-or-less "accurate" perception ($\wedge$) and part is projection or misperception or "hallucination" ($\sqsubset$) and part is some mixture of the two ($\wedge$)—

But only those who are extremely unbalanced mentally see "pure" hallucinations with no source in the sensory-sensual world.

So, in considering cases like these, I do not easily believe that the towns of Sunderland and Charleston and Memphis were totally mad and seeing things with no counterpart in actuality.

And I wonder, if we did not, all of us, have strict imprinted and conditioned programs about what is "real" and what is "unreal," would those folks have tuned in something less remarkable than reported, or something even more remarkable?

10 November 1965 St. Louis *Post-Dispatch*—a rain of *cookies*. They fell in a restricted area, covering a house, a garage and the yard between. No airline could be found that acknowledged loss of a cargo of cookies.

5 March 1888 Madras *Mail* (India)—a rain of bricks, or things that looked like bricks. Worse: they fell *inside* a room, and in the presence of thirty investigators.

February 1974 *Bulletin of the Shri Aurobindo Center* (India)—another fall of bricks, or things that were identified as bricks, inside various rooms of the Aurobindo Ashram.

And is it Fundamentalism or racism that will cause some to be more skeptical of these last two stories, because they come from India, than of other, equally remarkable stories, from London or St. Louis?

Being modeltheists, the Fundamentalists of course reject any model but their own Eternally True Model; but why are they always especially sarcastic and suspicious when Oriental or African sources are quoted? Bronowski, we noted, said frankly that the Japanese are incapable of seeing the world "objectively"—i.e. the way he saw it—but how many Fundamentalists think that, too, but are too politic to say it openly?

Autumn 1984 *Fortean Times* No. 42—a reported fish fall in the

Newham section of London. The Fortean correspondent made his own investigation and includes photos of some of the fish (But Photos Can Be Faked, You Know). He also found that some fish had fallen, or had appeared to have fallen, in nearby Canning Town. Asking specific questions, he found nobody who had actually seen the fish fall: the fish had been found under circumstances that made it *seem* they had fallen.

This recalls the "mad fishmonger" once suggested by a *Nature* correspondent to explain a similar "fishfall" in England around a hundred years ago. Charles Fort looked up the news stories and then wrote a hilarious description of how the "mad fishmonger" would have had to operate to scatter all the fish in that case. Since that case happened at high noon, Fort calculated it would have required the Mad Fishmonger to have a dozen colleagues all of whom were equally mad and also had the strange capacity to remain unseen by citizens who were not too oblivious to notice the fish themselves.

In this current case, the fish were found in the morning, so maybe it *was* a Mad Fishmonger; maybe he was even inspired by reading Charles Fort. He came around at night and planted the fish in Newham and then rushed over to Canning Town to deposit some there, too. Sure: that makes sense, sort of. Like all the TUURs and GSs and MSs and photo-fakers, he must have been part of the Vast International Conspiracy to create the unfair impression that the Fundamentalists cannot yet explain everything.

Unless the fish arrived in a more mysterious manner. It is amusing— or annoying: as you will—to think that, in similar cases people "see" the fish falling, while in this case they spontaneously "deduced" that the fish fell, as if there is some block against certain perceptions, or imaginations, about other ways such Damned Things might arrive.

STTUE, Persinger-Lafreniere, op. cit. p. 41—1901 Scotland: ribbons of light seen in the sky before an earthquake—1919, Indiana and Michigan: "UFOs" with earth tremors—1930 Japan: rainbow colors near the ground before an earthquake—1951 Washington State: in the town of Paco, the street lights were on when the power was not on—1956 Mexico: report of a tree, from which flames were seen blazing, but which did not itself burn.

Ibid, p. 42—small "UFOs" called "ghost lights" seen in the Chinata Mountains of Texas since Indian times—more "ghost lights" seen in Joplin, Mo. since 1951—Suffolk County, Virginia: "ghost lights" also appeared in 1951 and have been coming back regularly ever since—

Gonzales, La.: also afflicted with "ghost lights" since 1951—Silver Cliff, Co.: ghost lights since 1956.

And *Ibid* again, p. 43—short wave radio band picked up by a heater in Dallas, Tx.—music from a local radio station picked up by a drain pipe in a kitchen, Wayne, N.J. 1940—broadcast from a local Texas station picked up in many parts of England, 1954—March 1962 Huntington W.V.: telephone operator picks up part of a Merry Christmas call from the *previous* December—

Colin Wilson, *Criminal History of Mankind, op. cit.*:

Wilson presents a theory of the Violent Male, backed up by criminological and historical data from the past 3000 years, and some current anthropological data on our earlier ancestors.

He claims the Violent Male basically acts like Van Vogt's Right Man: he can never admit he might be wrong about anything. His ego definition, as it were, demands that he is always Right, nearly everybody else is always Wrong, and he must "punish" them for their Wrongness. He despises the "softness" of "emotions" and thinks most people are fools. As such, he sounds like the Authoritarian Personality described by such psychologists as Fromm and Adorno; what makes him Violent is a particular savage intensity of what I have called *modeltheism*. The Right Man, in addition to the above traits, has a basically paranoid attitude toward people: he thinks they are all rotten; they have all cheated him; they are always cheating; they are sneaks; they are liars; they are, in fact, *rotten bastards*. He is going to be the rottenest bastard of all to get back at them.

I think most of us have felt that way, if only briefly, in moments of acute grief, bitterness and despair. Although we may not know the jargon of physics, we remain sane because we sense vaguely that such a *model* does not include all data; we cheer up, eventually, and notice the good things about people again; we become optimistic, again, to some degree, and make an effort to be agreeable and friendly: we leave the Anger Model behind, and wonder how we could have been so self-centered and self-pitying to have thought that way at all, even for a few moments.

The Right Man *stays in* that Anger Model most of the time, virtually all the time—especially if this becomes an intellectual fad. If he relaxes a bit, it doesn't last long: at the first inconvenience or diappointment, the Anger Model makes sense to him again: everybody is deliberately being nasty and cheating. He will have to punish them again.

Wilson emphasizes that this model describes not only many, many infamous criminals, but quite a few of the more infamous statesmen and churchmen of history, who were not *called* criminals only because they were powerful enough to define what was "crime" in their society. Since these types have a strong power drive, most of history, as Wilson sees it, is Criminal History, the record of the crimes of one type of male.

This analysis is in remarkable agreement with that of those Feminists who are not Fundamentalists and do not project this model onto all males. Wilson seems to be describing the historical syndrome that they call Patriarchy.

Milton said once, poetically, that whoever murders a book, murders a man. Psychologists would mostly agree that that is symbolically true. Destroying a book, like the psychotic behavior of slashing a photograph, expresses rage at the person who wrote the book or the person in the photo. One cannot help wondering, at this point, about those who burned the books of Dr. Reich or conspired to suppress the books of Dr. Velikovsky.

Here we might think again about Dr. Bruner's cat who was able to "edit out" sound *at the ear-drum*. These processes must be considered, not vaguely "psychological," but concretely neurological. We receive around 10,000 sensory signals per minute and edit out (probably) more than 9,990 of them, to tune in or concentrate attention on less than 10 signals that seem "important" to us. The other 9,990-plus signals are "unconsciously" classified as "meaningless" or "irrelevant"; they are not "consciously" suppressed because they never reach the "conscious" centers of the brain. (It is extremely likely that, if the majority of sensory signals did reach the "conscious" centers, we would be so overwhelmed with data that we could not act at all. It seems plausible to think that the mechanism of psychedelic drugs involves inhibiting *inhibitors*—turning on circuits that are habitually turned off—and the subject is, then, perceiving, maybe, 20 to 100 signals a minute instead of the usual 10. This itself is startling enough to produce hilarious laughter, profound awe or acute anxiety, especially on first dosage.)

The Right Man, and especially the Violent Man, is then, according to Wilson's theory, simply turning *off* even more signals than is neurologically normal. Specifically, he has been conditioned or imprinted, or has conditioned himself, to suppress as "irrelevant" or "meaningless" the kind of signals that usually evoke compassion, charity or tolerance, in most of humanity. In his reality-tunnel, the only signals that reach the cortex are those confirming his thesis that People Are Rotten Bastards who need to be punished. This mental "set," however appalling socially and historically, is no more "peculiar" neurologically than the mental "set" that allows an artist to see what others ignore while simultaneously ignoring the social Status Game signals that others notice so painfully and acutely, or the "set" which makes certain art works comprehensible (because we have *learned* to decode their symbolism) while it sees other kinds of art as "meaningless" jumbles. Sometimes it takes quite a while to *see* a new type of signal: which is why even "cultivated" Europeans once saw Chinese painting as "crude" and heard Chinese music as "weird."

We have argued that Fundamentalist Materialism—as distinguished, once again, from liberal materialism—basically asserts the remarkable proposition that *no other reality-tunnel* except that invented by one group of white people in the past 300 years has anything of value in it at all. Michell and Rickard (op. cit. p. 7) refer to this as "mental imperialism," and it is not hard to suspect that the rudyards again are kipling and haggards ride once more in the way Fundamentalist Materialists react to Oriental or African or other, non-white reality-tunnels. I once read a diatribe against Dr. Reich (not written by Mr. Gardner, in this case) in which Reich was called "Swami." This was supposed to be funny, because Hindus are supposed to be funny in the Fundamentalist reality-tunnel. That there might be other kinds of "science" than Western culture knows is unthinkable; that yoga might be a "science" is absurd. And yet yoga is based on specific instructions to *perform certain operations and observe the result*: hold a certain posture for a certain time, together with a certain mental state, and observe what happens to you. That could be considered scientific method without stretching the metaphor too far. It is certainly remarkable that those who are most contemptuous of yoga have never tried its experiments, just as those who are most contemptuous of Reich have never tried his experiments.

East-West/South-North, by Peter Okera, Parade Press, Harrowgate, England, 1983—Mr. Okera, a Black African by birth, was educated as a physicist in England and worked on various UN committees. He tries to identify three types of human cultures. He calls the first *Dionysian*, and finds it chiefly in Asia and Africa. The second type, *Apollonian*, is found around the Mediterranean. The third he calls *Thorian*, and finds dominant in modern Europe and America.

The Dionysian culture produces humans whom Mr. Okera calls *inunituals* (pronounced in-UNITE-uals): persons who feel themselves united with all around them. The Thorian culture produces *individuals* (pronounced in-DIVIDE-uals, in a Joycean pun that might be greater than the word): persons who feel themselves separate from all around them. The middle, Apollonian cultures, he says, produce persons who swing between the in-UNITE-ual mode and the in-DIVIDE-ual mode.

Mr. Okera argues that Thorian in-DIVIDE-uals are the most *intolerant* type of human beings. He says they seem tolerant to themselves, but seen from outside—from an African or Asian perspective—their chief characteristics are dogmatism, robotism, bullying, and violence.

That's only his perspective, of course, but current news seems to indicate that a great many Africans and Asians have that view.

It also seems that the cultural type that Mr. Okera calls Thorian is quite a bit like Mr. Van Vogt's Right Man and also like the Male Chauvinist Pig of Feminist polemic. I wonder again if it is only a coincidence that the Citadel is largely made up of economically privileged white males.

And I wonder also—

Quite a bit of this book has been devoted to arguing that certain plausible inferences from Bell's Theorem—inferences being considered seriously by many physicists—deserve to be thought about, and are not absurd (even though unfamiliar to our culture) and are not necessarily crazy. And it seems that non-white people have been arguing that—trying to express the in-UNITE-ual perspective, trying to say that in-DIVIDE-ual reality-tunnels are not the only reality-tunnels—for many centuries now, without success.

It seems that the Right Man does not hear. He shuts such signals off at the ear-drum.

The territorial marks he has made—his grid for dividing what others see as one whole—is *real*. It is not inside him, but outside. It is the real grid of the real world. Any other grid is All Wrong.

And is "mental imperialism" too strong a word?

A social field might be considered a type of energy-field that is highly variable.

People get together and agree to produce a certain field effect called the Jupiter Symphony and it is "meaningful" to them.

Other people, not so consciously, "agree" to perpetuate a certain kind of social game. This game defines social space—how close they stand, who may actually touch another, etc.—depending on the game rules, or definitions of class, caste, hierarchy, etc. Certain perceptions are reinforced by playing the game, and other perceptions are taboo or "unthinkable." Over generations, this kind of social game becomes a group's reality-tunnel or emic reality or *culture*.

If there is any validity found in models which consider "consciousness" a social field effect, some games produce in-UNITE-uals who feel connected across space, and other games produce in-DIVIDE-uals, who feel that separation in space is "real" because their game defines it as such.

If consciousness may be considered a non-local field effect, Dionysian or in-UNITE-ual social games will encourage awareness of, and possible use of, these non-local field effects.

Thorian or in-DIVIDE-ual social games will cause a withering of non-local awareness and of non-local field effects. If such field effects occur at all, they will be felt as disturbing and may trigger actual disturbances, including hallucinations and manias.

This is, of course, only speculation.

Why is it possible to predict how certain in*divi*duals and groups will react to such speculation?

If "the sum total of all minds is one" (Schrodinger)—if "mind is a metaphor for mind" and we create ourselves, as we create our other grids, by metaphor—if our "minds" merge into, and are aspects of, "group-minds," "group-realities," sociological fields—if these fields are aspects of larger biological fields and genetic programs (as they might be, if the Sheldrake and sociobiological models both have some validity)—if these trans-time evolutionary fields are aspects of non-local physical fields of the sort contemplated by quantum mechanics—if hardware is local but software is non-local—

Then the in-UNITE-ual perspective—the perspective of most non-white societies, and of many artists and most women within white societies—may not be crazy, or perverse, or "mystical," or delusory, or inferior, or "primitive."

The Right Man may merely be a domesticated primate who takes his territorial marks too literally.

Maybe.

I'm still not insisting. I am only asking. Like all ignorant men I don't know much, so I ask a lot of questions.

Maybe, we all begin as modeltheists—incapable of criticising our own neurological programs. What we see and feel and measure is

What Is Real. Our grids and models are experienced *out there*, not our creations, "objective." Animal behavior indicates that is the evolutionarily "normal" mode of behavior. A dog and a cat do not sit down and ask "What is Real?" They react, automatically and mechanically, to whatever model has been imprinted and conditioned.

Then, maybe, some of us become capable of neurological self-criticism. We actually sit around and ask each other, "What is Real?" And, if we push this habit of criticism and caution, this agnosticism, far enough, we come to—Nietzsche's Chaos and the Abyss.

And maybe, beyond that, we eventually see a Transcendental Unity, a wholeness, an at-one-ness.

I think maybe Mr. Okera goes a bit too far in his glorification of the Dionysian, and much, much too far in his denunciation of the Thorian. There are some in-DIVIDE-ual values that I, as a libertarian, cherish and would not want to see thrown out in a general reversal to in-UNITE-ual modes of thinking/feeling. Alan Watts, Fritjof Capra and Theodore Roszack, like Mr. Okera, seem to me to often fall into the very error of dualism—mechanical either/or choices—that they denounce as the major sin of the modern West.

In general, what Peter Okera calls the Dionysian is isomorphic to Joyce's [—which includes, in addition to Cain and Satan, such historical figures as Napoleon, Shakespeare, Parnell etc., the Irish in general, the non-white races, and "artistic" and "intuitive" modes of apprehension.

What Okera calls Thorian is similarly isomorphic to Joyce's /\ —which includes, in addition to Abel and the Archangel Michael, such historical figures as Wellington, Sir Francis Bacon, Gladstone, etc., the Anglo-Irish ruling class of Joyce's time, the white race, and "rational" and "political" modes of thinking/feeling.

These stark contrasts—the [or Dionysian, and the /\ or Thorian—seem to be virtually identical to the split in the brain between the holistic right hemisphere and the linear-analytical left hemisphere. Dionysian or [-type cultures are dominated by the right hemisphere of the brain, and Thorian or /\ -type cultures by the left hemisphere.

Like Joyce, I think that the conflict between these two brain-functions is not likely to be resolved by the triumph of either [or /\ —Dionysian or Thorian—but by the imergence of a unified type including both—Joyce's /[, which Okera also recognizes as the Apollonian mean.

Maybe just as the West badly needs to integrate the long-repressed

Dionysian ($\sqsubset$) holism, the East badly needs to recognize that tradition of civil liberties for the individual ($\wedge$) that has never appeared in any non-Western culture. Maybe then, as both sides approach Apollonian balance ($\wedge\sqsubset$) neither will perceive the other, any longer, as lop-sided to the point of perversity and madness.

Maybe.

I don't know. Unlike the modeltheists and Fundamentalists and Right Men of all sorts, I have had no *gnosis*, no Inner Certainty. I remain *a-gnostic*. I go on wondering, and asking questions.

More mysterious frogs:

9 September 1981 Capetown *Argus* (South Africa)—Mrs. Maggie Hendricks vomits them. I mean, she appears to vomit them.

A police sergeant avows that he personally saw, or hallucinated, Mrs. Hendricks upchuck a frog "the size of a man's hand."

That's a bit stranger than having the little bastards fall out of the sky, isn't it?

Mrs. Hendricks also appears to spew forth nails and bits of broken bottle-glass.

She also appears to puke tadpoles and balls of hair and knife-blades.

Mrs. Hendricks alleges that she has had this unique problem for over a year. She also alleges that an invisible man visits her and makes indecent proposals. She does not specify what indecencies are proposed by this invisible visitor. Maybe he wants her to upchuck an elephant next. It is her understanding—her reality-tunnel—that all this is happening because she rejected the advances of a witch-doctor shortly before these afflictions fell upon her.

Sounds like what happened to Mr. Kellerman after *he* offended a witch-doctor, only nastier.

Probably just religious hysteria, of course. She worried about the witch-doctor's revenge until she started hallucinating.

But what about the policeman who saw Mrs. Hendricks regurgitate a frog the size of a man's hand?

Maybe he doesn't exist. Maybe he was invented by TUUR, who has moved to Capetown recently.

I devoutly hope so.

19 October 1981 London *Daily Telegraph*—tourists returning from the shrine of the Blessed Virgin at Fatima, Portugal—where 30,000 saw the "divine light" or UFO in 1919—oh, you already know this is going to be the worst yet—

The bus driver allegedly went into a trance. His hands allegedly clasped, as if in prayer, while he remained entranced. The bus appeared to drive itself, at speeds that appeared to the passengers around 50 miles per hour, without crashing into anything or running off the road—

And it appeared to drive that way for 20 miles. Then a voice spoke—or some clever trickster performed a feat of ventriloquism, as Mr. Randi will undoubtedly tell you—but, anyway, the alleged voice allegedly said, "I am your brother, Archangel Michael. God Himself had the grace to drive the bus as a test of faith for our brother, the driver."

All 54 passengers signed an affidavit, saying they thought they saw and heard what they thought they saw and heard.

The Buddhist says: the mountains are real. The mountains are not real. The mountains are both real and not-real. The mountains are neither real nor not-real.

The fruit is orange, to ordinary perception. The fruit is not orange, to Galileo's analysis. The fruit is both orange and not-orange, to those who recognize that the existential and the scientific grids each have a kind of validity. The fruit is neither orange nor not-orange, to those who recognize that all grids are human inventions.

I don't know what the hell happened on that bus, but I wish I had been there. I wonder if social, and other, fields are as potent as I sometimes suspect, and I wonder a great deal about whether I would have seen what the visitors to the shrine saw.

3 October 1933 London *Morning Post*—a phantom train reported several times in Tortuna, Sweden. It appeared to run on tracks where "real" trains ran, but not at times when the "real" trains were running.

The *Post* adds that a similar phantom train had been reported in Lapland two years earlier. That accursed thing was even worse. It ran where there were *no* tracks, and it not only startled human observers but allegedly caused stampedes among the reindeer.

Mysteries, by Colin Wilson, op. cit. p. 198—an experiment on "ESP" by Dr. Gertrude Schmeidler, at Radcliffe College, 1942. As usual, those who believed in ESP scored above chance in guessing hidden cards. We know the materialist objections to this, which is why we mostly haven't bothered citing such research: it was trickery by the subjects or it was sloppy research technique by Dr. Schmeidler. Of course. But in this case—

The ones who did not believe in ESP scored significantly *below* chance.

That is, they did not guess as well as any ordinary group would guess.

Were *they* cheating, too? Or are all reality-tunnels maintained in much the same way, by the same unconscious "decisions" to turn synapses off or on to accord with beliefs?

Then there is this:

30 December 1985 *Brain/Mind Bulletin* (Los Angeles)—a new study by Dr. Persinger, he of the wobbling magnetic and gravitational fields.

Persinger took 25 "well-documented" cases of "intense" paranormal experience from the records of University of Virginia researcher Ian Stevenson. These were 25 experiences in which people thought they were having what we call non-local awareness, or what is sometimes called "ESP" or that damned "precognition." Each case involved a relative who was in danger, and the "hunch" or whatever it was, was later confirmed as accurate.

Before examining Dr. Persinger's work, let us remind ourselves of the Fundamentalist verdicts on Stevenson's original 25 cases. The Religious Fundamentalist says demons did it. Since demons are not-tuned-in for most of us (I hope), we can pass that by as a relic of bygone times. The Materialist Fundamentalist says it was a series of coincidences. There is no way of proving or disproving such a proposition, but it is soothing to some minds, even if "meaningless" according to strict Logical Positivism.

Persinger examined the geomagnetic activity on the days when the 25 eerie events occurred. He discovered that in all 25 cases geomagnetic activity was "less than the mean for the month" and "considerably" less than during the seven days preceding and following.

25 out of 25 is 100 percent.

So, then—either "demons" or "coincidences" (take your pick) have an affinity for becoming active during low geomagnetic activity.

Or else the non-local fields possibly involved in such happenings are more "open" when not interferred with by heavy geomagnetism?

And here's another odd bit, which was sent by a friend and arrived while I was correcting the galleys for this book:

20 September 1986 *Philadelphia Inquirer*—corn has been falling out of the sky in an area northwest of Denver, Colorado.

According to the *Inquirer*—or according to TUUR, now working for the once-respectable *Inquirer*—corn has been falling off and on for about four years now. "I'd probably have a ton, if I'd picked it all up," says Gary Bryan who lives (allegedly) in the town of Evans.

The local sheriff rules out the remarkable segregating whirlwind, as there are no corn silos, or other plausible sites in the area, where the whimsical whirlwind could be picking the corn up, he says. He finds the matter "pretty confusing."

I'm sure nobody at CSICOP is confused. They know it's all either trickery or hallucination. As for me, I wonder a bit—as usual.

Sometimes pinto beans fall with the corn, the newspaper says.

I don't know whether that makes it more—or less—confusing.

All that seems fairly sure is that ice and frogs and lizards and other odd things fall out of the sky at times, or people who aren't Fundamentalist Materialists have a strange propensity for hallucinating that such things fall out of the sky. Either there are strange lights up there frequently, or people have a strange propensity for faking photographs of UFOs. You pays your money and you takes your choice.

Haunted People, by Nandor Fodor, Signet, New York, pp. 154 ff—In the early 1930s in a farmhouse called Doarlish Cashen on the Isle of Man lived James T. Irving, and his wife and children, and Gef.

Gef appeared to be shy and reclusive, like many of us eccentrics. He appeared to hide in the walls and never made what are called personal appearances. But he talked to anybody who cared to converse with him. Gef identified himself as a "very, *very* clever mongoose."

On the other hand, Gef was even more immodest on other occasions. He is alleged to have identified himself—maybe after he had a drop taken—as "the eighth wonder of the world," "the Holy Ghost," and "the fifth dimension." I swear, whatever the Fundamentalists say about me, I have never been that drunk.

Well, hardly ever.

When sober, Gef would put on psychic demonstrations for callers. For instance, they would toss coins and catch them. Gef would cry out "heads" or "tails." Fodor alleges that Gef was very accurage, but he does not quote statistics, as if that matters in a case like this. If statistics were quoted, the Fundamentalists would merely prove that you could get the same result by cheating.

Objects appeared to fly around when Gef was performing.

Fortean Times, Summer 1980—more on Gef. Harry Price, the "psychic investigator," came to the Isle of Man to speak with Gef, who apparently had an even lower opinion of Mr. Price than the Fundamentalists have. The appearance was rude and uncouth in that case: Gef appeared to urinate on Mr. Price's shoes.

Maybe he was just tired of guessing "heads" or "tails" for such persons. Maybe Dr. Fodor had taxed his patience.

Another investigator, identified only as Wylder, spoke at length with Gef and decided the little fellow was a mongoose after all, and not the Holy Ghost or the fifth dimension. Said Wylder, "The mysterious powers of animals are only beginning to be understood."

After the Irvings sold the farm and left, the next owner shot an animal on the property. It was a mongoose. If it was Gef, it didn't have time to shout, "Stop—I'm really the Holy Ghost!" If it wasn't Gef, it was another of our odd coincidences.

Drop out all the rest of the Gef saga and that detail alone—a mongoose on the Isle of Man—is rather tame, after what we've been reading lately. You see? It would have seemed highly mysterious only a few chapters ago, but now we're becoming accustomed to appearances of things that appear to bounce around as non-locally as quantum "particles." The virginity of our epistemology has been lost, and we are in danger of becoming intellectually promiscuous. Soon we will have no standards left and will let in any damned thing that comes along. It started when we asked if maybe Kelley did not really fake those "orgone" photographs, and soon we were wallowing in astrology. Now Gef. Next it will be Catholic statues that bleed.

Phenomena, Michell and Rickard, op. cit. p. 20-21—several accounts of Catholic statues that appeared to bleed. I refuse to reprint any of it. Everybody's reaction to that sort of thing is altogether too predictable. The Catholics will believe it, the Fundamentalists of both varieties will know it is all Papist humbug, and the agnostics will chortle at the thought of how mechanical those reactions are. Only the super-agnostics will wonder if their own reactions are equally mechanical.

Instead—

Probe India, August 1981—a statue that *menstruates*.

In the temple of Mahadeva in Kerala, a statue of the goddess Peravali occasionally gets the curse. The priest finds her loincloth stained, or so he alleges. The statue is then removed for three days and secluded. Afterwards, it is dressed in a fresh gown and returned to the altar. This has happened seven times in three years, according to the priest.

Maybe goddesses have longer periods than mortal women?

A spokesman for the Rationalist Association of India is quoted. He told the *Probe* reporter that the staining was caused by "chemical disintegration of the granite" of the statue. He was only mildly discombobulated when the reporter informed him the statue was not granite but metal. Well, then, he said, it was chemical disintegration of the metal.

If the damned thing had been wood, I suppose he would have said—chemical disintegration of the wood.

I suppose chemical disintegration was involved, as I suppose fish were involved in our fish falls; but I wonder still—why chemical disintegration in such a, as it were, suggestive spot? Why do the Catholic statues "bleed" from the appropriate places?

22 April 1949 *Science*—a fall of fish in Biloxi, Miss.—but that is getting common-place to us. In this case, however, there is the same "coincidental" aspect as in the selective "chemical disintegration" of certain statues: Dr. A.D. Bajkov, a well-known ichthyologist, was in Biloxi that day and was personally bombarded. Like many of our stories, it would make a great surrealist painting.

I think of the stones that seem personally aimed at one target. I think of the withering-away of ordinary notions of "space" and "time" and "separation" in the dream-state, and in many kinds of psychosis, and in quantum mechanics. I think of persons so "eccentric" that they dare to doubt the Idol of our time, Fundamentalist Materialism, and conduct their own little experiments in the manipulation of things that *appear* separated, such as one "mind" and another, or an allegedly isolated "mind" and an allegedly isolated set of "material objects."

6 July 1937 East Anglian *Daily News* (England)—a large rock in Stone Farm, Blaxhall, seems or appears to be growing.

A Mr. William Barber is interviewed. He claims to have proceeded scientifically in investigating the appearance. He says he has measured the Damned Thing repeatedly over a 15 year period and it has grown 2½ inches in that time.

Another case of instrumental error, no doubt.

Mr. Alfred Plant is interviewed. He utters further Heresy: "When I first saw it as a boy a kitten could just sit under it. Today a cat could get under it and so could a dog."

From *Phenomena*, Michell and Rickard, op. cit. p. 96-103: 230 cases described in Leroy's *La Levitation* of Catholic saints who appeared to float off the ground on occasion. Most famous is Joseph of Copertino who appeared to do this so often that his superiors continually moved him from one monastery to another, to avoid crowds of curiosity-seekers— Case of Francis Fry, cited in Aubrey's *Miscellanies*: Fry appeared, in 1683, to fly over a tree and land in a hay-stack, in Barnstable, Devon—Case of Antonio da Silva, cited in *The Unknown* by Clark and Coleman: da Silva disappeared from one town in Brazil, on 5 May 1969, and reappeared in another 200 miles away on 9 May, saying he had been picked up by a UFO—Case of Benjamin Bathhurst, English diplomat, cited from Baring-Gould's *Historical Oddities*—According to witnesses, Bathhurst was walking around his coach one day in 1809. He never arrived on the other side. He was never found. He never came back. He appears to have, well, really disappeared, as it were.

Nature 36-119—something that appeared to be charcoal appeared to fall in Orne, France, 24 April 1887.

Lit. and Phil. Soc. of Manchester 2-9-146—another seeming fall of something that seemed like charcoal in Allport, England, 1827.

Scientific American 35-120—seeming fall on 13 October 1839 of something that "resembled anthracite coal." There were about five cubic feet of it.

21 September 1877 New York *Sun*—W.H. Smith saw what appeared to him to be a winged human being over the sky of Brooklyn.

Zoologist July 1868—another ambiguity, at Copiapo, Chile. It appeared to be an airship with lights and a noisy motor, according to some. It appeared to be a gigantic bird with reptile-like scales, according to others.

37 years before the airplane.

Fortean Times Fall 1984—on 1 January 1984 (New Year's Day) a dud nine-inch shell of World War II vintage crashed into the backyard of Fred Simmons, 79, in Lakewood, California. Neighbors reported a whistling sound before it hit, but nobody saw an airplane.

The shell appeared real to Sheriff's Deputy Wes Slider when he examined it.

A trans-time New Year's Day present?

9 March 1984 *Guardian* (England)—another of our wandering crocodiles. This one was seen in a Paris sewer and ten firemen were summoned, who thought they saw it, too. They thought they struggled with it and managed to truss it up in ropes and remove it.

15 April 1957 *Sunday Express* (England)—a fall of 1000-franc notes in Bourges, France. The *Express* says there were "thousands" of them.

STTUE, Persinger and Lafreniere, op. cit. p. 140-143:

May 1832: "millions" of mice suddenly appear in Invernesshire, Scotland.

August 1955: an empty lake in appropriately-named Dry Lake, California, suddenly fills with water. Shrimp found in it.

And I think it is curious that "ESP" is hallucinatory in the Buddhist reality-tunnel as well as in the Fundamentalist Materialist reality-tunnel, although for different reasons.

To the Fundamentalist, "things" have a "real existence" and "real separation" in "real space" and "real time," and therefore "my" "mind" is localized in "my" "head" and cannot make any link with "another" "mind" if they are truly "separated" in "space" and "time."

To the Buddhist, as to Schrodinger, the sum total of all "minds" is one, and no separation is "real." Hence, so-called "ESP" does not exist as a thing in itself or a "transmission" between "minds"; instead so-called "ESP" is just a partial awakening from the illusion that makes us believe in "separations." Such a partial awakening, to the Buddhist, remains in the area of hallucination, because it still assumes the "minds" are "real" and the "separation" is "real."

Of course, if we take the Buddhist metaphor seriously for a few moments, and try to think of a non-dual or non-local existence or a unified continuum—

Then any damned Po game makes sense; that is, you can insert a Po between any two allegedly separate things or areas of knowledge and there will be a valid perspective gained.

It would work, presumably, even with something as absurd as our game several chapters back of

UFOs Po Rabbits

In an early novel, *Illuminatus*—written in collaboration with Robert J. Shea—I created a character, Joe Malik, who is abducted by the crew of a UFO and later initiated into an odd religious sect, Discordianism, which gives him the holy name, U. Wascal Wabbit, taken from the Bugs Bunny cartoons (in which Elmer Fudd is forever calling Bugs "You wascal wabbit!")

Harmless comedy, of a surrealist flavor.

15 October 1975 Chicago *Tribune*: a mysterious cattle mutilation 50 miles northwest of Chicago. In addition to the slaughtered cattle, there was also a beheaded *rabbit*. Police are said to be "investigating" reports that a UFO was involved.

A UFO and a sinister rabbit story—as if my book were coming alive—

London *Fortean Times* No. 28 (1977)—article by Nigel Watson, "Strange Encounters in Yorkshire," deals with a family that has repeatedly seen UFOs while rabbit-hunting.

Coincidence again. Of course.

I have these stories, originally, from MEBON—the Mutual Easter Bunny Observation Network. This may well be no more than a parody of the better-known MUFON—the Mutual UFO Network.

Martin S. Kottmeyer, the founder of MEBON, explained in a letter to me that the idea behind this remarkable organization came from the writers who have suggested that *human expectations* create UFO sightings. Now, there are two schools of thought who both share that opinion, but who otherwise contradict each other totally. For convenience, these may be very loosely called the Reductionists and the Surrealists. The Reductionists say that human expectations create UFOs by making people hallucinate, and that's all. The Surrealists say that human expectations *really* create UFOs, so to speak; phrases that the former group despises—you know, phrases like "psycho-kinesis" and "synchronicity" and "mind-matter interaction"—get tossed around happily by the more exuberant theorists of the group I call Surrealists.

Mr. Kottmeyer and his friends in MEBON decided to check the hypothesis that human expectations might create *Easter Bunny* sightings. When they started searching the literature and sending out enquiries, they did not find any unambiguous E.B. sightings, but they did find something a bit fey.

They found, in fact, conjunctions of rabbits with UFOs. They have named this new field of study, or this satire on the human love of correlations, *lepufology*. We should, of course, decide whether these conjunctions should be interpreted Reductionistically or Surrealistically by unprejudiced examination of the data itself, but if I know anything about human beings, most of us will decide on the basis of whether we are temperamentally Reductionists or temperamentally Surrealists.

Whether we want to look at it Reductionistically or Surrealistically, here are some more lepufological correlations from the Mutual Easter Bunny Observation Network (MEBON):

November 1978, *Flying Saucer Review*, p. 17—A UFO seen stealing baby rabbits from a hutch.

UFO Phenomena and B.S. edited by Haines, p. 83: a Close Encounter in which the observer asserts the UFO occupant looked like a giant rabbit.

10 October 1981, *Saucer Gear*—letter claiming that the Pennsylvania State Game Commission is investigating the "mysterious" disappearance of rabbits from that State.

More from MEBON, this time quoting MUFON — at the 1984

MUFON UFO Forum, one Budd Hopkins played a tape of another UFO abductee, or a woman who thought she was an abductee. Under hypnosis, she reported the usual UFO abductee story, whatever one thinks of that, but there was an interesting detail: before she encountered the Ufonauts she saw "hundreds" of *paralyzed rabbits*.

But of course I started this damned nonsense myself, with the UFO/Wascal Wabbit joke in *Illuminatus*, and how can I take seriously one of my own jokes? Po is supposed to increase creativity, not gullibility.

MEBON again, citing *The McMinnville Photos* by Dr. B.S. Maccabee: a Mrs. Trent of McMinnville saw a UFO while out in the yard feeding her rabbits. She has photos, but of course photos can be faked . . .

MEBON citing John McPhee, *Basin and Range*—a giant white UFO seen immediately after a group of jackrabbits dancing in the road.

Dancing?

Common Ground (English magazine) No. 7 p. 5—Bunnyman is a myth or hallucination or an unknown entity often reported in parts of southern England. One recent witness saw Bunnyman immediately after seeing a UFO. Bunnyman spoke and said "Please pray for me."

It would take a very extreme aggravation and exacerbation of whatever is wrong with me before I take *that* one seriously for a moment.

MEBON, citing a book called *The Humanoids*—a farmer in Isola, Italy, 1954, reported a cigar-shaped UFO which landed in his yard. Three dwarfs got out, took all the rabbits from the farmer's hutch, and returned to the craft, which took off.

Some readers are beginning to believe extraterrestrials come here chiefly to obtain the makings for rabbit stew; others are barely able to control their anger at a writer who presents such nonsense and asks us to think about it. But, again, I am not asking you to judge the reports at all, but to *observe your own reactions to them.*

"Fear is the father of the gods," said Lucretius. But the gods are cunning and subtle; in the ancient world, when many began to misbelieve in them, some disguised themselves as Platonic Ideas and were able to survive another thousand years in that form. (In some Chairs of Philosophy they still survive.) Others, more cunning still, became General Principles and *A Priori Truths* and eventually evolved into the "known physical laws" worshipped by Prof. Munge. But by this sign ye shall know them: great anxiety is aroused by him who challenges them, and their priests are full of fury and malice against such an heretic.

And what anxiety would shake our being—what Chaos and Abyss would open before us—if we thought for a moment there might be extraterrestrial rabbit-hunters around or that southern England possesses a giant rabbit who speaks English and wants us to pray for him?

MEBON citing *The World's Greatest UFO Mysteries* by Blundell and Boar—case in which UFO sighting is proceeded by "a curious menagerie" crossing the road: seven rabbits, a raccoon, a possum and several cats.

Obviously, in the new science or new idiocy of lepufology we are approaching the area of dream and myth; however, as James Joyce once remarked, since we already spend one third of our lives there, we ought to give that half-world some serious attention.

Books like Vallee's *The Invisible College,* Coleman and Clarke's *The Unknown,* Vallee's and Hynek's *The Edge of Reality,* Jung's own *Flying Saucers,* etc. have all stressed a link between UFOlogy and Jung's alleged "collective unconscious." All are uncertain, to say the least of it, about how this link functions and what, in any given case, should be called "hallucination" or "psychokinesis" or filed under Jung's catch-all of "synchronicity." With this in mind and the reassuring thought that we are only looking, here, at the dark side of our species' mind, let us press on into the murk for a few steps at least.

MEBON—A Bugs Bunny cartoon on 1952, "Hasty Hare," has Bugs abducted by Ufonauts; this preceded the claims of human abductions in Ufology.

The film, *Monty Python and the Holy Grail* (1975) not only has shots in which the Grail looks like a UFO, but also introduces a *Killer Rabbit* whom we shall later encounter escaped from humorous fantasy into consensus reality, more or less.

A rabbit appears at the UFO landing site in Spielberg's 1983 film *E.T.*

The Firesign Theatre comedy album "Not Insane" includes a letter from a rabbit postmarked "Deep Space."

In the novelized version of Spielberg's *Close Encounters of the Third Kind,* rabbits run across the road before the hero's second sighting of a UFO.

May 1979 *Analog* (science-fiction magazine) has a letter by one C.V. Haroutunian satirically arguing that the Easter Bunny could be an extraterrestrial utilizing a technology far in advance of our own.

Michigan Quarterly Review 18:200 contains the following from the transcript of the flight of Apollo 11:

> *Mission Control:* **An ancient legend says that a beautiful Chinese girl named Chango has been living on the moon for 4000 years. . . . You might look for her companion, a large Chinese rabbit . . .**
> *Michael Collins:* **We'll keep a close eye for that bunny girl.**

MEBON's wonderful comment is worth reprinting: "Though one may be inclined to dismiss this conversation as a jest, it should be remembered that all the astronauts on the moon exhibited conspicuous hopping behavior."

And before we abandon this absurd subject—so intriguing to Surrealists, so infuriating to Reductionists—let us chew on this conjunction: James Earl Carter was the only President to be a UFO witness. He also had an encounter, later, with a Killer Rabbit.

WASHINGTON August 29, 1979 (Associated Press)—"A 'killer rabbit' penetrated Secret Service security and attacked President Carter on a recent trip to Plains, GA. according to White House staff members who said that the President beat back the animal with a canoe paddle."

The story goes on that "reports are unclear about what became of the rabbit," and that some White House staff members had been skeptical about the incident, saying that rabbits do not swim and are not that dangerous, anyway. A photo had been taken, AP goes on, and President Carter ordered an enlargement to confound the doubters. The photo was allegedly convincing. A White House skeptic is quoted: "It was a killer rabbit. The President was swinging for his life." But the White House *declined to make public any photographs;* I italicize this because it is the sort of governmental behavior that always arouses acute suspicion among UFOlogists.

The next sentence of the AP story is even more sinister and should attract the avid attention of Conspiracy Buffs everywhere, whether or not they have previously been concerned with UFOs and Killer Rabbits:

> "There are certain stories about the President that must forever remain shrouded in mystery," Rax Granum, the deputy White House press secretary said today.

Was the C.I.A. involved? Was it a matter of National Security? Had the Killer Rabbit originally been hired to assassinate Fidel Castro and then turned on his employers? These questions should be faced squarely by all those who devoted so many years to the Umbrella Man in Dealey Plaza. (The chap who opened his umbrella—on a *sunny* day!—just before the shots that killed John F. Kennedy.)

Journal of Psychohistory Vol. 7 No. 1 (Summer 1979), article "The Assassination in Dallas: A Search for Meaning," by James P. Johnson, notes that:

Harvey Oswald and Killer Rabbit each have 12 letters.

(But that looks like forcing the data. Very well: *Lee* Harvey Oswald and *The* Killer Rabbit each have 15 letters. See?)

Count down 3 letters from H.O. (as in Harvey Oswald and you get K.R. (as in Killer Rabbit).

Jimmy Carter and John Kennedy have 11 letters each.

Both presidents were democrats.

Kennedy was killed in a Ford. Carter defeated Ford to become President.

Plains and Dallas have the same number of letters, and both are on the 32 degree of latitude. (For the benefit of anti-Masonic theorists, I add that 32 is a sacred number to Freemasons.)

Photos were withheld in both incidents.

Both incidents happened in the third year of the presidencies of the victims.

Neither killer rabbit was ever brought to trial.

I might add that Harvey Oswald, in the Marine Corps, had the nickname Ozzie Rabbit, according to Kerry Thornley, a witness who served in the same Marine regiment.

MEBON notes that the attack on a semi-mythic ruler of England by a killer rabbit in *Monty Python and the Holy Grail* occurred four years before this attack on the ruler of the U.S. by a killer rabbit.

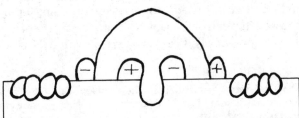

**DO NOT ADJUST YOUR MIND SET:
IT IS THE BOOK WHICH IS MALFUNCTIONING**

No, no, this will never do. Hold on, I'll get a grip on myself again. As Mason said to Dixon, you have to draw the line *somewhere*.

It's all right now.

None of this really happened, of course; it only *appeared* to happen. In the Real Universe, there are Eternal Laws, and "matter" is still solid—not made up of waves and energy-events and mysterious *quarks*—and every instrument reads only what is consistent with Law, and every person sees only what is consistent with Law, and the Right Man is always Right and can prove it.

And, despite grave reservations, I do not totally deny the existence of that Real Universe of Platonism and Fundamentalist Materialism. For all I know it exists—*somewhere*.

I just don't see any sign of it around here.

Ultimately, I think—or, in this imperfect world, I approximate toward thinking—that existence is just as Abyssmal as it seemed to Nietzsche.

I know a group of people, all of them with advanced degrees in medical or biological sciences, who think immortality—physical immortality—is possible in this generation. They not only *believe* that (which is a passive state) but are *doing* something about it. All of them are actively involved in what is loosely called "gerontological research," which is the study of what things cause the aging process, and all of them are hoping to find drugs or other techniques that will *reverse* the aging process and allow us to live indefinitely. I have written about some of these people in a previous book, *Cosmic Trigger*.

I also know a man who, in the year or so after the release of *The Exorcist*, performed 28 exorcisms of people who thought they were possessed by demons. He is a computer scientist with more than a passing interest in Jungian psychology and "the occult." His exorcisms were all successful. He did not argue with the "possessed" people, but accepted their reality-tunnel as real for them, and performed the kind of ritual which is supposed to cure "possession" in that reality-tunnel, and the rituals worked. The people were no longer "possessed." The exorcist remains cheerfully agnostic or Copenhagenistic about the whole business. He merely says ironically that the "demons" were an unimaginative lot.

I live in Ireland, a country where the majority of the population, according to a recent poll, believes that Jesus Christ was conceived parthogenetically and rose from the dead after being buried. They do not bump into walls, and they drive their cars about as well as Londoners or New Yorkers, and they do not seem particularly mad to me. Their reality-tunnel seems to work well enough, most of the time—as most reality-tunnels seem to work tolerably well, most of the time.

It seems to me that existence—at this point I have doubts about "the" "universe"—is a lot like a Rorschach ink-blot. Everybody looks at it and sees their own favorite reality-tunnel.

In science, where my favorite reality-tunnels are usually (but not always) to be found, every decade brings new shocks and surprises. When I was a child, there were no television sets in the United States outside experimental laboratories. During my adolescence, the Western world went through a non-violent revolution as breath-taking as the Industrialization of the 18th-19th Centuries, but in this case it happened in about five years, and TV sets appeared everywhere. While this electronic revolution was going on, I was reading a great deal of debate about whether we could ever fire a rocket to the moon; at that time, there were still "experts" who insisted it could *never* be done, and many, less conservative than that, sid it would not be done for at least a hundred years; I have quoted a few of those Dogmas earlier. Neil Armstrong walked on the moon while I was in my mid-30s and by now probes have visited all the inner planets of the solar system.

One of the researchers who are aiming for physical immortality, mentioned earlier, is Dr. Alvin Silverstein. In his book, *The Conquest of Death*, he quotes some figures—from French economist Georges Anderla—showing the *rate* at which scientific knowledge has been increasing in the past two milleniums. Anderla's statistics show that knowledge doubled in the 1500 years between the birth of Christ and 1500 A.D. It doubled again in the 250 years between then and 1750, and doubled again in the 150 years between then and 1900. It doubled again by 1950, again by 1960, again by 1968, and again by 1973—at which point Anderla concluded his study. All evidence on the horizon suggests that it has not slowed down but—aided by microprocessors—has probably accelerated even faster since then.

Going back to the birth of Christ, at that time only nine chemical elements were known, and it was not understood that they should be called elements. "Earth, air, fire and water" were thought to be "the" elements, then. By the time of the French Revolution, the modern definition of elements had emerged and about twenty of them were known and identified. In less than 150 years—by 1932—all 92 of the natural elements were known. Physicists have been creating new elements since then.

Some rough idea about causality has probably been around since the dawn of human intelligence, but the classic Western metaphor of *cause* only emerged after Aristotelian logic was combined with experimental method in the late Rennaisance. The first doubts about causality began among quantum physicists in the 1920s. Now, since non-local effects violate this model of causality, physicists are becoming accustomed to thinking of two kinds of principles, the causal (local) and the acausal (non-local).

The man and woman in the street knows enough about Relativity to tell you that a rod *shrinks* as it approaches the speed of light. While this is not quite correct—it contains the Aristotelian assumption that the length at the speeds we are accustomed to it the "real" length—but it is adequate for conversational purposes. It is astonishing knowledge, when one recalls that, in most cases, the great-grandparents of this man and woman in the street were illiterate peasants who thought the Earth was flat. By the 1990s—considering the proliferation of popularizations in recent years—the woman and man in the street will know enough about quantum mechanics to tell you that some events have causes and some things happen for other reasons, which is good enough for conversational purposes.

It would not surprise me at all if, in the same 1990s, the dream of physical immortality, now the exclusive possession of a few eccentric idealists, will also have reached the ordinary citizen; there are more and more articles about "longevity" appearing everywhere; even today. A large minority is taking daily vitamins or herbs that allegedly contribute to longevity.

When I was at University, hardly anybody had conceived of anything like a Guaranteed Annual Wage; the only ones I encountered who were writing about it at that time were the architect Buckminster Fuller and the "eccentric" poet Ezra Pound. Now it is a widely discussed option and articles about it appear almost every week.

The first article urging the practicality and desirability of space colonization appeared in *Physics Today* in 1973; now there is a nationwide lobby working for that goal in the United States, and the Russians seem to have plans of their own.

A group of idealists in California has a different lobby, promoting the

the idea that starvation can be, and should be, abolished world-wide by 1995. Since I no longer know what is "possible" and what is "impossible," I find this think-able, and I like to think about it. In my reality-tunnel, a world in which no child ever again starved to death would be a greater accomplishment than chaps from NASA playing golf on the moon. (Between the first and last drafts of this chapter, the LIVE AID concert brought this particular fantasy into the reality-tunnel of millions of people.)

My wife informs me that on RTE-radio this morning, she heard a gynecologist being interviewed. The gynecologist said it is now possible to preserve fertilized human embryos for 14 days and transplant them elsewhere. She (the gynecologist) said further that she expected in a few years it would be possible to transplant them into transsexuals who had been born male but converted surgically into females. This seems think-able and possible to me, too. I would not be stunned if, around 1993, some person, born male, would bring forth a living child, even though that has never before happened in human history.

The "horrors" of possible genetic engineering have been widely publicized; the possibility of genetically engineering future humans to be ten times, or a hundred times, more intelligent than we are, or to live a hundred times longer, is just as thinkable, and some of us may live to see it.

In the dawning world of surrogate mothers, test-tube babies, cloning, etc. *the very basic concept of "reproduction" is changing its meaning.*

It seems that the only things in the human world that are *not* changing rapidly are the reality-tunnels of various Fundamentalists—Roman Catholic Fundamentalists and Islamic Fundamentalists, Marxist Fundamentalists and Ecological Fundamentalists, along with the gents I have been satirising here, and accompanied by a few other varieties of modeltheists who devoutly believe they *know* what is possible and what is not possible. These Right Men—and, thanks to Feminism, we now have a few Right Women around, also—are, of course, all inhabitants of the "Real" Universe. They literally *live* in it, in a way similar to an actor "living" a role. They know the "Real" Universe, and they know its laws, and they know what is possible and impossible there.

Unfortunately their "Real" Universes, however different and baroque from outside, all have one thing in common. They have very little contact with the experienced universe, or existential struggle, in which the rest of us live.

I think that the last time any of us was really, deeply *satisfied* with a model—intellectually and/or esthetically and/or emotionally—we entered into a state of *hypnosis* in which that model became a "Real" Universe for us. I think that if we can never consider another model, we will remain hypnotized. I think—or I mechanically fumble toward the thought— that all animals are hypnotized that way by their models, and that humanity has been struggling for a long time toward an awakening from such hypnosis.

I suspect that existential "reality"—the "reality" we encounter and endure—always has the capacity to astonish us by being bigger and more complicated than any model we have made.

Whether it be "fact" or an appearance or—maybe—only a parable, I think there is much wisdom to be gained from one more Mysterious Tale:

16 October 1888 St. Louis *Globe-Democrat*—there were three nights of strange doings at a lighthouse in Point Isabel, Texas.

The first night, a shower of nails fell on and around the lighthouse.

The second night, there was another shower of nails.

The third night, a crowd of curiosity-seekers gathered to see the phenomenon.

Down came the nails.

Down, also, came clods of earth and oyster shells.

Beethoven's music, I think, is often like that. Just when you think you recognize the pattern in his creative acts, he surprises you by a variation. Is that, maybe, why we sometimes feel such music is closer to experienced reality than any *theory* we can devise?

CHAPTER EIGHT

CREATIVE AGNOSTICISM

(with further comments on the human brain, and how to use one)

One of the greatest achievements of the human mind, modern science, refuses to recognize the depths of its own creativity, and has now reached the point in its development where that very refusal blocks its further growth. Modern physics screams at us that there is no ultimate material reality and that whatever it is we are describing, the human mind cannot be parted from it.

Roger Jones, *Physics as Metaphor*

If, as Colin Wilson says, most of history has been the history of crime, this is because humans have the ability to retreat from existential reality into that peculiar construct which they call The "Real" Universe and I have been calling *hypnosis*. Any Platonic "Real" Universe is a model, an abstraction, which is comforting when we do not know what to do about the muddle of existential reality or ordinary experience. In this hypnosis, which is learned from others but then becomes self-induced, The "Real" Universe *overwhelms* us and large parts of existential, sensory-sensual experience are easily ignored, forgotten or repressed. The more totally we are hypnotized by The "Real" Universe, the more of existential experience we then edit out or blot out or blur into conformity with The "Real" Universe.

Concretely, the Violent Male—the extreme form of the Right Man—edits out the suffering and pain he causes to others. That is *only appearance* and can be ignored. In The "Real" Universe, the victim is only one of Them—one of all the rotten bastards who have frustrated and mistreated the Right Man all his life. In existential reality, a large brutal male is beating a child; in The "Real" Universe of self-hypnosis, the Right Man is getting his just revenge on the oppressors who have abused him.

We have repeatedly employed Nietzsche's metaphor in which existential reality is Abysmal. In one dimension of meaning, this merely asserts that it is endless: the deeper you look into it, the more you see. It has the *sense of infinity* about it, whether or not it is topologically infinite in space-time.

The "Real" Universe—the model which has become experienced as the real universe—is, on the other hand, *quite finite*. It is compact and tidy, since it has been manufactured by discarding all the inconvenient parts of existential experience. This is why those self-hypnotized by a "Real" Universe of this sort can be so oblivious to the existential continuum around them. "How could a human being do something so *cruel?*" we sometimes ask in horror when an extreme Right Man is finally apprehended. The cruelty was "only" in the world of existential appearances; it does not exist in the edited and improved "Real" Universe of the Right Man. In The "Real" Universe, the Right Man is *always* Right.

The ghastly acceleration of violent, inexplicable and seemingly "pointless" crimes by Right Men in this century—and their hideous magnification into mass murders and war crimes by Right Men in governments—indicate the prevalence of this type of self-hypnosis and what Van Vogt calls "the inner horror" that accompanies it. This "inner horror" is a *sense of total helplessness* combined with the certainty of always being Right. It seems paradoxical, but the more totally Right a man becomes, the more *helpless* he also becomes. This is because being Right means "knowing" (*gnosis*) and "knowing" is understanding The "Real" Universe. Since The "Real" Universe is, by definition, "objective" and "outside us" and "not our creation," we are made puny by it. We cannot *act* but only *re-act*—as The "Real" Universe pushes us, we push back. But it is bigger, so we will lose eventually. Our only defense is in *being Right* and *fighting as dirty as possible*.

This, I think, is in succinct form the philosophy of Adolph Hitler. It is the philosophy of the Marquis de Sade, and of any rapist or thug you can find in any prison in the world. Where Single Vision reigns—where The "Real" Universe is outside us and impersonal—this shadow-world of violence and horror follows in its wake.

This, probably, is why Nietzsche, who understood this pathology from within, raged against both the modeltheistic epistemology—denying The "Real" Universe entirely—and against what he called the Revenge motive. Even if The "Real" Universe were real, he said again and again, we could not know it, since all we know is the existential world of experience. Besides that, linguistic analysis indicates rather clearly that The "Real" Universe is our creation, made up of our metaphors and models. But his deepest attack goes at the *psychology* of The "Real" Universe and its connection to Revenge, and the *disguises of Revenge*. If a man feels overwhelmed by The "Real" Universe, he will seek to destroy what oppresses him. Since we cannot get at The "Real" Universe, revenge must be directed at symbolic targets in the existential continuum. The Will to Power—which Nietzsche held was essentially a will to self-overcoming: to neurological self-criticism in my terminology: to become *more* than one *was*—then becomes deflected into a Will to Destroy.

In the language of modern existentialist and humanist psychology, Nietzsche is describing the process by which we *shirk responsibility*. We seek revenge, but since we are only *re-acting*, The "Real" Universe made us do it. Any criminal will give you his own version of what Nietzsche is describing: "It was my mother's fault." "It was my father's fault." "Society was to blame." "I wanted to get even with all those bastards." "I couldn't control myself: I just went haywire." "They pushed too hard and I exploded."

Man as a re-active mechanism—the Materialist metaphor—is Man with a grudge. The most well-known, and probably the most typical, lines of verse of the 20th Century almost certainly are:

> I, a stranger and afraid,
> In a world I never made

This is the self-image of modern humanity: of the Right Man in particular, but of masses also of ordinary men and women who have internalized the Fundamentalist Materialist metaphor and made it the New Idol. Pessimism and rage are never far below the surface of most of the art of the Materialist age. The sad clowns of early Picasso—the frenzied monsters of his middle period—the defeated heroes and heroines of Hemingway and Sartre and Faulkner—the cosmic butcher shop of Bacon—the homicidal nightmare of such arch-typical films as *Dead End* and *Bonnie and Clyde* and *Chinatown*—the bums and thugs and the endless succession of self-pitying and easily-defeated rebels in virtually all the novels and plays and films that claim to be Naturalistic—the music that has increasingly become less a melody and more a shriek of pain and rage—the apotheosis finally achieved by Beckett: man and woman in garbage cans along with the rest of the rubbish.

Adolph Hitler read Nietzsche, mistook the diagnosis for prescription, and proceeded to act out the worst of the scenarios Nietzsche could imagine, ironically incorporating precisely that nationalism and anti-semitism that Nietzsche most despised. The world looked on in horror, learned nothing, and decided Hitler was a "monster." It remained hypnotized by the same materialistic biological determinism which, to Adolph, had justified both his self-pity and his revenge.

And so we stumble on toward a bigger Holocaust than the Nazis could imagine, complaining bitterly that it is "inevitable." The "Real" Universe will not give us a chance.

When I speak of The "Real" Universe being created by self-hypnosis, I do not intend anything else but psychological literalness. In the hypnotized state, the existential "reality" around us is edited out and we go away to a kind of "Real" Universe created by the hypnotist. The reason that it is usually easy to induce hypnosis in humans is that *we have a kind of "consciousness" that easily drifts away into such "Real" Universes rather than deal with existential muddle and doubt.* Everybody tends to drift away in that fashion several times in an ordinary conversation, *editing sound out at the ear* like Bruner's cat. As Colin Wilson points out, when we look at our watch, forget the time, and have to look again, it is because we have drifted off into a "Real" Universe again. We visit them all the time, but especially when existential concerns are painful or stressful.

Every "Real" Universe is *easy to understand*, because it is much simpler than the existential continuum. Theists, Nazis, Flat Earthers, etc. can explain their "Real" Universes as quickly as any Fundamentalist Materialist explains his, because of this *simplicity* of the edited object as contrasted with the *complexity* of the sensory-sensual continuum in which we live when awake (unhypnotized).

Being hypnotized by a "Real" Universe, we become more and more detached from the existential continuum, and are annoyed when it interferes with us.

"Real" Universes make us puny, however, because they are governed by Hard Laws and we are small compared to them. This is especially true of the Fundamentalist Materialist "Real" Universe, and explains the helplessness and apathy of materialist society. Vaguely, we know that we are hypnotized, and we do not even try to act anymore, but only re-act mechanically.

Since the criminal mentality derives from such hypnosis by a "Real" Universe and the *helplessness* and *rage* induced by such metaphors, the criminal becomes, more and more, the typical person of our age. When the "Real" Universe becomes politicized—when the hypnotic model is based on *"Us"-versus-"Them"* Aristotelian logic—the criminal graduates into the Terrorist, another increasingly typical product of the materialist era.

Against all this mechanized barbarism, existentialist psychology and humanist psychology—aided, perhaps not coincidentally, by the metaphors of quantum physics—suggests that other models of human existence are possible and thinkable and desirable.

In existentialist and humanist models—models influenced by the thought and experiments of researchers such as Maslow, Sullivan, Ames, Perls, Leary, Krippner, and many others—the human being is seen as both in-DIVIDE-ual and in-UNITE-ual, separated in some ways but connected with all things in other ways. How a human being experiences his or her world is not regarded as an immutable *"fact"* but as that human's *"interpretation,"* perhaps learned from others, perhaps self-generated. The "Real" Universe is regarded as a model—a linguistic construct—and we are stuck with existential experience, which may or may not mesh with our favorite "Real" Universe.

According to existential-humanist psychology, where the materialist says "I perceive," it would be more correct to say *"I am making a bet."* Concretely, in Ames's cock-eyed room, we "make a bet" that we are seeing something familiar to us. If allowed into the room and asked to touch a corner of the ceiling with a pointer, we quickly discover the *gamble* in every act of perception. Typically, we hit almost everything *but* the corner in our first attempts—the walls, other parts of the ceiling, etc. A strange thing happens as we go on trying. *Our perceptions change—* we are making a new series of bets, one after another—and gradually we are able to find the corner we are aiming for.

The same sort of thing happens in any psychedelic drug experience, which is why existentialist-humanist models became more popular with psychologists after the 1960s. The same sort of thing, again, happens in meditation—clearing the mind of its *habits*—and that is why so many psychologists of this tradition have been involved in researching what happens, physiologically, to those who meditate.

When we return to the ordinary world of social interactions after such shocks as the cock-eyed room, LSD or meditation, we observe that the same processes are going on—people are making bets about which model fits best at a given time—*but they are not aware of making bets.* They are—it must be repeated—*hypnotized* by their models. If the models do not fit very well, they do not revise them but grow angry at the world—at experience—for being recalcitrant. Most typically, they find *somebody to blame*, as Nietzsche noted again and again.

Edmund Husserl, who was as important as Nietzsche in pioneering this kind of existential analysis, points out that, where in the materialist metaphor consciousness appears *passive*, once we recognize the gamble involved in every perception, consciousness appears very *active* indeed. Nobody is born a great pianist, or a quantum physicist, or a theologian, or a murderer: people have *made themselves* into those things by actively selecting what types of perception-gambles they will make habitual and what types of other experience they will edit out as irrelevant. It is no surprise, from this perspective, that the world contains Catholic reality-tunnels, Marxist reality-tunnels, musical reality-tunnels, materialist reality-tunnels, literary reality-tunnels, *ad infin*. It is a mild surprise, almost, that any two individuals can superimpose their reality-tunnels sufficiently to communicate at all.

This surprise vanishes when we remember that none of us was born and grew up in a vacuum. We "are," socialized as well as "personalized"—in-UNITE-uals as well as in-DIVIDE-uals. Even the most "creative" of us will be found, most of the time, "living" in a social reality-tunnel manufactured of elements which are, in some cases, thousands of years old: the very language we speak controls our perceptions (*bets*)—our *sense of "possibility."*

Nonetheless, the process of socialization or acculturalization—the Game Rules by which Society imposes its group reality-tunnel on its members—is only statistically effective. Every individual seems to have a few eccentricities in her or his private reality-tunnel, even in totalitarian states or authoritarian churches. The alleged conformist—the typical "bank-clerk," say—will reveal some astonishing creative acts in his or her private model, if you talk to such a person long enough.

In short, consciousness, in this model, is not a passive receptor but an active creator, busy every nanosecond in projecting the art work that is an individualized reality-tunnel and is usually *hypnotically dreamed of* as The "Real" Universe. This trance, in most cases, appears as deep as that of anybody professionally hypnotized to repress pain during surgery. The criminal—we return to this point to stress that these observations are not academic but urgently existential—*repressed sympathy* and *charity* just as "miraculously" as the patient *repressed pain* in the above example. We are not the victims of The "Real" Universe; we have *created* the particular "Real" Universe that we happen to dwell in.

This existentialist-humanist psychology thus comes around to the same conclusion as the majority of quantum physicists: *whatever we are talking about, our mind has been its principle architect.* "Nothing is real and everything is real" as Gribbin says. That is, in this model, *nothing* is absolutely real in the philosophical sense, and *everything* is experienced reality to those who believe in it and *select* it in their perception-gambles.

If we recognize some validity in these observations and try to "wake" ourselves from the hypnotic *trance of modeltheism*—if we try to recall, moment by moment, in an ordinary day that The "Real" Universe is only a model we have created and that existential living cannot be compressed into any model—we enter a new kind of consciousness. What Blake called "Single Vision" begins to expand into multiple vision—into conscious bet-making. The person then "sees abysses everywhere," in Nietzsche's deliberately startling metaphor. (Blake says it more soothingly when he speaks of perceiving "infinity in a grain of sand.") The world of living experience is not as finite, or static, or tidy, as the trance called The "Real" Universe. Like Godel's Proof, it contains an infinite regress. In talking to another human being for two minutes "I" experience and create dozens of gambles (reality-tunnels) but never fully know that person anymore than the quantum physicist "knows" if the electron "is" a wave, or a particle, or a "wavicle" (as has been suggested), or something created by our acts of seeking. The other person's "mood" or "self"-at-the-moment, similarly, now seems friendly, now bored or unfriendly, now shifting too fast to be named, now something I have *helped create* by the act of seeking to tune in that person.

As the Buddhists say, the other person and indeed the whole continuum of experience now seems to "be" X and not-X and both X and not-X and neither X nor not-X. All that seems like relative certainty is that whatever I think I "know" about a person or a whole world is just my latest *gamble*.

One begins to perceive that there "are" *at least two* kinds of consciousness. (There seem to be many more.) In "ordinary consciousness" or hypnosis, models are considered The "Real" Universe and projected outside. In this state, we "are" modeltheists, Fundamentalists, and mechanical; all perceptions (gambles) are passive mechanical acts. We "unconsciously" (neurologically) edit and select bits of existential experience and admit them to The "Real" Universe only after they have been processed to accord with the "laws" of The "Real" Universe. Being mechanical and passive, we are also, or experience ourselves as, dominated by The "Real" Universe and pushed here and there by its brutal impersonality.

In this existentialist-humanist mode of consciousness, on the other hand, we "are" agnostic, and consciously recognize our models as our creations. In this state, we "are" model-relativists, "sophisticates" and actively creative; all perceptions (gambles) are actively known as gambles. We consciously seek to *edit less* and tune in more, and we look especially for events that do not neatly fit our model, since they will teach us to make a better model tomorrow, and an even better one the day after. We are not dominated by The "Real" Universe since we remember that the linguistic construct is just our latest *gamble* and we can make a better one quickly.

In the first, materialist mode of consciousness—as Timothy Leary says—we are like persons sitting passively before a TV set, complaining about the rubbish on the screen but unable to do anything but "endure" it. In the second, existentialist mode of consciousness, to continue Leary's metaphors, we take responsibility for *turning the dial* and discover that there is not just one "show" available, that choice is possible. The tuned-in is not *all* of existence; it is only—the tuned-in.

To ask which mode of consciousness is "true," after experiencing both, seems as pointless as asking whether light is "really" waves of particles, after seeing the two-hole experiment.

In fact, the emphasis on "choice" and "creativity" in existentialist-humanist psychology has an exact parallel in the two-hole experiment. Many physicists think the best metaphor to describe that experiment is to say that we "create" the wave or particle depending on which experimental set-up we "choose."

The wave/particle complimentary seems to mirror the existential experience of consciousness even more closely when we examine it. The ordinary consciousness of the "self"—in the vernacular sense, with no technical philosophic doctrine implied—is much like a particle: "solid," "isolated," "real," encapsulated by the skin and more or less static. When one becomes detached enough for *neurological self-criticism*—for revising models as one goes along—the "self" appears more like a process and even a wavy process: it "is" a *succession* of states, rather than a state itself (as Hume noticed) and these states come and go in a wave-like manner, "flowing" between "inner" and "outer." As one observes them come and go, one learns to choose desirable states, at least to the same extent that the two-hole experiment "chooses" waves or particles.

One of the best ways to learn to experience the wave-aspect of consciousness, of course, is listening to music, especially Baroque music, with one's eyes closed. Much quicker than Oriental meditation, this makes one aware of consciousness's wave-like flowing aspect, and of its synergetic nature. At its richest, as in meditation, consciousness appears to become the object of its attention; "there is no separation between me and the music," we say. This simple experience, available to all, makes clear that in-UNITE-ual and flowing modes of consciousness are existentially as "real" as the in-DIVIDE-ual "particles" that we normally experience as our "selves."

In Dr. Leary's *Flashbacks* (Tarcher, Los Angeles, 1983) he writes the latest account of his celebrated and controversial "drug research" with Massachusetts convicts in the early 1960s, in which, statistically, many "criminals" became "ex-criminals," and the recidivism rate dropped dramatically. Leary emphasizes, as he always did, that there is no "miracle" in any drug *per se*, but in what he calls the *set* and *setting*—the preparation for the drug experience. This included an explanation, in simple terms, of the main points of existentialist-humanist psychology. During the drug experience, not unexpectedly, music was played. Some criminals wept, some laughed uncontrollably, some sat in silent awe: all were receiving more signals per minute than usual, and *understanding* how signals are usually edited. In a phrase, they were given the opportunity to look at materialist consciousness from the perspective of existentialist consciousness. It is not surprising that many of them thereafter "took responsibility" and ceased robotically repeating the imperatives of their old criminal reality-tunnels.

Nor is it surprising that Dr. Leary, like Dr. Reich, was subsequently denounced, slandered colorfully and, finally, imprisoned. The ideas we have been discussing—the ideas that, in a sense, were being tested in the convict rehabilitation research—are profoundly threatening to *all* dogmatists, not just to materialistic dogmatists. Powerful churches, political parties and vested (financial) interests, for example, have a strong desire to program the rest of us into the particular "Real" Universes that they find profitable, and to keep us from becoming self-programmers. They want to "take responsibility" for us, and they have no wish to see us "take responsibility" for ourselves.

Materialism-in-the-philosophical-sense is very much supported by materialism-in-the-economic-sense.

To summarize:

Consciousness is not a *given*, or a *fact*. Our mode of consciousness seems historically to have been determined by neurological (unconscious) habits. When we become aware of this, and struggle against the inertia of habit, consciousness continually mutates, becomes less particle-like and "fixed," spreads like a flowing wave. It can more between the poles of pure in-DIVIDE-ualism and pure in-UNITE-ualism, and between many other poles, and can become increasingly "creative" and "self-chosen."

Since there is no explanation for these experiences of consciousness-altering-consciousness, or self-programming, in the materialist model, we can either reject them as "hallucinations" and "appearances" if we wish to retain the materialist model at any cost, or we may supplement the materialist model by recognizing that, like all models, it describes *sombunall* of Universe, whereupon we may choose a more inclusive model, which in this case seems to be supplied at present by existentialist-humanist psychology, quantum mechanics, and the thought of philosopher-psychologists like Nietzsche, James, Husserl and Bergson.

In the "Real" Universe, all things are determined, including us and our thoughts.

In the experienced world, things come and go incessantly and some come and go so fast that we can never know why; causal models fit only *sombunall* of experience. There is a sense of flow, process, evolution, growth, and of what Bergson called "the perpetual upsurge of novelty." In this experienced world, and not in abstract theory, we are faced by apparent decisions continually. We make them and we experience the sense of choice as we do so. We can never know how much such *choice* is "real" absolutely, but since we can never know anything else absolutely, we make do on probabilities.

In the "Real" Universe we are re-active mechanisms; in the experienced world, we are creators, and The "Real" Universe is just another of our creations—a dangerous one, with a tendency to hypnotize us.

Concretely, on any ordinary day, we may observe ourselves contacting the experienced world continually, merging with it, actually breathing its molecules in and out, eating and excreting other parts of it. It "passes through" us as often as we "pass through" it. Since we edit and orchestrate the signals that make up our personal share of the experienced world, we are never separate from it or from *responsibility* for it.

Neurological research during the past two decades has rather clearly demonstrated that the passive consciousness in which there is a "Real" Universe "out there" is characteristic of left-brain domination. Correspondingly, any method of moving into the flowing-synergetic-holistic mode of consciousness—with meditation, or with certain drugs, or by the process of Zen-like attention described in the previous pages—leads to an increase in right-brain activity. Presumably, if we stayed in the flowing right-brain mode all the time we would become, in Mr. Okera's term, Dionysian.

It is more amusing, and more instructive, I think, to *orchestrate* one's consciousness, by "dialing" the TV set—choosing which mode one uses. This way one learns the best, and worst, of both hemispheres of the brain. One also can learn, with self-experiment, that there are other modalities besides right and left. There seems to be a top-bottom mode also, connected with the degree of possible *delay* we can tolerate: the bottom or old brain seems to be reptilian in its reflexes, the top or new brain more easily visualizes a multiple-choice reality-labyrinth in place of the either/or of pure reflex. And there even *seems* to be a front/back polarity: the frontal lobes *seem* to fine-tune the intuitions in the general direction of that damned and *verboten* "ESP."

In short, it appears to those who try the experiments/experiences of yoga and humanistic psychology, that what is tuned in is a function of how we use our brains habitually, and what is not-tuned-in may, in many cases, become tuned-in, with practise in neurological reprogramming.[1]

I go to a pub and talk to another man. He is *experienced* deeply part of the time, and shallowly another part of the time, depending on the *quality* of my consciousness. If I am very conscious, meeting him can be an experience comparable to great music or even an earthquake; if I am in the usual shallow state, he barely "makes an impression." If I am practising alertness and neurological self-criticism, I may observe that I am only experiencing him part of the time, and that part of the time I am not-tuning-in but drifting off to my favorite "Real" Universe and editing out at the ear-drum much of what he is saying. Often, the "Real" Universe hypnotizes me sufficiently that, while I "hear" what he says, I have no idea of the *way* he says it or what he means to convey.

I walk down the street and, observing my state of consciousness, I see that I am in contact with experienced reality *part* of the time only. Some trees are quite beautiful, but then I realize that I have passed other trees without noticing them. I have drifted off into The "Real" Universe again and edited out a large beautiful hunk of the experienced world. The trees did not cease to exist; they were simply not-tuned-in.

One who remains alive and alert to the experienced world knows *where he is, what he is doing* and *what is going on around him.* It is truly startling, at first, to practice neurological self-criticism and notice how often one has lost track of such simple matters as that. It is even more startling to notice that one is walking among hypnotized subjects who, most of the time, have completely lost track of such matters and are telling themselves stories about The "Real" Universe while editing out vast amounts of the experienced world.

When the mathematician Ouspensky was studying with Gurdjieff, he found it very hard, at first, to understand this unique human capacity to forget where one is, what one is doing, and what is going on around one. He was especially dubious about Gurdjieff's insistence that this "forgetting" was a type of hypnosis. Then, one day, after World War I had begun, Ouspensky saw a truck loaded with artificial legs, headed toward the front. Educated as a mathematician and trained in statistics, Ouspensky remembered that—just as it is possible to calculate how many persons will die of heart attacks in a given year, by probability theory—it is possible to calculate how many legs will be blown off in a battle. But the very calculation is based on the historical fact that most people most of the time will do what they are told by Superiors. (Or, as some cynic once said, most people would rather die, even by slow torture, than to think for themselves.) In a flash, Ouspensky understood how ordinary men become killers, and victims of killers. He realized that "normal" consciousness is much like hypnosis indeed. People in a trance will do what they are told—even if they are told to march into battle against total strangers who have never harmed them, and attempt to murder those strangers while the strangers are attempting to murder them. Orders from above are tuned-in; the possibility of choice is—not-tuned-in.

War and crime—the major problems of our century and chronic problems of our species—seem, to the existentialist-humanist psychologist, the direct results on drifting off into self-hypnosis, losing track of experience and "living" in a "Real" Universe. In the Real Universe, the Right Man is *always* Right, and the blood and horror incidental to proving that is only an appearance, easily forgotten. Besides, the Right Man knows that he is only a re-acting mechanism and ultimately The Real Universe itself is to blame for "making" him explode into such furies.

In existential experienced life, we notice that we are making *bets* and *choices* all the time, and are responsible for being alert and aware enough to make them intelligently and to revise them when necessary. We cannot blame everything on The "Real" Universe, since it is only a model we have created to deal with experienced life. If the model is not good enough, we do not blame it but revise and improve it.

Ultimately, existentialist psychology agrees with neurology (and sounds remarkably like quantum mechanics) in stressing that there is no model that is not an expression of the values and needs of the model-maker, no description that is not also an interpretation, and hence no "objective observer behind a glass wall" who is merely watching what happens. In short, the whole traditional language of "the thing out there," "the image in here," and "the mind" separate from both is totally inadequate to describe our experience, and we need a new holistic or synergetic language. The search for this new language—for "a new paradigm"—is increasingly acknowledged in many other disciplines, these days, as it becomes obvious to more and more researchers that the old models have outlived their usefulness.

The "jargon" suggested in parts of this book—the strange new terms used in place of old terms—is a groping and fumbling, and it is meant to be suggestive and poetic rather than precise. The new paradigm has not quite emerged yet; we see only its broad general outlines.

The human brain, from the viewpoint of perception theory and existentialist psychology, appears much like a very unique self-programming computer. It chooses—usually unconsciously and mechanically—the *quality* of consciousness it will experience and the reality-tunnel it will employ to orchestrate the incoming signals from the experienced world. When it becomes more conscious of this programming, its creativeness becomes truly astounding and has been called meta-programming by Dr. John Lilly.

In meta-programming or neurological self-criticism, the brain becomes capable of deliberately increasing the number of signals consciously apprehended. One looks casually, in the normal way, and then looks *again*, and *again*. Dull objects and boring situations become transformed—partly because they "were" dull and boring only when the brain was working on old mechanical programs—and, without being too lyrical about it, the synergetic unity of observer-observation becomes a *thrilling* experience. Every experience becomes the kind of intense learning that usually only occurs in school when cramming for exams. This state of high and *involved* consciousness—called awakening by the mystics—seems perfectly normal and natural to the brain that has been programmed to watch its own programming. Since, in the existential world of experience, we have to make *bets* and *choices*, we are consciously "cramming" all the time, but there is no special sense of stress or anxiety involved. We are *living* time instead of passing time, as Nicoll said.

The brain, it seems, works best under pressure. The soldier being decorated for bravery often says "I don't remember doing it—it all happened too fast." Even in situations less terrifying and punishing than war, most of us have had flashes of this staggering efficiency and rapidity of brain processes in emergencies. It seems very likely that habitual feelings of "helplessness" and "inadequacy" derive chiefly from our habit of wandering off into The "Real" Universe and not being electrically involved in *where we are, what we are doing,* and *what is going on around us.* In crises, this wandering off or hypnosis is not permitted: we are urgently aware of every detail of the experienced field. Some people develop a suicidal habit of seeking danger—mountain climbers and other sportsmen, for instance—just to enjoy this state of rapid brain functioning and High Involvement again and again. Metaprogramming or neurological self-criticism, developed as a *habit* to replace the old *habit* of wandering off to "Real" Universes, creates that kind of "ecstasy" more and more frequently, and it appears that one has never been using one's brain before but only *misusing* it.

Concretely, two people can "be" in the same existential situation but experience two very, very different reality-tunnels. If they are both modeltheists or Fundamentalists, these different reality-tunnels will both be experienced as "objective" and each will *react* passively. If both are in heightened consciousness—seeking more and more signals every minute—both reality-tunnels will still be different, but each will be experienced as a *creation* and both persons will be *involved.* It is more likely in the second case they will be able to communicate clearly and understand one another; in the former case, they may fall into violent quarrel about who has the "real" reality-tunnel and the Right Man will have to punish the other for "error."

It seems that when "God" or "nature" or "evolution" presented us with a human brain, we were not given instructions on the operation of this marvelous device. As a result, most of our history has been an attempt to learn how to use it. In learning that this involves *taking responsibility* and *being involved* we seem to be learning, also, lessons that are not merely technological but esthetic and "moral." Once again, it seems the experienced world functions holistically and our separation of it into separate grids—"science," "art," "ethics"—is more confusing than helpful.

To use the brain efficiently—to be aware of where one is and what one is doing and what is going on around one, and to take responsibility for one's bets or choices—seems to increase "intelligence" and "creativity." That is hardly a surprise. Whatever our technical definitions of these mysterious functions, it is obvious that they are somehow connected with the number of signals *consciously* apprehended, and with the rapidity of the *re*vision process. When one model is held statically between ourselves and experience, the number of signals drops, no *re*vision occurs, and "intelligence" and "creativity" correspondingly decline. When many models are available, and when we are consciously *involved* in our choices, the number of signals consciously apprehended increases, and we behave more "intelligently" and "creatively."

But the same process of involvement, responsibility, *conscious* choice, etc. also increases those faculties that are traditionally called esthetic and moral. *There is no separation; experience is a continuum.* What we see and experience tells us the most intimate truths about who and what we are as well as disclosing increasing richness of "meaning" in every existential transaction. To quote Blake again,

> The Fool sees not the same tree the wise man sees.

Once again, it appears that the materialist model of mechanical consciousness covers *some but not all* experience, and it excludes precisely that part of experience which makes us human, esthetic, moral and responsible beings.

One may suspect that this is why the materialist age has become increasingly inhuman, ugly, amoral and blindly irresponsible.

One may suspect that this is also why the Citadel—the economically entrenched section of the New Fundamentalism, which serves and is fed by the Warfare State—increasingly draws most of the brain-power of most of the living scientists in the world to the single task, as Bucky Fuller said, of delivering more and more explosive power over greater and greater distances in shorter and shorter times to kill more and more people.

To the existentialist-humanist, the "Real" Universe is not forcing us to behave collectively that way. Ultimately, Irrational Rationalism—the reality-tunnel of Dr. Frankenstein and Dr. Strangelove—is a social invention. Ultimately, "The Communists are plotting to enslave us" is a Game Rule of the cold war; it permits every Russian act—however conciliatory it may appear to neutral observers, however it may seem to aim at *detente*—to be defined as another trick. Ultimately, "The Americans are plotting to destroy us" is a similar Game Rule of the Politburo. The "Real" Universe where this madness appears as sanity is our collective creation. In existential experience, we are only making bets, but we have become hypnotized by our models and we walk toward Armaggedon thinking The "Real" Universe makes it impossible to stop and try a better game.

Like cattle going to slaugher—or like Ouspensky's soldiers going to have their legs blown off—we do not stop to remember who we are, where we are, and what is going on around us.

The resistance to hearing the women at Greenham Common is not unrelated to the resistance to "bizarre" information we have been examining. There are economic as well as neurological reasons why Dr. Reich and Dr. Leary went to prison, while Dr. Teller, Father of the Hydrogen Bomb, is a recognized Authority on The "Real" Universe, rich, honored and praised throughout the Citadel.

1 A variety of exercises to test these general conclusions for yourself can be found in my book, *Prometheus Rising*.